DREAMS OF TOTALITY

Dreams of Totality

Where We Are When There's Nothing at the Center

Sherry Salman

Spring Journal Books
New Orleans, Louisiana

© 2013 by Spring Journal, Inc.
All rights reserved.

Spring Journal™, Spring: A Journal of Archetype and Culture™, Spring Books™, Spring Journal Books,™ Spring Journal and Books™, and Spring Journal Publications™ are all trademarks of Spring Journal Incorporated.
All Rights Reserved.

Published by:
Spring Journal, Inc.
627 Ursulines Street #7
New Orleans, Louisiana 70116
Website: www.springjournalandbooks.com

Dickinson, Emily: Trustees of Amherst College from *The Poems of Emily Dickinson*, Thomas H. Johnson, ed., Cambridge, Mass.: The Belknap Press of Harvard University Press, Copyright © 1951, 1955, 1979, 1983 by the President and Fellows of Harvard College.

Cover Image: *Infinity Mirrored Room—Filled with the Brilliance of Life*, by Yayoi Kusama, installed for the Kusama Exhibition at Tate Modern, 2012. © 2013 Yayoi Kusama/Yayoi Kusama Studio, Inc., and Tate, London.

Back Cover and About the Author Photographs: © 2013 China Jorrin.

Cover design and typography by
Northern Graphic Design & Publishing
info@ncarto.com

Text printed on acid-free paper
Library of Congress Cataloging-in-Publication Data Pending

To Woodley and Sophie—
for your boundless love and dignified forbearance

Study what thou art,
Whereof thou art a part,
What thou knowest of this art,
This is really what thou art.

—Salomon Trismosin, *Splendor Solis*, 1535

Contents

List of Figures xi

Acknowledgments xv

Introduction 1

Part I: Imagining Totality

Chapter One
    Womb and Tomb: Opening and Closing 17

Chapter Two
    Poison and Panacea: A Universal Medicine 67

Part II: Of Human Things

Chapter Three
    Psychology's Dreams 91

Chapter Four
    Society's Dreams 123

Chapter Five
    Sacrifice: Blood Payments and Open Wounds 149

Part III: Nothing at the Center

Chapter Six
    Masking and Unmasking Imagination:
    Virtuality and Its Transgressions 173

Chapter Seven
    The R_x 189

Bibliography 199
Figure Credits 207
Index 211
About the Author 222

Figures

Figure 1: Folio #129 from C. G. Jung,
  The Red Book: Liber Novus 31

Figure 2: The Callanish Stones, Isle of Lewis, Scotland 35

Figure 3: Mummy Cave, Canyon de Chelly, Arizona, USA 35

Figure 4: Rotating Magic Circle, from Tiphareth Designs,
  by Julianus Nightfire, a virtual reality product from
  Second Life Marketplace, 2010 36

Figure 5: *Saturn Devouring His Son,* by Peter Paul Rubens (1636),
  oil on canvas, Museo del Prado, Madrid 39

Figure 6: Borobudur, Java, Indonesia 40

Figure 7: *The Dream,* by Henri Rousseau (1910), oil on canvas,
  Museum of Modern Art, New York 41

Figure 8: *Figures for a Trance Diviner: Couple,* Baule, Cote d'Ivoire
  (19th-20th century), wood, pigments, bead, and iron,
  Metropolitan Museum of Art, New York 43

Figure 9: *The Creation of the World and the Expulsion from Paradise,*
  by Giovanni di Paolo (ca. 1445), tempera and gold on
  wood, Metropolitan Museum of Art, New York 45

Figure 10: *Down at the Rapture with George* (artist unknown),
  www.crutchoftheweak.com 46

Figure 11: *Vitruvian Man,* by Leonardo da Vinci (ca. 1492), pen
  and ink on paper, Gallerie dell'Accademia, Venice 49

Figure 12: *The Chakras of the Subtle Body*, by Kangra (ca. 1820), gouache, heightened with gold, on paper, in the collection of Sven Gahlin, London 52

Figure 13: *Jacob's Ladder* or *Jacob's Dream*, by William Blake, a figure in the bible (Genesis 28:12) painted for Thomas Butts, the British Museum, London 53

Figure 14: Romanesco broccoli fractals (photograph taken with a Canon D60 camera and 28-135 mm lenses) 55

Figure 15: *Dismemberment of Watakame*, by Jose Benitez Sanchez (1973), yarn painting with wood, beeswax, and wool yarn, Juan Negrin and Wixarika Research Center, Mexico 56

Figure 16: Human embryonic stem cells, from the laboratory of Guoping Fan, California Institute of Regenerative Medicine, University of California, Los Angeles 57

Figure 17: *Sibyl and Medicine Bowl* or *Yassi Society Figure*, Sherbro, Sierra Leone (19th-20th century), wood, University of Pennsylvania Museum of Archaeology and Anthropology, Philadelphia 71

Figure 18: *Ifa Divination Tray*, Aja-Fon region, Benin (early 17th century), wood, Ulmer Museum—Weickmann Collection, Ulm, Germany 73

Figure 19: Helix Nebula, photographed by the Hubble Helix Nebula Team, NASA 82

Figure 20: *The Creation of the World* (closed front panels of *The Garden of Earthly Delights*), by Hieronymus Bosch (1504), wood, Museo del Prado, Madrid 93

Figure 21: "The Blue Marble, East," NASA (2002) 94

Figure 22: Advertisement on the *Hindu Business Line* website (2005) 95

Figure 23: Freud's Consulting Room,
　　　　　Freud Museum, London 96

Figure 24: *Brain Story*, by Rachel Napaljarri Jurra (1994), acrylic on
　　　　　linen, Alice Springs, Australia 99

Figure 25: *Moscow at Night*, photograph by
　　　　　Alexey Kochemasov 126

Figure 26: *The Wheel of Time, Kalachakra* (17th century, Tibet),
　　　　　mineral pigments on cloth, Rubin Museum
　　　　　of Art, New York 133

Figure 27: *Narcissus*, attributed to Michelangelo Caravaggio
　　　　　(c. 1597–99), oil on canvas, Gallery Nazionale d'Arte
　　　　　Antica, Rome 137

Acknowledgments

Many people and institutions were very generous with their time, with permission to reproduce works of art and illustrations, and with permission to excerpt from my previously written material. I am grateful to the Rubin Museum of Art (New York), Yayoi Kusama Studio, Inc. (Tokyo), the Metropolitan Museum of Art (New York), the Prado Museum (Madrid), Galleria dell'Accademia (Venice), Gallery Nazionale d'Arte (Rome), Harvard University Press, artist Rachel Napaljarri Jurra and C. San Roque for the Petrol Link Up Substance Misuse Prevention Project of the Commonwealth of Australia, Guoping Fan's laboratory at the California Institute for Regenerative Medicine at the University of California in Los Angeles, aviator and photographer Alexey Kochemasov, photographer Kenro Izu, Second Life artist Julianus Nightfire, Taschen Books, Murray Stein and Open Court Books, and Bob Hinshaw, publisher at Daimon Verlag. I would not have found the images from Africa had it not been for *Art and Oracle: African Art and Rituals of Divination* (New York: Harry Abrams, 2000)—the catalogue of an outstanding exhibit at the Metropolitan Museum of Art in New York curated by Alissa LaGamma. And I want especially to acknowledge all the assistance I received from Ami Ronnberg, curator of the Archive for Research in Archetypal Symbolism (ARAS) in New York, and the entire ARAS staff.

Without my colleagues and students in the Jungian Psychoanalytic Association I would never have written this book. Thank you all. I also want to acknowledge my friends and colleagues Patricia Finley and Beverley Zabriskie for their support. Author Hilton Obenzinger of Stanford University was very encouraging and very generous with his editorial wisdom. Thank you also to John Peck and Sonu Shamdasani for sharing information about Jung's mandala in *The Red Book* and to Paul Smyres for his help with formatting several of the illustrations. A special thank you to my brother Charles Salman for his understanding and meticulous reading of a preliminary manuscript and to Priscilla Rodgers for her ongoing enthusiasm and for the film we made together on imagination that debuted at the first Art and Psyche Conference in San Francisco.

And thank you to Siobhan Drummond and especially Nancy Cater of Spring Journal Books.

My heartfelt gratitude continues to go out to family and friends who respected and adjusted to my preoccupation.

INTRODUCTION

One night during the autumn of 2008, just before Barack Obama's election to the presidency of the United States, I was flipping through a magazine in New York's Penn Station while waiting for my train home. Amid all the excited press, a passage about contemporary culture caught my eye. "A recurrent vision swirls in the shared mind of the Net, a vision that nearly every member glimpses, if only momentarily: of wiring human and artificial minds into one planetary soul."[1] Reading those rhapsodic words written by the founding editor of *Wired* magazine I was reminded of another legendary net, one described seventeen hundred years earlier in a third-century Buddhist sutra—the jeweled net of Indra which hung suspended above the god's palace. A brilliant gem glittered at every knot, each one reflecting the images of the others, twinkling and sparkling like stars in an infinity of night sky.

Flipping forward, I scanned the next article, which was about al-Qaeda's "networks of terror." A fundamentalist monster, threatening an end to the Western dream, wove this net of hidden threads imagined as encircling the world in a sinister web. So there was the other side, the darker side of those beatific visions of interconnection and totality. At the same time that the World Wide Web seemed to promise the reality of an enlightened global village, networks of terror, mass epidemics, and global meltdowns seemed to threaten an end to the planet. Yes, I reflected to myself—with a smile for both the stunning correspondence and my clever discernment of it—there really is nothing new under the sun. Looking up, I saw that my train was boarding and hurried off.

That night I had a dream. And although this book is not a book about dreams in the usual sense, it did begin with one. I dreamed that I had woken up in a hotel in Prague, a city I wanted to visit but hadn't been to yet. It was dawn. Sitting up and looking out through a large window, I could see an old cathedral in the central square. There was something or someone atop the cathedral spire, an animal. It began singing. I thought that it must be a rooster crowing, but then realized that couldn't be—it would have had to be an enormous rooster. Then I saw that it was a winged dragon with the body of a seahorse, a kind of living weather vane. As I watched, the dragon flew off the steeple and began circling the city, around and around, mile after mile, in widening rings. He went in and out of my sight as he got closer to the hotel. I struggled to open the window. It gave way just as the dragon appeared in front of me. His head filled the entire window frame. The air smelled fleshy, almost overpowering, his scales rumbled as he breathed. Placing his forearms on the open windowsill, he looked at me through big dark eyes, and speaking wordlessly, asked, "Do you want to hear the story about the story before I go?" In the way of dreams, I silently indicated yes, and as he began to sing the story to me, my alarm clock went off and I woke up.

Astonished, my first thought was that the dragon looked like images I had seen of what the medieval alchemists called the quicksilver aspect of Mercurius, what we would describe today as the mutable quality of the imagination. My next thought was that this dragon was a hippocampus—a mythological creature whose name means horse-shaped sea monster. The hippocampus is also the name for a seahorse-shaped structure in the brain that is heavily implicated in processing emotions, learning, and dreaming—something I remembered from my grad school days in neuropsychology. I'm never actually awake at dawn if I can help it, and so I wondered about the dream's dawn setting. Was it signifying the start of another day, the sunrise that roosters routinely announce, or was it the dawning of a new day, the beginning of something different? If the latter, what was new and why the urgency?

My work as a psychoanalyst has taught me that the propensity we have for imagining wholeness and significance has taken on the same forms and design across history and cultures—like the similarity between Indra's net, the World Wide Web, and the networks of terror that I'd thought about the day before. I also assumed that there was something at the center of our psyches, at minimum an orienting perspective on psychological and cultural life that moves us centripetally toward integration—albeit through some nasty cycles of destruction, like many a Yeatsian "rough beast." Why then was this creature going off center, departing the place over which he presided, even leaving town altogether? And what was the story about this story that I had only just begun to hear?

One of my favorite of C. G. Jung's quips appears in a letter he wrote to Miguel Serrano, a diplomat and esoteric philosopher who had his own bizarre brand of esoteric Hitlerism that had deemed the Führer the last avatar from a golden age. It was 1957, and Jung was already an old man. When Serrano asked Jung about the goal of achieving an ideal and whole personality—an image that Jung termed the *Self* and that Serrano would have considered a godlike state—Jung replied, "I believe that the thing I call the self is a dream of totality."[2] I like to think that Jung was a bit annoyed, that his cryptic statement was a veiled way of saying that there are no totalities or conditions of wholeness, whether of self, of man-gods, or of anything else. To think otherwise is an illusion, a dream in the sense of a wish. There is, however, a process at play. The integrative and constructive process that Jung was alluding to—what I refer to here as dreaming of totality—is one of the ways our imagination creates and imposes cohesion on our experience and helps us to adapt to changes in ourselves and to a changing environment. Whether it be in the form of nostalgia for a fantasized golden age, or in the search for a missing other who will make us complete, or as a dream of globalization or a wired-in consciousness that will unite humanity—the imagination seems to work to make things whole.

Humanity has always fashioned these dreams of totality, visions of utopias and dystopias, of perfect worlds and apocalyptic end-times, of holy lands and holy wars, of universal saviors and of evil agencies. We have put our faith in revelation and in hyperrealities, in gods of testaments and in gods of technologies. Our bright and dark dreams of totality are the powerful products of our propensity to fashion a sense of wholeness and meaning out of disparate data, to contain our conflicted feelings, to protect and defend what we value most highly, and to explore new adaptations in response to changing environments. We create images of totalities—whether they are of God, of a self-organizing universe, of an integrated self-identity, or even of a Buddhist empty center. These images power and drive religious beliefs and practices, sociopolitical paradigms and programs, artistic movements and expression, and all manner of conceptual systems—including humanistic and psychological theories and therapies of identity, self, and health.

Dreams of totality are called up within us in response to distress, and they appear without fail during times of conflict and change—with a do-or-die, beautiful, horrific, or even holy-feeling numinosity. Dipping down into nonverbal types of awareness and cognition, dreaming of totality takes place at deep levels of emotion and mind, at hippocampal levels of psychological processing. This is why no one can escape their power and allure. And while it is universally acknowledged that the inability to dream of totality—to mobilize processes of integration and creative imagination—is a catastrophe on the order of a black hole in the mind and heart, it is equally true that dreams of totality can also result in the coercive foreclosing of imagination. When "gone bad," when humanity's dreams of totality have become totalitarian, they have destroyed many more people and civilizations than any plague or epidemic in human history.

It seems our imaginations have always had this provision to dream of totality—to construct all manner of narratives, metaphors, and images of wholeness that serve to give a center and meaning to individual and collective life. However, with the stirrings of postmodern sensibility and the explosion of communications technology, the previously unthinkable possibility that there might be nothing at the center of either individual or collective life is upon us—and there is no going back. Our contemporary dreams of totality—the ones through which we live and breathe—are no longer reliably located anywhere. Instead, they seem to shift and change shape, are deferred and referred, appearing and disappearing in ways that feel fragmented and chaotic. As national borders and identities become radically destabilized, for example, fears of immigration—of contamination by the disenfranchised—proliferate in reaction. With the collapse of traditional boundaries and centers comes the creeping paranoia that the enemy is now anywhere and everywhere, a "fact" that seems self-evident to us in both our fantasies and the realities of globalization and life on the virtual frontier.

Cultural and individual identities are also shifting quickly. Family life has changed shape overnight, people occupy multiple social roles, and the approaching sensibility of geophysical and cosmopolitan citizenship might require that animals and even plants have rights to life and liberty—if not the pursuit of happiness. Biological identity is up for grabs as we create new hybridized species and accept that we can change our gender. The restless, shape-shifting aspects of psychological life have come to the fore, and without firm centers and identities to rely on, we experience both the freedom to transgress boundaries in a creative way and great difficulty recognizing harmful boundary transgressions. That which contains us now (if uneasily)—rapidly updated information, globalization, virtuality, and multiple and shifting identities—may be a new type of cultural experience. The all-seeing eye of imagination no longer beholds a monomythic totality, but rather, blinking and updating, it skims lightly over the surface of everything, like the virtual map of Google Earth.

At the same time, our tendency to dream of totality is being colonized and even corrupted by the relentless spinning of images by the multimedia culture and the infotainment industry. The psyche is so saturated with prefabricated images that imagination struggles to breathe. Reality TV is our contemporary *fascinosum*. In a particularly disturbing gesture, the American Psychiatric Association's working group for the new *Diagnostic and Statistical Manual of Mental Disorders* (DSM-5) sought to classify introversion (but not extroversion) as a troubling indicator of a potential personality disorder. Despite astounding technological and social advances, much of the postmodern landscape—at least from our current vantage point—seems to be characterized by dissociation and a proliferation of ruptures. No matter where we look, or where we try to place our feet, no matter how connected we are or how much we love, fault lines are opening everywhere. Even the planet itself appears to us to be coming undone. And as the boundaries between cultures and between selves become more fluid, hard and fixed centers of psyche, nationalism, and dogma form in reaction. These compensatory dreams of totality arise in the form of fundamentalisms—which in America have even shifted into the cultural mainstream.[3] These encapsulated and idealized religious and cultural dogmas defend sacred and literalized texts, aiming to purify contaminating influences. The twenty-first-century twist comes into play when the media culture magnifies these fundamentalisms into full-blown spectacles.

Because there seems to be nothing at the center of contemporary life we can become embroiled in a desperate search for fundamentals, attempting to take refuge in doctrine of all sorts, or in a nostalgic clinging to what we perceive to be essential. Even the dream of a global village, a planetary population happily wired together in the Web, can turn fundamentalist. Just as fundamentalisms can hybridize—such as the sort of spiritual nationalism that grips America when identified with a redeemer fantasy—fundamentalism and image spinning often come together in powerful ways. The blockbuster film *Avatar*, for example, which purported to look forward to an idealized and simple (albeit psychedelic) life for its message of hope and salvation inadvertently fell backward into a quaint dream of totality, a Rousseauesque fantasy valorizing tribal (but benighted) societies in perfect quasi-spiritual tune with nature, a misleading fantasy of perfect union that was made sacred and projected uneasily onto the future. This form of tribal living could, of course, never be sustained in the reality of twenty-first-century living, if for no other reason than tribal societies don't allow for individual freedoms and choice, being held together instead by highly stratified ranks and social status, not to mention transcendental entities. Unobtainium indeed.

But mesmerized by all manner of media spectacles we often give up and give way to a casual relationship to truth or to a privileging of a faux subjectivity and the costume parade of manufactured images that it wears. "Have it your way" the slogan goes—which really means have it the corporate way, with a sprinkle of style and a dash of bling, accessorizing that has also been determined by market indicators. We are desperate for something that feels like authenticity and desperately in love with artifice. Where this often ends is in a dissociative numbing. As imagination fragments into manic images, dissolves into endless spin, we finally collapse exhausted, saying, as we do in America, "whatever" and "it's all good."

As the links in our dreams of totality are breaking apart, as what contained us before no longer does, several things seem to be happening at once. Encapsulated fundamentalisms of all sorts—religious, political, social—arise in compensation, struggling vigorously to restore order, especially as new dreams like globalization and the virtual world of the Web are pressing forward and taking over our collective imagination. Many people revel in the destruction of the old forms in a kind of gleeful or righteous apocalyptic nihilism. Many are lulled into passivity by the spectacles of disaster and undoing celebrated by the media industry, perhaps our contemporary form of the bread and circuses that characterized the Roman Empire before its fall. But as our anxiety rises, there's also an opportunity for something new. The breaking up of dreams of totality begins where there are weak links in the fabric of experience, where so-called dysfunctional or disenfranchised elements of individual or social life create tension at the boundaries of a system, where tricksters and transgressors, as Lewis Hyde wrote in *Trickster Makes This World*, "slip the trap of culture."[4] As things begin to fray, what was left out or is newly emerging pushes to be incorporated. We construct our own cosmologies, and we also break them to bits when they no longer express the realities of living. And it's all happening very fast right now.

There have been many nostalgic laments and cynical diatribes and much reactionary mysticism in response to our increasingly high-stakes contemporary mosaic. This book is not any of those. Instead, it offers my own bit of disruption, a different optic on the shift in our dearly held dreams of totality that inform, or fail to inform, the life of contemporary individuals and societies. The more we believe that stability and structure are the greatest virtues, the crazier we are going to feel in today's rapidly changing world. Our unmoored and digitized selves are as legitimate—and also as partial—an image of ourselves as children of God. What I will argue is that it is precisely when our cherished dreams of totality fall away, and especially now when there is less and less at the center of psychological experience, that the imagination's provision to dream of totality is revealed and can come fully into its own, slipping the traps of both disintegration and fundamentalism. The psychological and social movements between opening up and closing off, between emancipation and prohibition, may be less a law of history and more a basic property of imagination. We are now in a position to see that.

The "we" in this book are Westerners and those living in developing societies, and we are also Americans—at least symbolic ones—to the extent that the American pattern of multiplicity and rapid change is taking hold everywhere. America itself is also symbolic in this context because America was founded in a dream of totality that contained both the inclusive promise of a diverse democracy and the insularity of religious doctrine right from the start. We are also those everywhere who feel the emotional push-pull between fragmentation and fundamentalism, who want to grapple with contemporary life in a different way, who don't want to be swallowed by the image industry and give up their imaginations, and who don't want to be waging constant war on this and war on that.

As an activity that delivers a critique of social norms by deconstructing and reconstructing personal and collective myths, in true subversive and trickster fashion dreaming of totality allows us to forge surprising connections and promotes empathy with what is forgotten, censored, thrown out, disfigured, or newly emerging. At least at the start. For although dreams of totality open up new individual and collective possibilities, they also close possibilities down. When they reify they become poisonous, hardening up into terrorizing matrices—becoming stranded in a transcendent dimension or in the dead zone of fundamentalisms of all stripes, becoming either totalitarian or "rotten with perfection."[5] Throughout history, dreams made reality in this manner have become loci for the coercive implementation of power. In this sense, Freud was right when he proposed, in *The Future of an Illusion*, that the fiction of religion functioned as a coercive arm of civilization, quelling the antisocial trends that threatened the status quo. From this point of view, the postmodernists were also right to deconstruct and mock the meaning of meaning, with its significations of wholeness, self, totality, and truth; these too can become imprisoning. I will argue though that Freud, for example, and our contemporary antireligion crusaders, particularly Richard Dawkins and Christopher Hitchens, are throwing the baby out with the bathwater. For if we live in the psyche only like fish in the water, without appreciating how and why imagination creates our images of totality, then the religion/science debate is doomed to oscillate between polarized narratives of blind faith and the most literal kind of empiricism.[6] Sociobiologist Edward O. Wilson, for example, in his afterword to *From So Simple a Beginning: The Four Great Books of Charles Darwin*, confessed to finding it "surpassingly strange" that 50 percent of Americans polled in 2004 did not believe in evolution by natural selection and did not even believe in evolution at all, and that in fact 60 percent accepted the prophesies in the book of Revelation as truth.[7] It may be disturbing, but it's not really that strange.

As is especially evident with respect to the great religions but applying equally to those for whom science is a god, dreaming of totality works like a universal medicine for both society and individuals, what the ancient

Greeks called a *pharmakon*. But as with most drugs, dreams of totality are both poison and panacea. The art is in the dosing. Too much is toxic, too little does nothing for the ailment. Dreaming of totality reinforces a movement toward radical democracy in the psyche and society when it promotes inclusion and transgression—the panacea—but it can also harden into reactionary totalitarianism or an apocalyptic mysticism—the poison. In keeping with the dual nature of its ubiquitous symbol, the circle or sphere, our dreams of totality can be inclusive and also exclusionary. They are both womb and tomb, a subversive kiss or a locked down embrace, visions of possibility or the elaborate coffins for the soul and society that prohibit the imagining of new worlds.

When a dream of totality loses its charm it ceases to feel like an eternal truth and slips into the relative time of history and culture—and the truths of a moment in time always have ragged edges and missing pieces. However, when it's active, a dream of totality feels like the most profound container and expression of our individual and communal desires, of our values and our visions. They are not given up without a fight. Our struggles with the loss and betrayal of our dreams of totality and with the emptiness that's left when they unravel cut to the very roots of identity and substance, bringing us face to face with fury, fear, and despair—with everything that appears hostile—and this is hard to bear. The loss of our dreams can lead to a vengeance-driven repetition compulsion of blood payments, where "what goes around always comes around." Traditionally, these are the terrorizing sacrificial rituals of exorcism, scapegoating, or denial that have been implemented to keep paradigms of totality intact.

But whether we like it or not, reality and new life always tear holes in the fabric of our dreams at their weakest links, revealing what is right outside the boundaries of the prevailing system. What we do when that happens, whether we sacrifice and let go or harden up and clamp down, is usually the decisive factor in psychological, and even societal, vitality. What I will suggest is that we are in a better position than ever before to allow our dreams of totality their weak links, their slippage and their fault lines, and that the strong emotions this evokes in us can leave an open wound, a wound that fosters healing instead of foreclosure. Rather than decreasing the tension between what is in and what is out of our dreams of totality, bearing with the tension by sacrificing completeness can open another kind of fault line, a fault line that can become an open wound of empathy and communion with what appeared as the other.

Making room for fluidity and transgression is key to preserving the creative function of dreaming of totality, while at the same time breaking up its compulsive tendency toward rigid foreclosure of experience and imagination. Contemporary developments provide a new opportunity in this regard, as the transparency of virtual reality, for example, could provide this radical openness, despite its potential dangers, its gaps and omissions, its dissociative draw, its shape-shifting and even its duplicity. By drawing us into the flow of ongoing psychological life and into the multiplicity of its images, virtuality could encourage the individual and collective stability that dreams of totality provide to reside more lightly, but also more fully and firmly in the imagination. Participating in the virtual experience, which is simultaneously real and imaginary, discourages identifying with particular images or paradigms. However engaging, its origin in the imagination still shines through.

Freely transgressing boundaries, allowing for both loving and losing our dreams of totality, virtuality could open things up beyond their margins of fixed identities—of self, of social norms, of religions or scientific models—helping us to sacrifice our attachments to the literality of particular paradigms. This form of sacrifice would not require belief in supernatural agents or entities, sacred taboos, or the bloody death of scapegoats, whether animal or human. The sacrifice of authority we are experiencing in contemporary life promotes an acknowledgment of chaos, of limitation, and of artifice—and also a reorganization that consciously acknowledges complexity.

The tense and critical moment in which we live is ripe for the emergence of new dreams of totality, and they are appearing everywhere, including the images of a limitless virtual frontier and a globalized population. As always, these images and paradigms of totality give body to the imagination as it seeks new solutions to contemporary dilemmas, and they contain strong emotions. However, as history continues to show, the dangers of literalizing any total visions, or exiling them into an unreachable and transcendent dimension of an afterlife or a virtual life, are ever present.

Neither virtuality nor its geopolitical analog, globalization, are panaceas. There is plenty of poison in both to go around. For example, as the corporate media industry drew a tighter and tighter circle around what was deemed newsworthy, that which was left out or pushed out took shape in the blogosphere—with all of its misleading and attendant claims on truth. A related conundrum often arises as to whether or not the mingling of genres so characteristic of contemporary culture and of peoples (that is, multiculturalism) is a postmodern form of dilettantism, perhaps even an opportunistic con, or whether there really is something new and more inclusive going on at the margins between order and disorder. This book is also a challenge to this sort of either/or quandary that induces a characteristic quartet of symptoms: anger, anxiety, dissociation, and idealization. Our contemporary dreams of virtuality and globalization, if appreciated as symbols, embody—if we can even use that word—the paradoxical and ambivalent *pharmakon* of totality as we experience it now. This book provides a road map for navigating between the twin poles of idolatry and iconoclasm—preserving the creativity of dreaming of totality while at the same time loosening its often deadening grip.

As we will see in what follows, the divinely inspired and transcendent sensibility behind dreams of totality gave way over time to the dominance of humanism and psychology, to the exalted individual creator who dreamed his or her own dreams of totality. This has now given way to a perception that we the dreamers are decentered players in a universe of depthless and reproduced signifiers, in which sensibilities of totality, centers, and meaning seem to have no place. Postmodernism has delivered its resounding insult. As Richard Kearny wrote in *The Wake of Imagination*:

> Disseminated into the absolute immanence of sign-play, the imagination ceases to function as a creative centre of meaning. It becomes instead a floating signifier without reference or reason—or to borrow Derrida's idiom, a mass-produced postcard addressed "to whom it may concern" and wandering aimlessly through a communications network, devoid of "destiny" or "destination."[8]

As images flood and glut collective life, dreams of totality seem both threatening and threatened and are still emerging on the margins of virtual illusion. This often engenders feelings of powerlessness that give rise to images of a postmodern wasteland, where the multiplicity of the self and the disappearance of truth have become dominant motifs of contemporary life. We are in danger of underestimating both the power and the purpose of imagining totality. But there is no way back to a sensibility of wholeness in the old mythic-ritualistic sense—those dreams have come and gone.[9]

A sentimental or righteous clinging to images and programs of totality in the form of various isms—religious, political, psychological—is a defense against that loss. So is a nostalgic longing to return home to a golden age of culture or values.

I will argue that setting dreaming of totality free from fixity is a matter of individual integrity and social ethics—a pressing matter on an order of magnitude with any religious prescription for living a good and proper life or the most deeply felt pleas of science and the humanities for freedoms of mind and heart. In the complexity and crush of contemporary living, just as there is no longer anywhere to throw out our unwanted garbage, there is also less and less of a sacred inner chamber in which to take refuge with one's chosen dream of totality. Even images of totality qua images may be starting to lose their postmodern luster, as we are now invited to know dreaming of totality apart from its particular images and representations. Given the current situation, there is a possibility of placing one's faith in a capacity of the human mind and heart which was always provided for but may only now perhaps be realized: deliverance from the boundaries of self-preservation into radical interactivity with our shared human imagination—into the unknown self, the approaching other, and the emerging dream.

Amid the welter of postmodern relativity and artifice, among the multiplicity of genuine images and the collective's reproductions, at the same time that we are confronted with nothing at the center of our dreams of totality and the vigorous fundamentalisms that confront this development, there is an opportunity to come to terms with imagination. One of the most difficult but essential projects of contemporary life is to dissolve dreams of totality into a larger solvent—the imagination. In the same way that the individual artist gives way to what the alchemists called "the Art"—changing one form or state of being into another—what I hope to convey is that holding to that solvent, the imagination, is the solution.

Part I explores the imagination, the sharing of emotional and cognitive essentials it provides, and the ways in which totality has been imagined across cultures and throughout history. This is followed by looking into the "call and response" dynamic of generating images of totality in response to chaos or distress, how we eventually become entombed by them, and how we then deconstruct those images and paradigms when they no longer serve adaption. This unfolds into a discussion of how dreams of totality function as both poison and panacea for individuals and cultures. Part II provides a perspective on dreaming of totality with respect to the psychological and social narratives of the Western dreams of self, identity, culture, and community. First up are psychology's images and narratives of wholeness and unity, particularly its big dreams of interiority and identity. This is followed by an exploration of dreams of totality that take sociopolitical form, the great paradigms and movements through which we view history and the isms: totalitarianism, capitalism, fundamentalism, and globalism. This moves into a discussion about the relationship between sacrifice and dreaming of totality, and the progression from blood payments to open wounds that contemporary living demands. Part III focuses on where we are now, including an exploration of virtuality and its transgressions, the masking and unmasking of imagination in contemporary culture, and a symbolic perspective on dreaming of totality—including a prescription, a psychological R_x, for taking the medicine of totality when there's nothing at the center.

It used to be said about living that "it's not whether you win or lose, but how you play the game"; now we need to come to know more about what games we're playing.

Notes

[1] This excerpt from Kevin Kelly, *Out of Control: The Rise of Neo-Biological Civilization* (New York: Perseus Books, 1994), originally appeared in the May 1994 issue of *Harper's Magazine*.

[2] Miguel Serrano, *C. G. Jung and Herman Hesse: A Record of Two Friendships* (New York: Schocken Books, 1966), p. 50.

[3] As Robert Lifton pointed out in *The Protean Self* (New York: Basic Books, 1993), American fundamentalism drew on the tradition of American Bible centeredness and was a correction of sorts to both liberal theology and secular culture.

[4] Lewis Hyde, *Trickster Makes This World: How Disruptive Imagination Creates Culture* (New York: Canongate, 1998).

[5] Michael Hyde, *Perfection: Coming to Terms with Being Human* (Waco, TX: Baylor University Press, 2010), p. 4.

[6] There has been an ongoing discussion in Jungian theory about whether we live in the psyche, unconsciously as it were, like fish in the water, whether we are conscious of the water as fish are not, or whether

we live within another psychic condition altogether. For those interested in following this discussion, see Jung's work on alchemy: *Psychology and Alchemy*, vol. 12, *The Collected Works of C. G. Jung* (Princeton, NJ: Princeton University Press, 1953); *Alchemical Studies*, vol. 13, *The Collected Works of C. G. Jung* (Princeton, NJ: Princeton University Press, 1967); *Mysterium Coniunctionis*, vol. 14, *The Collected Works of C. G. Jung* (Princeton, NJ: Princeton University Press, 1963); and *The Practice of Psychotherapy*, vol. 16, *The Collected Works of C. G. Jung* (Princeton, NJ: Princeton University Press, 1954). See also James Hillman, *Healing Fiction* (Woodstock, CT: Spring Publications, 1998), and *Re-Visioning Psychology* (New York: Harper Paperbacks, 1977); and Wolfgang Giegerich, "The End of Meaning and the Birth of Man," *Journal of Jungian Theory and Practice*, 6(1).

[7] Edward O. Wilson, ed., *From So Simple a Beginning: The Four Great Books of Charles Darwin* (New York: W. W. Norton, 2005), p. 1479.

[8] Richard Kearny, *The Wake of Imagination* (London: Routledge, 1988), p. 13.

[9] Wolfgang Giegerich has written on this theme in *The Soul's Logical Life* (Frankfurt: Peter Lang, 2001); and *Technology and the Soul: From the Nuclear Bomb to the World Wide Web* (New Orleans: Spring Journal Books, 2007).

Part I

Imagining Totality

Chapter One

Womb and Tomb:
Opening and Closing

> Imagination is more important than knowledge. For knowledge is limited, whereas imagination embraces the entire world, stimulating progress, giving birth to evolution. It is, strictly speaking, a real factor in scientific research.
> —Albert Einstein, 1931

> Rose, oh pure contradiction, desire,
> To be no one's sleep under so many
> Lids.
> —R. M. Rilke's epitaph, 1925 (translated by John Mood)

Imagination and the Sharing of Essentials

In their particular completeness, dreams of totality have punctuated the story of humanity's creative imagination. They are the stuff of history and cultures—a living record of symbols that have left traces of the evolutionary path of the human mind and heart. Their representations are among both the oldest in human history and the newest, ranging from archaic magic circles that protected sacred space to the all-seeing "eye of God," from stories of paradise lost and found to the long-sought beloved's kiss which makes us feel complete, from our fantasies of apocalyptic end-times to our dreams of social cohesion in the World Wide Web. Dreams of totality rest under, hover over, and surround our consciousness. And we believe in our dreams wholeheartedly, give them our full commitment and grant them complete credence. We put our fate in our symbolic creations, with the unwavering faith that they bring coherence and meaning into the world.

In *The Lexus and the Olive Tree*, journalist Tom Friedman invoked the powerful image of globalization to explain the organization and dynamics of the contemporary world. Globalization, he wrote, is "the inexorable integration of markets, nation-states and technologies to a degree never witnessed before."[1] According to Friedman, globalization has its own defining features and dominant ideas, its own perspective and its own rules: integration, deregulation, speed, connectivity, and free-market capitalism. It has its own power structures, the global financial markets, and its own defining demographic—Americanization. The technologies of digitization and the Internet are the sine qua non of globalization, allowing people, nations, and corporations to reach around the world very fast and also allowing world events to reach people, nations, and financial markets equally speedily. The collapse and intermingling of boundaries within and between politics, cultures, nations, disciplines, and media are also a big part of the globalization picture, and Friedman observed that globalization even seems to have its own special set of anxieties—fear of rapid change, a sense of potential danger from unseen enemies, and the uncomfortable feeling that no one is in charge.

There is a great deal of argument about what globalization is and about whether it will open up possibilities for a better world or close those down, perhaps inadvertently.[2] What is clear is that Friedman, for example, was looking at the world through a particular lens. Deeply ambiguous, both hailed as the solution to the world's ills and feared as a harbinger of the end, if ever there was a super story, a master metaphor and a mega system, a dream of totality writ large—globalization is it. As an image, it informs the way we think about things and make decisions; as a story it both reveals and conceals the realities of experience. And imagination of this kind, as Einstein said, is more important than knowledge because without imagination there is no knowledge, there is no relationship to reality.

This may seem counterintuitive at first, since we usually associate imagination with flights of fancy, with precisely what isn't real, with something suspect, or with something mysterious and romanticized called "creativity." But recent work by cognitive psychologists tells a different story, a story about imagination as the central engine that drives our experience and structures what is meaningful. The world of metaphor and imagination is not just a pretend world, or a protection against unconscious infantile urges, or a space in the mind filled with secondary products of instincts or neuronal detritus. On the contrary, images and metaphors are pregnant with meaning, the prime movers of both psychological and social life. As Andrew Samuels pointed out in *The Political Psyche*, "imagery runs relationships, evokes the goal of the instinct, promotes conflict, engenders emotion and infects institutions."[3] From our perspective here the question is: How does a powerful image like a dream of totality do this?

First off, rather than imagination being the antithesis of rationality, it may actually be the basis for rational thinking, the process by which we begin making sense of our experience. Cognitive psychologists like Mark Johnson have explored the idea that image schemata like verticality (derived from the experience of standing upright after crawling), containment, or center-periphery awareness are recurring patterns of body-based perceptual interactions that get translated into metaphors.[4] They become cognitive structures, translated from one domain into another. So, for example, the body-based image schemata of verticality comes to mean "up is more," or the bodily experience of containment is translated into a psychological metaphor of "in or out." We then use these metaphors as a basis for reasoning and the construction of meaning. One of the points that cognitive psychologists are making is that rationality is not an abstract mental experience. It stems from embodied experience, and the link between bodily perceptual experience and reasoning is what we call imagination. Another way to say this is that imagination organizes and synthesizes body-mind representations into coherent symbolic packets that we then use as a basis for rational thinking.[5]

The symbolizing function of the mind takes note of patterns of emotions and experience, of similarities and differences between things. These patterns are continuously being reorganized into images, analogies, stories, and networks of correspondences and metaphors that resonate with one another. This perception of patterns allows potential trajectories of future possibilities in the form of predictions to be generated. The ancients had their own version of this network of patterning called the "sympathy of all things," or *correspondentia*. They imagined most phenomena as being linked up in series, the same substance, for example, existing on different planes that were linked to one another by their correspondence and significance. This sensibility was expressed in symbol systems like astrology, in the Hermetic maxim "as above, so below," and in the various correspondences between gods, planets, colors, elements, and so forth—the goddess Aphrodite, the planet Venus, the color green, the metal copper, and the quality of desire, for example, all being aspects of the same principle. We have our subjectively oriented modern rotation, expressed in ideas like "as within, so without."

Returning now to the image of globalization, we can understand it not only as a sociopolitical construct but as a symbolic image, a blend of metaphors that have been derived from body-based image schemata like containment, balance, symmetry, and center-periphery. The powerful conceptual blend that we call globalization becomes a metaphor itself, a rich narrative that makes a deep translation of experience and also structures it. In their book *The Way We Think: Conceptual Blending and the Mind's Hidden Complexities*, Fauconnier and Turner make the point that the brain makes and unmakes "integration networks," but that "very few of the networks tried out in the chambers of brain and culture actually survive. A network that does survive takes its place in individual or collective memory and knowledge."[6] The most impressive conceptual blends attain the status of what C. G. Jung identified long ago as archetypal images.

A dream of totality like globalization is probably a variation on such an archetypal image or integration network, and it's taking its place in history with others of its kind, with dreams of wholeness like the kingdom of heaven or the idea of man as a microcosm of the universe. At the very heart of globalization lies the intimation of wholeness, one of the most powerful conceptual blends. The global village has undertones of balance, symmetry, and multiple links, of everything humming along smoothly on the wings of free markets, democracy, and the World Wide Web. The feeling of containment—of being either happily or grudgingly "in" or longingly or resentfully "out" of the global network—is palpable. Another factor central to the metaphor of globalization, one of its "defining anxieties" as Friedman suggested, is the feeling that there is no center anywhere and consequently no way to measure a metaphorical distance between center and periphery. Globalization seems both entirely boundless and utterly complete. From a rational perspective this makes no sense; from an imaginative perspective it makes all the sense in the world.

If, as Jung wrote, "the image is a condensed expression of the psychic condition as a whole," then an image like globalization is one of the ways that the contemporary mind has given form not only to its propensity to think and feel in wholes, but to its overall condition in the moment.[7] It's important to emphasize at this juncture that dreaming of totalities like globalization is a property of the psyche, not a metaphysical construct of oneness and unity or an impulse toward perfection or an empirical fact. Nor is it a hidden compass, pointing to the one true north of psychological or social life—the developments and accidents of science and history are equally real. Dreaming of totality works more like a telescope that zooms in and both organizes and distorts experience into images of wholeness that bring together our perceptions of events with our thoughts and feelings about them, orienting us, regulating our reactions, needs, thoughts, and desires, and cooking up adaptations to our changing experience.

One of the central implications to come out of the work on image schemata, metaphors, and conceptual blending is that the traditional boundary between rational and nonrational types of thinking is collapsing. Cognitive fluidity has taken center stage. So we need to think about dreaming of totality as something distinct from the pejorative "irrational" (which can come to mean delusional) and more as a mode of thinking that combines limbic and cortical brain processes, bringing together the expression of emotions, the rewriting of memory and experience, and executive functioning—something not unlike ordinary dreaming. This kind of blended thinking has been referred to in literary and artistic contexts as mythopoetic thinking. Poets use mythopoetic language when they choose a word that evokes a myriad of related images, thoughts, and feelings. Visual artists use form and color to evoke feelings and thoughts; musicians use sound. Psychologists use mythopoetic thinking when they amplify dream images or behavior with corresponding images and metaphors from humanity's various symbol systems, like mythologies. Anyone who wants to understand or influence behavior at a deep emotional level employs it or uses its rhetorical trope, metonymy—where one thing is merely substituted or used as reference for another in a faux mythopoetic sleight of hand, for example, Wall Street walked off with our money.

The mythopoetic imagination penetrates deeply into the heart of things, making connections and meaning out of events and experience. It does more than translate information from body-based schemata into rational thinking. The dreams of totality that imagination creates, while they often have an appealing spatial quality of satisfying roundness that may hail from an image schemata, also have a poetic and dramatic intensity, even a hallucinogenic aesthetic beauty or what appears as an unassailable logical completeness. They exert a pull of desire and longing to which we succumb or resist. Their narratives are mythic in scope and depth. They emerge from the mind wrapped in paradox, with a feeling of grace but also of certainty, with a magical mysterious intimation of revelation and also with the "aha" of discovery. Our imagination is concerned with very substantial things, precisely with the things that matter to us most. And as we will see in what follows, periods of stress and strain that challenge our survival set the stage for this type of mythopoetic thinking to come to the fore and offer solutions.

I think it was Aristotle who said that metaphor is the hallmark of genius and that all people carry on their conversations with metaphors. Genius then is not only a rare gift or a state of possession by a voice that speaks without reason, from "out of your mind." It's more like the free play of ordinary imagination that comes up with new arrangements of ideas and images. While it is, for example, the genius of the logic of scientific methodology to offer partial explanations designed to be disproved, it is the genius of imagination to offer comprehensive and complete visions. As we will see, these imaginary constructs are also subjected to continuous critique and revision by the same processes that created them. Although some people are better at playing than others, imagination is an essential and shared faculty of mind. Many have argued that the flow of images and information dispensed by digital technology potentially available to everyone will encourage conceptual blending and the play of imagination in a radical and democratizing way, although it remains to be seen whether what's created are simulacra or genuinely new arrangements. In any case, we are now in a position to understand imagination not as something utterly subjective, but as something public that we all have in common and share with one another, even as the faculty that allows us to communicate and understand one another.

From this perspective, what we think we understand is less a set of facts and more an event both private and public. There is no god's-eye view of reality, but there are shared cognitive processes that lean toward shared human perspectives. Our propensity to translate experience into images of wholeness doesn't just make meaning out of experience. Whether symbolic or actualized, these images also act as theories of mind, providing access into the minds of others, promoting a sharing of emotional and cognitive essentials. Which brings us back to the question: How does a powerful image ruin relationships, engender conflict, and infect institutions?

In August 2010, Arianna Huffington posted a piece entitled "Sarah Palin, 'Mama Grizzlies,' Carl Jung, and the Power of Archetypes" on the *Huffington Post*:

> I've been thinking about this paradox: the most important political ad of 2010 so far did not play on television, and came from someone not currently running for any office. It was Sarah Palin's latest web video, "Mama Grizzlies." . . . Among the choice sound bytes:
>
> "It seems like it's kind of a mom awakening . . . women are rising up."
>
> "I always think of the mama grizzly bears that rise up on their hind legs when somebody is coming to attack their cubs."
>
> "You thought pit bulls were tough? Well, you don't wanna mess with the mama grizzlies!"[8]

Huffington noted that it didn't matter that the video was devoid of public policy solutions, because people responded not to Palin's lack of policy expertise but to her use of symbols.

The evocation of "mama grizzlies" rising up and taking over the country, ridiculous as it was at one level, also resonated deeply in the imagination. Bears sleep through the winter, which is likely one reason they appear in myths about death and rebirth. What emerges from the dead zone of winter is hungry, scary, and powerful. Fierce and protective, bears take care of their own. They were sacred to the virgin huntress Artemis—one wrong move into its sphere and the bear tears you limb from limb. In Norse legend, frontline warriors were called berserkers— covered in bearskins, they entered a trance-like state of fury, roaring frightfully and leading the charge into battle. In North American Winnebago and Pawnee lore, bear shamans and their grizzly bear spirit guides perform initiation ceremonies of dismemberment and evisceration. One such spirit vision of death and rebirth was described by cultural anthropologist Paul Radin in *The Road of Life and Death*:

> Finally, these grizzly-bear spirits danced . . . They would tear open their abdomens, then making themselves holy, heal themselves. Or, they would shoot bear-claws at each other and stand there choking with blood. Then, making themselves holy, they would cure themselves.[9]

The essentials that are shared through the image of mama grizzlies rising up embrace killing rage, power, self-protection, and healing via destruction. In the case of the mama grizzlies video, the maternal tendency toward protection and birth was strong-armed into a grizzly parody of threatening revenge against the political party then in power and a takeover of its terrain. This particular sharing of essentials was taking place during a period of national crisis: the mama grizzlies video was released at a time when there was record unemployment and economic upheaval in North America, the fault lines in free-market capitalism were opening up, and the global climate crisis was accelerating. Under such conditions of distress, emotional and psychological boundaries become very permeable. New narratives take hold easily, berserk or not.

All great mythopoetic stories and images are vehicles for what cognitive psychologists call "narrative transport," an immersion into an altered state of mind that fosters a sharing of essentials. New observations from the field of neuroscience about how mirror neurons work are starting to uncover the physiological mechanisms by which these sharing of essentials between people might happen. Studies using functional magnetic resonance imaging (fMRI) have discovered that certain neurons found thus far in humans, primates, and birds fire both when performing an action and when merely observing another performing that action. These neurons mirror the behavior of others as though we ourselves were doing the acting. There is much speculation in the scientific community about mirror neurons mediating imitation, language, empathy, and theories of mind. Neuroscientists are beginning to talk in terms of "shared intersubjective space," with a consequent "memory of mankind" being available via something like a mirror neuron system.[10]

What we do know for certain is that all mammals have the capacity to transmit very fast, even automatic emotional communications. This may be another neurophysiological basis for the transmission of emotions from person to person. We can even imagine some sort of evolving or nested relationship between phenomena like mass hysteria and unconscious contagion—where feelings and thoughts pass from person to person often undetected—and the capacity for empathy wherein connection becomes more conscious. The sharing of emotional essentials that happens when instinctive reactions are set off is part and parcel of the creation of metaphor and psychological experience. The imagination creates images and symbols that express these essentials in new and different ways. A potent image is potent precisely because it links our subjective emotional experience with the emotional and cognitive experience of others.

Those big images like dreams of totality that emerge to contain and restructure the threats posed by fragmentation and change are powerful markers of the moments when imagination gives form to the wilderness of experience. In the words of postmodern narrative theory, they are markers of the moments that the story is yielded up. For individuals, these images bespeak our own particular solutions which often take mythic form, like the search for the beloved other or its opposite, self-containment. For societies, they are the cultural paradigms that organize collective experience into meaningful wholes. And on top of our mammalian ability to transmit emotional signals rapidly, we can now transmit visual signals via the Internet, using sites such as Facebook and YouTube, that awaken those emotions and transmit them without even being physically present. Add the media's love of spectacle to the mix, and the sharing of essentials that can take place in contemporary life is perhaps unprecedented in human culture. We can sense that this is changing the way the game is played, maybe even changing the game itself.

The Call and Response

In 2008 people everywhere were saying, "He's the one"—but they weren't talking about the messiah of a triumphant second coming or about Neo, the reluctant millennial hero of *The Matrix*. This wasn't religion or science fiction—it was politics, and "the one" was a man who would become the forty-fourth president of the United States, Barack Obama. "Obama mania" was spreading through the world, bringing with it both a fresh and an age-old dream of hope and redemption. The old king had died—in the form of former president George W. Bush—and the new king appeared poised to preside over the twenty-first-century Camelot, the global cybervillage.

Our imagination works hard to fashion images and stories that contain us, especially during times of uncertainty in response to a need for reorganization. They appear in the right spot at the right moment—hitting the mark and penetrating into the heart of the matter. For as mythology and history have shown, there is a consistent and enduring call and response dynamic in the human imagination, a pattern of lost and found: the disappearance of a dream of totality is always followed by a search for what will restore unity—the return of Persephone and spring after the darkness of grief and winter, the risen and transfigured Christ, the next incarnation of the Dalai Lama, or a new societal paradigm like globalization.

This call and response dynamic seems to be part of how imagination works, and the dreams of totality that emerge do so either with a sense of unshakeable certainty, feeling completely and self-evidently right, or sometimes with a quieter grace. When old systems become reified or when they no longer hold our experience adequately, they start to break down. They come apart at the edges between order and disorder, at the places where weak links in our images of totality are starting to fray and give way. As we will see in what follows, all sorts of compelling imaginary figures and actual persons make an appearance in these openings. They personify the breakdown and reconstruction process, and they usually take the form of psychopomps who will lead us into new territory or tricksters who upset the established systems. Disenfranchised elements of individual and social life—what had been left out of the old order—transgress the boundaries set by the old dream, reconfiguring it and leading the way to what's next. Obama, for example, ignited and captured the transgressive boundary-breaking element in the collective imagination during the time preceding his first election in 2008—his ancestry was racially mixed, he was young, and he was a cosmopolitan and global citizen with a corresponding worldview—he had all the qualities of a leader for the new globalized world or, depending on your point of view, of the Antichrist heralding the end of an era.

When collective mind-shifts are taking place, we find ourselves in an interregnum of sorts, a vulnerable and dangerous period between one psychosocial reign and another, a period during which the values and structures that contained us are disappearing. When the symmetry of an established system begins to break down, it feels as if the givens of one's world have tilted, twisted, or fall apart. The tensions that are felt during the interregnum create further openings in the psyche as the boundaries between people and institutions become fluid and permeable, and in reaction also harden up. This is a situation that generates new unifying symbols and ideas and also presses for the regressive restoration of old forms.

We know that danger sets off instinctive responses such as fight or flight and fosters movements toward affiliation and bonding. We go to war to protect boundaries and causes, or we flee the scene entirely. We build and rebuild communities. We shut down or we open up, often both in turn. The dangers of the interregnum require being conscious and discriminating about the back and forth movements between progressive and regressive visions and paradigms all of which answer the call for reorganization. It's a special moment and a dangerous time, because the dreams of totality that emerge during an interregnum will create the molds and set the stage for the corresponding events and players that appear in reality, in the reality of our individual lives and on the world stage, as was the case with Palin and Obama.

Taking a close look at one person's situation—Carl Jung's breakdown and recovery and its correspondence with the collective turmoil of World War I—will make it clearer how the mythopoetic imagination weaves together the twin strands of distress and relief to fashion a dream of totality in response to the need for more inclusive containment. Jung had formally broken with Freud in 1912 over their significant differences about the function of symbolization. The two were unable to agree to disagree. As Jung (quoting Hamlet) famously wrote at the end of his last letter to Freud on January 6, 1913, "The rest is silence."[11] The break left Jung professionally alone in an atmosphere that was still hostile to psychoanalysis. In the autumn of 1913 while on a train trip in Switzerland, Jung had a vision that Europe was being engulfed in a catastrophic flood.

> In October [1913], while I was alone on a journey, I was suddenly seized by an overpowering vision: I saw a monstrous flood covering all the northern and low-lying lands between the North Sea and the Alps. When it came up to Switzerland I saw that the mountains grew higher and higher to protect

> our country. I realized that a frightful catastrophe was in progress. I saw the mighty yellow waves, the floating rubble of civilization, and the drowned bodies of uncounted thousands. Then the whole sea turned to blood. This vision lasted about one hour. I was perplexed and nauseated, and ashamed of my weakness.[12]

The vision was repeated a few weeks later.

> In the following winter I was standing at the window one night and looked North. I saw a blood-red glow, like the flicker of the sea from afar, stretched from East to West across the northern horizon. And at that time someone asked me what I thought about world events in the near future. I said that I had no thoughts, but saw blood, rivers of blood.[13]

Being a psychiatrist, Jung was afraid that he might be "hopelessly off" or, as he wrote to Mircea Eliade many years later, "doing a schizophrenia."[14] Dreams and visions continued to assail him. Increasingly worried about his sanity, but also wondering whether there was something else going on inside himself, Jung took action and decided to engage more directly with his dreams and visions. In the evenings after the day's work was done, he began inducing trance states and having conversations with the characters that emerged in his fantasies. Every night he wrote down everything that happened, all of which he later transcribed, illustrated, and set down more formally in his infamous Red Book, the record of his engagement with what he called "the spirit of the depths," with what was inexplicable and painful in himself, and with what was under the surface of collective life.[15] Almost half a century later Jung would write of this period, in his autobiography, "The material brought to light from the unconscious had, almost literally, struck me dumb."[16] At the time, compelled to press inward but seriously shaken, Jung resigned his position at the university, although he continued to see patients.

World War I broke out in August 1914, and Jung, relieved on his own behalf, became convinced that his visions of a sea of blood were not signaling an impending psychosis—at least not his. He came to the conclusion that unconscious processes in him had grasped the possibility of the oncoming war, that his visions were precognitive. Jung felt that "because I carried the war in me, I foresaw it," namely, that somehow there was a correspondence between his internal strife and the war in Europe.[17] He redoubled the exploration of his fantasies in order to understand the connection between his personal turmoil and the collective events engulfing Europe.

In the midst of this, Jung was called up to carry out his mandatory tour of duty in the Swiss military service. Stationed in Château-d'Œx, his duties as commandant were to take care of the British prisoners of war who had been captured by the Germans and interned there. It was at Château-d'Œx, while confronting the traumas of war—what we would presumably identify today as post-traumatic stress disorder—that Jung began drawing mandalas, sketching twenty-seven of them into his military notebooks. At the time he didn't know exactly what he was doing, only that it helped. It would be several years until Jung came in contact with sinologist Richard Wilhelm, translator of the *I Ching* and *The Secret of the Golden Flower*, who introduced Jung to the mandalas of the eastern tradition. At the end of his life, Jung wrote about his experience at Château-d'Œx in *Memories, Dreams, Reflections*:

> While I was there I sketched every morning in a notebook a small circular drawing, a mandala, which seemed to correspond to my inner situation at the time. With the help of these drawings I could observe my psychic transformations from day to day. Only gradually did I discover what the mandala really is: "Formation, Transformation, Eternal Mind's eternal recreation." . . . My mandalas were cryptograms on the state of myself delivered to me every day.[18]

Much of Jung's experience with the centering function of the mandala symbol would find its way into the Red Book, which became Jung's mythological diary, a testament to his personal cosmology and the state of his soul, and a commentary on the psychosocial situation of the Europe in which he lived. He showed the Red Book to friends and colleagues, and he encouraged his patients to embark on similar endeavors, but he never published it. After his death, the Red Book was tucked away in a Swiss bank vault. It was finally made public and published in 2009.

In the years immediately after Château-d'Œx, Jung wrote only two important published papers. This period of outward restraint ended with the publication of *Psychological Types* in 1921, in which he described the many different modalities—introversion, extraversion, thinking, intuition, feeling, sensation, and their combinations—through which people perceive the world, themselves, and others, as well as how we express these perceptions. The overarching point was that there are many roads to Rome, many subjective paths to an objective awareness of our shared psychology.[19] This was the same year in which Jung painted an unusual mandala in the Red Book, a great black serpent emerging almost explosively out of the night sky, its body weaving in and out of the arms of a luminous sixteen-pointed star (figure 1). An eight-pointed star sits at the center of the large one, and within that a four-pointed star inside a circle forms an even smaller nexus. In the lower right corner, Jung painted a man who looks like he's standing on a rooftop with his hands raised up to the great beast. The scene evokes an experience of intense light and creative energy at the core of darkness, a kind of nonlocal "big bang" of psychic energy.

The picture is cryptically referred to in a section of the Red Book called "The Gift of Magic." Jung's annotation about it reads: "The gifts of darkness are full of riddles. The way is open to whomever can continue in spite of the riddles. Submit to the riddles and the thoroughly incomprehensible. There are dizzying bridges over the eternally deep abyss. But follow the riddles."[20] The painting itself may be an answer to one of those riddles, the one that Jung was trying to solve within himself: How can there be light at the core of darkness (his breakdown; the war)? And how does submitting to darkness yield up this light, a combustion and release of energy that Jung likened to the "gift of magic"?

Jung's experience of personal turmoil and the war in Europe were both interregnum periods followed by radical reorganization. Before his breakdown, Jung was a successful (if somewhat ambivalent) dragon-slaying hero of his time, doing battle with the monsters of the unconscious, or attempting a Faustian bargain and appropriating those monsters in the service of ego enhancement. That adaptation had begun to fail him—the old king (including Freud) had failed—and the spirit of the depths took over. As Jung wrote of this experience in the Red Book, "the God becomes sick if he oversteps the height of the zenith. That is why the spirit of the depths took me when the spirit of this time had led me to the summit."[21] In the serpent mandala, which is near the end of the Red Book, there is something new afoot, even a reversal of the traditional serpent-hero motif found in myth and fairy tales. Instead of a serpent being slain by a hero, Jung painted a scene of submission, the little man seeming to give himself over to the dynamics of psychic energy and imagination, to what was called

Figure 1: Folio #129 from C. G. Jung, *The Red Book: Liber Novus*.

in Jung's day the "serpent power"—the seemingly magical property that the imagination has to renew and transform the psyche.[22] This may have been personified by the conjunction of the black serpent and the light. It is tempting to speculate that Jung experienced what Wolfgang Giegerich has described as "releasing ourselves, without logical safety nets, into the freshness and newness of each present moment and into the atomic subjectivity of ourselves—in order to discover in it, only in it, our true universal humanness."[23]

A large part of what Jung experienced during the Red Book years was the way that the "atomic subjectivity" of himself met the outer world in a startling congruence that he would later call synchronicity. Jung had read William James's *Varieties of Religious Experience* very carefully and was taken with James's notion of psychic fields. Always interested in the scientific developments of his time, Jung had also met with Einstein and was familiar with the theory of special relativity. It was Einstein, he later remarked, who had started him thinking about the relativity of time and space in regard to psychological life and about how these might be psychically conditioned.[24] Revelations about quantum mechanics were also in the air; Heisenberg's work with uncertainty and the conditionality of reality vis-à-vis the observer was not far off. And most striking, the atomic aspect of the serpent mandala may have anticipated the collaboration that would start nine years later between Jung and Wolfgang Pauli, the theoretical physicist whose work on spin theory in quantum mechanics earned him a Nobel prize. Although Jung was not Pauli's analyst, he analyzed 1,300 of Pauli's dreams, and they worked together on the idea of synchronicity and the nonlocality of psychic energy.[25] A model of the psyche that featured the interconnectedness of matter and psyche was eventually born, and Jung had fashioned a new dream of totality that seemed to contain his experience of himself and of the world he lived in. At this point he returned to psychological equilibrium, and by 1930 he stopped working on the Red Book.

Closing Down and Opening Up

As we have seen, dreaming of totality creates new connections between things and heals rifts, replacing those rifts with a more functionally intact system, often with a larger scope of awareness than was available previously, as was the case with Jung's Red Book mandalas and the new theories of synchronicity and the nonlocality of psychic energy. But that is not always how a dream of totality works. Other aspects of Jung and

Pauli's collaboration, for example, tell a different story. According to Jung, one of the culminations in the unconscious material of Pauli's that Jung analyzed was Pauli's vision of a grand and complex world clock. This world clock had a mathematical point at its center and was an image, Jung wrote, "of the most sublime harmony . . . that made a deep and lasting impression on the dreamer," and by which "the center and its periphery represent the totality of the psyche and consequently the self."[26] The vision was, in Jung's words, "a turning point in the patient's psychological development. It was what one would call—in the language of religion—a conversion."[27] Jung goes on to say that

> if you sum up what people tell you about these experiences, you can formulate it this way: They came to themselves, they could accept themselves, they were able to become reconciled to themselves, and thus were reconciled to adverse circumstances and events. This is almost like what used to be expressed by saying: He has made his peace with God.[28]

But in this case, Jung was wrong. Not long after he had the vision of the world clock, the problems for which Pauli initially sought treatment returned. He started drinking again, and his troubles with relationships continued, as did his paranoia. How was it that a vision of totality like Pauli's world clock did not have a lasting or containing effect on the difficulties he experienced? One possibility is that the vision was signaling not acceptance or reconciliation as Jung thought, but rather a closing down of engagement, an avoidance of dynamic entanglement with what was outside the clock's periphery (in quantum theory entanglement is the phenomenon of particles remaining responsive to one another even after they have separated). Jung had been avidly interested in the purity of Pauli's dreams, and he had sent Pauli to a novice analyst for treatment imagining that in doing so, the analysis would not interfere too much with the unfolding of Pauli's unconscious material. Was this move on Jung's part also an avoidance of engagement with what Jung referred to in Pauli's case as "the chaos of the personal psyche and its dramatic entanglements"?[29] Together, they may have created an exclusionary magic circle around themselves that protected them both from engaging with one another emotionally. It is to this aspect of dreams of totality that we turn now.

Magic Circles

Creatures of the deepest imagination, sublime and monstrous, revolutionary and reactionary, dreams of totality function as a birthing ground for new conceptions of cosmos, society, and self, but when the process becomes reified or is co-opted, a dream of totality becomes a killing field, a coercive system of exclusion and suppression, closing off and prohibiting new developments. A classic and extremely destructive example of this was the Nazi dream of unification and purity. This dream of totality closed the weak links in the national identity of a Germany fractured and weakened after World War I. Nazism was fundamentalist, even millenarian—Hitler was famously enamored with the fantasy of a thousand-year Reich and with the Götterdämmerung, the mythical twilight of the gods when massive apocalyptic destruction would run rampant at the end of the world. The Nazi dream functioned to exclude and scapegoat, invoking inviolate myths and rituals, becoming threatening in itself and constituting its own danger and distress. It's worth noting that Jung didn't see this coming either. Although his enchantment with the magic circle of National Socialism wore off completely when its diabolical aspects rose unmistakably to the foreground, Jung's failure to engage quickly and effectively against the ensuing Nazism has had lasting and bitter consequences for psychoanalysis.[30]

We can get a better understanding of the opening up and closing off effects of dreams of totality by looking at the alpha and omega images of wholeness: the magic circle and its sophisticated cousin, the mandala. A magic circle was originally a round area marked out physically to contain energy and provide protection for the purposes of ritual magic. Both individuals and cultures draw the equivalent of magic circles around themselves to protect their integrity and homogeneity from intrusion and contamination. These can take the forms of designated sacred spaces, defended national borders, inner circles of like-minded people, even cases of rigid self-identity. No matter what the form or specific function, magic circles protect what is within their borders and exclude what's felt to be disturbing or unwanted. They are one of humankind's oldest ritual symbols, familiar to us as ancient standing stones like those shown in figure 2, a circle in Scotland built circa 2700 BC, which may have marked the entrance to a burial cairn or functioned as an astronomical calendar. The form repeats itself in many cultures—figure 3 shows the Mummy

Figure 2: The Callanish Stones, Isle of Lewis, Scotland.

Figure 3: Mummy Cave, Canyon de Chelly, Arizona, USA.

Figure 4: Rotating Magic Circle, from Tiphareth Designs, by Julianus Nightfire, a virtual reality product from Second Life Marketplace, 2010.

Cave, an ancient Pueblo village of ceremonial rooms in Canyon de Chelly, Arizona, within the Navajo Nation. Echoing into contemporary culture, figure 4 shows a magic circle available from the marketplace for use on a virtual reality website called Second Life.

The psychology of the magic circle state of mind is characterized by totems and taboos, by dos and don'ts, by omnipotence and a sense of magical connection to truth, by creative introversion, and often by fear and paranoia about what lies outside the circle. Within its boundary everything is felt to be whole and connected, timeless and held together by the liminal magic of the circle. What lies outside the circle is profane, threatening, and chaotic.

The magic circle is also a metaphor that describes the way individuals and groups begin to experience a stable center of identity and agency. It is psychologically and culturally primitive—in the sense of immature—because in its isolation it often mistakes itself for the whole. To go back, for example, to the early days of psychoanalysis, in *The Secret Ring: Freud's Inner Circle and the Politics of Psychoanalysis* Phyllis Grosskurth brings to life the cast of characters in Sigmund Freud's secret committee, a committee formed to "safeguard" Freudian thought, one aspect of which was to monitor Jung. From Freud's point of view, Jung—having been Freud's chosen heir apparent—had broken ties with his loving father in a series of intense and bitter betrayals. In response to Jung's defection, Ernest Jones, a loyal Freudian, proposed that a secret committee be formed as a guard around Freud. Freud, in a letter dated August 1, 1912, responded:

> What took hold of my imagination immediately is your idea of a secret council composed of the best and most trustworthy among our men to take care of the further development of and defend the cause against personalities and accidents when I am no more.[31]

In 1913, as Grosskurth tells us,

> the five members of the Secret Committee—Jones, Ferenczi, Abraham, Rank, and Sachs—met in Vienna. There they were bound together by their secrecy against the world, their faith in Freud's theory, and their personal devotion to the leader. Freud told Ferenczi he was very happy with his "adopted children" [*angenommene Kinder*].[32]

To seal the bond, the "adopted children" received antique intaglios from Freud, which they had mounted onto gold rings. Freud's was engraved with the head of Zeus. The intaglios, which were traditionally used as seals on contracts, now bound the secret committee together in a ring of eternal fidelity to their leader and his cause. It's not clear whether Jung actually suspected that a secret committee was forming, but the emotional climate would surely have added a sense of urgency to the distress he began feeling in 1913. Everything was coming apart, and Jung began creating a magic circle of his own. He withdrew into his fantasy life, found refuge and renewal in the symbol of the mandala, and began working toward new therapeutic models and methods, all of which was chronicled in the Red Book, a magic circle in its own right.

All the charismatic psychoanalysts—even more recent thinkers like Heinz Kohut and Jacques Lacan, who explicitly stressed the idea of multiplicity and many selves—ended up with followers and disciples whether they wanted them or not. One aspect of such discipleships is a tendency to attempt to stop time dead in its tracks and keep what has been revealed within the magic circle of the beloved leader. This is a malignant situation, but also an archetypal one, a creation myth of sorts, albeit a violent one. Figure 5 is a painting by Rubens known as *Saturn Devouring His Son*. The mythology behind it is that the Titan Kronos (Saturn), fearing that one of his children would overthrow him, ate each one of them moments after they were born. His wife finally hid the sixth child—Zeus—giving Kronos a stone wrapped in swaddling to eat instead. Zeus thrived in his hiding place on Crete, soon returning to overthrow his father as foretold, by making Kronos so violently ill that he threw up Zeus's brothers and sisters, including Hades, Poseidon, Demeter, and Hera. Thus the great Olympians were vomited into being.

As we will see in what follows, there is a pattern in the psyche whereby what has been disenfranchised or is just emerging gets swallowed back and then violently disgorged when too much has been excluded and forbidden. Or in a variation of this theme, what is threatening may seem to be benignly "eaten," that is, assimilated or integrated—but nevertheless stuffed into a magic circle in a totalizing way. The fundamentalist position pictured by this devouring pattern is never free from violence because it always has to keep that which is other out of sight, creating an uneasy and thwarted situation that is rarely free of impending destruction. This dynamic forms the backstory of many a revolution.

In addition to imagery that defines space and place as a magic circle, the sensibility of the magic circle state of mind is also described by temporal metaphors, for example, by the timeless myth of eternal return. As Mircea Eliade argued in *The Myth of the Eternal Return*, in this fantasy of totality there is no progressing toward anything new or more inclusive, nowhere to move on to. Instead, the dominant imagery is of an ebb and flow of eternal archetypes that recur cyclically. On a grand scale, for example, conceived and lived within the worldview that "as above, so below," the great imperial cosmologies of the ancient world imagined that there were intricate connections between earthly life and the divine stage stitched together by myriad correspondences which rendered social constructions that were complete, timeless, and sacred in their order. Their preeminent cities, such as Babylon, Delphi, Jerusalem, and Borobudur (figure 6), all reflected fantasies not only about sacred space, but also about sacred time and creation, deriving their character from participating in the eternal unity of a divine world. Their sacred temples, often organized around an extraordinary natural feature like a mountain, a spring, or a huge rock, were imagined as being the center of the whole world, the place

Figure 5: *Saturn Devouring His Son,* by Peter Paul Rubens (1636), oil on canvas, Museo del Prado, Madrid.

where heaven, hell, and earth came together—a world navel or axis mundi. Every consecrated place coincided in space and also in time with the divine center of the world—timeless and outside of history.

Figure 6: Borobudur, Java, Indonesia.

Moving alongside those great imperial cosmologies were great cosmic cycles of time and history, such as the Mahā-Yuga (4.32 million years) imagined in Indian mythology. Or, moving much faster, the Western astrological precession of the equinoxes, which could take 26,000 years to complete, with each smaller astrological age lasting about 2,200 years and expressing its own character—Aquarius, the water-bearer (which we're approaching in contemporary time), for example, having a different spirit than Pisces, the fishes, which presided over the Christian era. We are presumably no longer "in the water" awaiting redemption; we now carry the water ourselves. While there are dangerous, even revolutionary dawns and twilights, interregnums that connect the various ages together, in the magic circle of eternal return there is no notion of meaninglessness, nothing absurd or annihilating happens, there is no blind suffering or capricious fate.[33] Everything fits into a system of regeneration and repetition; there is truly nothing new under the sun.

Psychological and emotional life reflects this magic circle of cyclical time and periodic renewal when we long to "get back to basics," "come home," or feel that we cycle contentedly (or fatally) around fixed determinants and themes of our particular givens and circumstances. This can become quite romanticized, as depicted in Rousseau's last painting, *The Dream* (figure 7). Here, the simplicity of primitive nature and of (natural) woman are idealized and reflected in a dream of totality that gripped the collective imagination at the turn of the twentieth century, a century in which the secrets of the natural world were being revealed and also exploited in ways unimaginable before. In regard to this, it's interesting to note the huge success, at the turn of the twenty-first century, of *Avatar*, a film that extols the virtues of a humanoid species in perfect tune with nature. Both nostalgic and futuristic, *Avatar*, like *The Dream*, also looks backward to an idealized tribal life for its message of hope and salvation but projects this longing for essentials into a technological future. In tandem with our utopian projections onto cyberspace and the virtual global village, there is a corresponding nostalgia for a simple and magical solution to the uncertainty and complexity of living.

Figure 7: *The Dream,* by Henri Rousseau (1910), oil on canvas, Museum of Modern Art, New York.

This dynamic can be refreshing if cured with grains of salt, but misleading and childish in the worst sense if it becomes entrenched and sacralized. It is part of our wise ancestor mythology and fantasies and of our dreams of a perfect ecology and is bound up with our symbolization of death and renewal. For example, figure 8 shows two wooden figures, a couple from the Baule people in Cote d'Ivoire, Africa. Diviners used these figures to bring the ancestor spirits out of the bush and into the village. According to custom, the ancestor spirits of a village group were flattered and attracted to the idealized figures and came to inhabit them. Thus invested with power, the figures became oracles that could be consulted for their ancestral wisdom. "From a Baule perspective," writes Alisa LaGamma, "human experience evolves out of and remains inextricably tied to the ancestral world (*blolo*)—referred to as 'the village of truth.'"[34] This village of truth includes the present extended generation of villagers, the next generation not born yet, and up to five generations of ancestors. The oldest of these ancestors merges with the forces of nature, spirits, and the gods.

In psychological terms this can be likened to an unfolding field of psychological relationships between generations and with the land, a kind of "Great Family Unconscious," linking village and psychological life both backward and forward in time.[35] In the psychology of the village of truth, going forward always means going backward as well. It's still a relatively closed systems approach, and we find a variant of it in models of family therapy that make reference to intergenerational dynamics. It's also in the background of many depth psychologies, in their assumption that childhood fantasies and psychoanalytic fantasies about childhood are not just concerned with recovering lost memories or inner children but with finding origination and new beginnings in the "older generation," in imagination—an ancestral type of thinking informed less by actual predecessors and more by our shared creative imagination. Many psychologists work with dreams in therapy because dreams provide a way to consult with this archetypal ancestry of mythopoetic thinking, which in turn allows us to dream our story forward into the next generation, into the next chapters of life.

This sharing of essentials continues to inform our postmodern dreams of a world community, or what Robert Lifton, in *The Protean Self*, called "a psychological field that expands toward species consciousness."[36] In this hyper-inclusive dream of totality, rather than the ancestors blending with

Figure 8: *Figures for a Trance Diviner: Couple*, Baule, Cote d'Ivoire (19th-20th century), wood, pigments, bead, and iron, Metropolitan Museum of Art, New York.

the spirits of nature and the gods to maintain continuity of experience, the movement goes the other way into the future—toward those who haven't existed yet or who do exist now but in other places on the planet. Or put another way, in the imagery of a species self, the ancestor souls are and will be everywhere, almost a high state of mystical oneness, but this time brought about by twenty-first-century communications technology.

It is seductive to speculate with Lifton that "only the unbound imagination can press toward a species mentality" and that it will do so by "transcending time and space—to contain simultaneous elements of highly diverse cultural places."[37] This is not to say that such a thing won't happen, but it is to say that the image of a species self can also function emotionally and psychologically like a magic circle, excluding what doesn't fit into its elevated picture, acting as a hedge against dissociation and chaos or defending against the more troubling aspects of transcending time and space. Much the same can be said about our more simplistic conceptions of ecology, in which the inevitable trash of human life is either pathologized and banished or romanticized into a golden vision of life-giving compost. But of course, our trash is also just garbage and will be everywhere—there is no longer an "out" where it can be put nor a magical recycling plant by the name of Eternal Return.

Breaking Up the Magic Circle

The moment humanity entered the scene as an active subject was (and still is) imagined as a precarious and unhappy state of affairs, and the former gods who presided over the magic circle are usually hostile to this decisive turn. This conflict, for example, occurred in earnest in Genesis between the Lord of paradise and humanity. Adam and Eve wanted a taste of knowledge and got it—by being expelled from the paradisiacal totality of the Garden of Eden and falling into the new myth of sin and redemption. Figure 9, a painting by Giovanni di Paolo (ca. 1445) called *The Creation of the World and the Expulsion from Paradise*, poignantly depicts the tension and grief we feel when one dream of totality collides with the beginning of another. The Lord is pictured rolling the world in the form of a zodiacal wheel right at the unhappy couple, who are still surrounded—but not for long—by the perfect four rivers and seven trees of the Garden of Eden. As humanity entered into its own imagination as an active player, the magic circle of eternal return was broken by our awareness of the possibility of stark and single acts of destruction—acts that seemingly would never be repeated again.

Figure 9: *The Creation of the World and the Expulsion from Paradise*, by Giovanni di Paolo (ca. 1445), tempera and gold on wood, Metropolitan Museum of Art, New York.

The terrifying possibility of the finality of events or human history entered our imagination fully blown as the image of apocalypse and end-time fantasies of destruction, timeless epiphany, or endless darkness. These apocalyptic fantasies actually come around periodically, echoed in the numerous end-time fantasies that still abound in contemporary life: the lackluster millennial Y2K fantasy, the always imminent arrival of Judgment Day, the end of the Mayan calendar in 2012, nuclear holocaust, even the more garish visions of a global climate meltdown. In these dreams of totality, sometimes intimations of rebirth peek through, sometimes it's just the bitter end, and sometimes we leave the planet, bound for heaven via the Rapture, as humorously depicted in figure 10. Some of us have even evacuated planet Earth, heading out, albeit dead, to a better world, hoping to join the ranks of more evolved ancient astronauts.[38] In any event, life as it was known before apocalypse comes to an end.

Figure 10: *Down at the Rapture with George* (artist unknown), www.crutchoftheweak.com.

One way to sum up for a moment before following the breakup of the magic circle is to note a pattern in psychological organization. First, the myth of eternal return is centered on the experience of eternal being, the myth of history on that of becoming; the former is rooted in the "paradise of archetypes," the latter in the "fall" of humanity into the myth of history and death.[39] Second, these two dreams of totality often balance one another, and when one takes hold of the collective imagination, it is not too long before the other appears. Definitive and limiting historical moments are usually followed by a resurgence of eternal archetypal gestures and images, something to keep in mind when we consider the paradisiacal attributions given to our own regnant dreams of totality: globalization, cyberspace, and a green world. This question is taken up in detail in part III, which explores the definitive moments—such as breaking the genetic code and the leap in locality made possible by computer processing and communication technology—that are being responded to by images of wholeness and integration.

Though we may now think about what is called, variously, God (Christianity), the Single One (Mayans), Brahman (Hinduism), the Most High (Judaism), the One God (Islam), or Tao (China) in different terms, such as the principle of self-organization attributed to the cosmos or the Web or emergent phenomena in nature and even of consciousness, humanity's dreams of totality do not disappear without a trace. Even the ancients envisioned the magic circle as eventually separating into delimited parts—often four or five parts—its timeless sovereignty giving way to discrete subjects and objects, to particular spaces and places, and into the history of particular times. Another way to describe this is that the unity of the One, what the ancients called the *unus mundus*, the imaginal and timeless "one world," breaks up and becomes what we experience as reality.

Many of the world-creating deities in the West were imagined as having manifested creation by portioning themselves into four spaces, four directions, or four elements. The Native American medicine wheel of the Great Spirit has four cardinal directions. The four evangelists—the ox, the lion, the eagle, and the angel—mirrored the four fixed signs of the zodiac—Taurus, Leo, Scorpio, and Aquarius—forming a specifically European square. The magic circle of origination often becomes squared, and this provides for another form of stability, one that acknowledges the facts and experience of particularities as a condition of potentiality becomes one of actuality. A startling example of this foundational image of totality—the One manifesting as a fourfold structure—finds reverberation in the modern discovery of the structure of DNA: that all animate life from a blade of grass to a human being is built from the same four components of genetic material. This fourfold matrix seems to close a circle in the imagination, providing as it does an uncanny echo of the fact that across many cultures and throughout human history the quaternity has been a universal symbol of the parts, qualities, and aspects of the "One" world-creating deity. As the old saying still goes (mythopoetically speaking), "God is a circle whose center is everywhere and whose circumference is nowhere."

This kind of number magic, when the One divides into symmetrical parts, is a signal characteristic of many older dreams of totality. Pythagoras had his theory of divine numbers, the number one, for example, being the source and the unity that everything arises from, and Philo equated the four rivers of Paradise with the four cardinal virtues: wisdom, courage, moderation, and justice.[40] Galileo opined that numbers were the speech of God; Pascal and Leibniz also heard God speaking in mathematics. We can also appreciate the connection between numbers and totality in the beauty and ideal wholeness of the human body as portrayed by da Vinci in *Vitruvian Man* (figure 11). Da Vinci was scrupulous in his description of the dimensions of the human body as conforming to both the square and the circle: the ideal arm span being equal to one's height formed a square, with a circle drawn around the square when the legs are parted. The center of the circle is at the navel, the connection to origination.

Although our ideas about the universe and ourselves have expanded from a geocentric magic circle to a more complex heliocentric world into a much less symmetrical cosmocentric model, numbers still resonate in our imaginations as expressions of symmetry, patterns, and fantasies about wholeness. This becomes especially apparent in storytelling, in which numbers symbolize ways in which we experience the creation of new worlds and experience. In fairy tales, for example, "once upon a time" suggests that first there was a one—a person, a place, or a problem, perhaps a bankrupt social institution like a kingdom.[41] Then an enemy or a conflict appears or the protagonist's longed-for romantic other shimmers just out of reach—as the two. The ensuing drama between the two becomes the third, and as the story develops there's also often a repetition of three—something happens three times, three wishes are granted, or the protagonist is given three chances. Three conveys a dynamic sense of process or expresses the dialectical third, as in "Goldilocks and the Three Bears," where the necessities sought were too small, then too big, and then just right. Threeness is a condition much less stable than the standoff of two or the solidity of four or five. As many fairy tales come to a close, the dramatic movement of three resolves into the fourth—the game ends, the lover or the treasure is found, or a solution to the problem is fashioned. The initial situation has developed, and the one is no longer where one was at the beginning; the ground map has changed, one's vision is expanded.

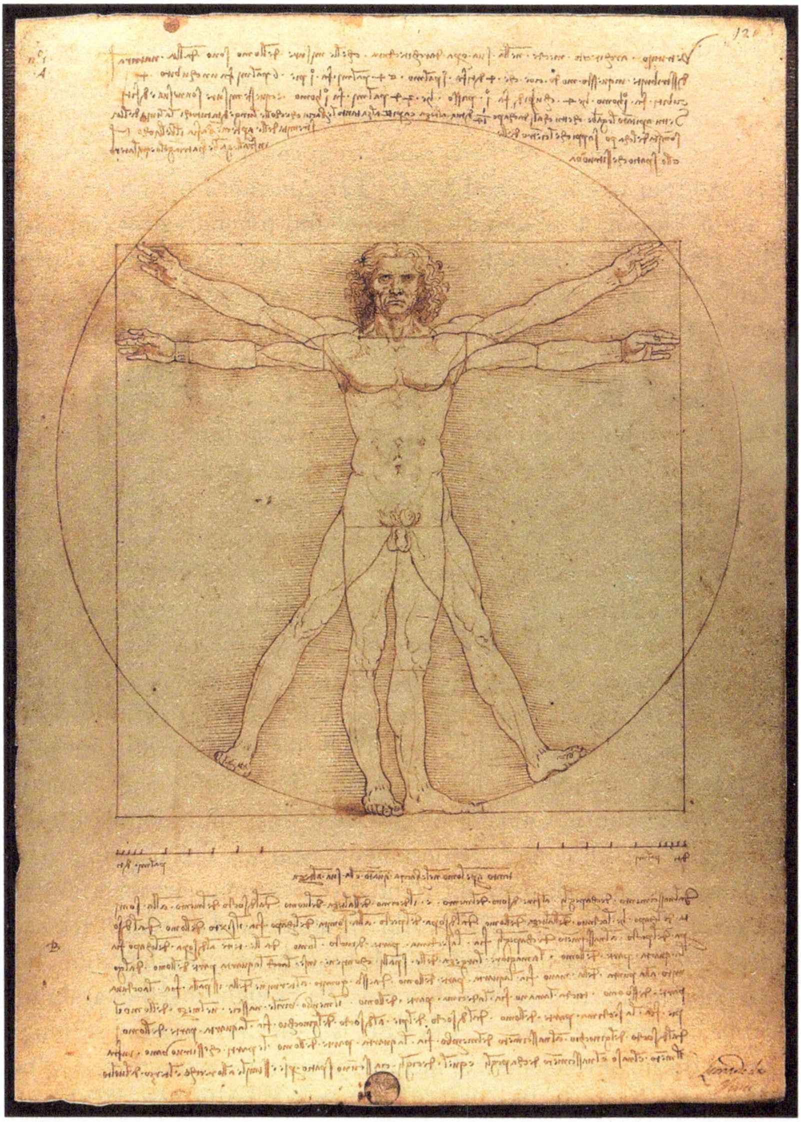

Figure 11: *Vitruvian Man*, by Leonardo da Vinci (ca. 1492), pen and ink on paper, Gallerie dell'Accademia, Venice.

The variations of number magic are endless. The same movement from one to four that we find in fairy tales was expressed long ago in a medieval spiritual precept attributed to a third-century alchemist, Maria Prophetissa: "One becomes two, two becomes three, and out of the third comes the one as the fourth."[42] Other numbers that appear in myths and stories, like the number seven (seven days of creation) and twelve (twelve houses of the zodiac) are formed from operations on three and four (3 + 4 = 7 and 3 x 4 = 12). Another rotation on this is found in Taoism, although the spiritual and psychological emphasis is different—the twoness of opposites (yin/yang) is imagined as being in harmony, not conflict, because each contains the seed of the other within itself. The harmony of the opposites is itself the third, and there is also a quaternity of four forming a one, which is the Tao, the way itself. What's missing for Westerners is the experience of conflict that usually gets us there. But no matter how it's derived, as Christopher Booker writes in *The Seven Basic Plots: Why We Tell Stories*, the fourth is often symbolic of the ability to "see whole."[43]

To sum up for a moment before we leave magic circles behind: numeric patterns often describe how initial states of undifferentiated unity imagined as magic circles divide and then come back together in a new form—as a unity comprised of fours, for example, or as a fourth—or as in the Taoist model, where unity differentiates by holding opposites within itself. In psychological terms, the recognition of the twos and threes of life, of particularities and limits, of conflict and of the need to integrate projections, to accept the reality of the other, both within oneself and in the reality of another person or situation does indeed constitute a considerable psychological achievement. And we also imagine these particularities, once they are differentiated, becoming reunited into an integrated whole. Although, the worlds of subject and object, what is self and what is other, are necessarily divided for the sake of adaptation, the old number magic tells us that they must be brought together again for the sake of health. Health, in this case, is a dream of totality in Jung's sense—a dream of wholeness, of inclusivity and interconnection, an echo of the ancient sensibility that all things are really one. With this formulation, we approach the omega image of totality, the mandala, in which particularities are both fully differentiated and imagined as belonging together. The mandala encompasses and protects totality like a magic circle; it is also, however, an image that unites warring conflicts and fragments of experience into a living whole.

Mandalas

The mandala is an iconic image of totality because it holds a differentiated wholeness within itself, seeing whole and setting things in motion according to the whole. Figures 1, 11, 12, 14, 15, 18, 25, 26, and 27 all have mandala-like features. The center of the mandala, traditionally imagined as the Tao, the palace, the rose, the lotus, the labyrinth, or the Way, expands into the shape of the universe and contracts into a still point of unity. Being "that which encircles a center," a mandala expresses the totality of center and periphery, the interconnections between cosmos, human beings, and Buddha Mind, the many contained in the one. When viewed in three dimensions, a mandala often has the form of a temple or palace, with a vertical axis mundi at its center. The axis of a mandala has also been imaged as being a natural feature, for example, the mythical Mount Meru over which Indra's net hangs or the spinal canal that centers the human body, as shown in figure 12.

As well as being a stable structure symbolizing differentiated wholeness, the mandala symbolizes the movement *toward* integration. Employing numbers and geometric forms in its construction, mandalas are used in many spiritual traditions as a visual aid for trance induction to promote an experience of wholeness—an experience of the simultaneity of evolution and dissolution, repose and tension, rest and motion. Mandalas can also be a pictogram of the soul's journey from the periphery of life's experience into a center of understanding. This sensibility of totality as a process has also been imagined in circular arcs of ascent and descent, as the ascending and descending paths of Kundalini yoga in Tantric and Taoist ritual practices, for example. Psychophysical energy is imagined as a sleeping serpent coiled up at the base of the spine, which when awakened winds its way up the spine, opening up various energy centers in the body and mind called chakras as it goes, rising finally to the top of the head. Once the kundalini serpent reaches the crown chakra, the point of universal awareness, it goes back down the spinal canal to complete the circle. In psychological terms, the circle made by these process-oriented mandalas depicts the movement of psychic energy from concrete embodiment to imaginal abstraction and back around again, in a process that encourages an experience of wholeness.

This motif is also hinted at in figure 13, *Jacob's Ladder* by William Blake, which depicts figures ascending and descending to and from the

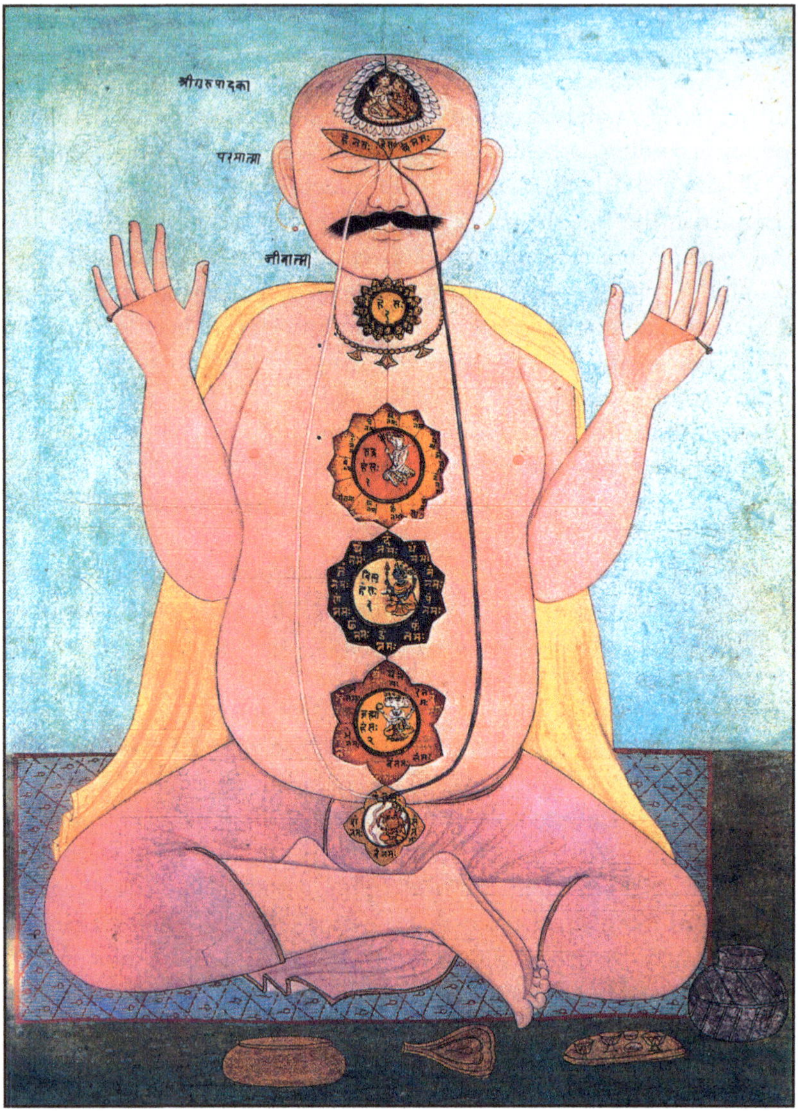

52   DREAMS OF TOTALITY

Figure 12: *The Chakras of the Subtle Body*, by Kangra (ca. 1820), gouache, heightened with gold, on paper, in the collection of Sven Gahlin, London.

sun. This up-and-down movement to the heavens and back to earth has been referred to in many wisdom traditions as "spiritualizing matter and materializing spirit." What this means is investing the everyday world, including ourselves, with a sensibility of the sacred and eternal (spiritualizing matter)—not in order to transcend it, but to disidentify from the idea that it is solely material and thus completely open to manipulation. The downward arc (materializing spirit) symbolizes the

Figure 13: *Jacob's Ladder* or *Jacob's Dream*, by William Blake, a figure in the bible (Genesis 28:12) painted for Thomas Butts, the British Museum, London.

embodied and actual living of what's felt to be sacred and eternal in the here-and-now of our experience—giving it concrete form, not leaving it stranded in a transcendent dimension. The imagination sees psychic energy as going both ways, although this tension can be hard to hold, and we often privilege one side over another. Science, for example, privileges the downward arc, while religion usually stresses the upward one.

We have seen that there is a tension in the image of totality between opening up and closing off, between inclusion and exclusion, between timelessness and historical time, between structure and stability as opposed to process and movement. Even though an image of totality like a mandala is often pictured as a stable, even preexisting condition of oneness, totality is never actually at rest for long. It's also a moving process, in which being on the path toward totality—the movement toward ever-increasing integration—is the goal. Even the mandala, that still point in a turning world, is meant to be navigated, to be moved through in the same way one would walk through a palace or through a labyrinth. It is even meant to be destroyed and created anew, as is enacted, for example, in a Tibetan Buddhist ritual during which an elaborate and large mandala that takes several weeks to make out of colored grains of sand is simply swept away when it is complete, and the sand poured into a river.

The One and the Many

The Tibetan Buddhist ritual of the sand mandala also expresses our experience of wholeness always breaking apart into smaller and smaller bits, disappearing into the flow of life, or multiplying into a plurality that is also one. The third image of totality we will look at, the "One and the Many," was the great enigma expressed by ancient Greek formulas like the golden ratio and the Golden Mean and found in the hermetic traditions of the Renaissance, and it resonates soundly in our contemporary psyches. The idea is that in the multiplicity of the many, a totality can be found, and that there's also a plurality in the oneness of totality. Totality shows up in the multiplicity of its own images, and conversely totality yields to an experience of multiplicity, for example, as the many faces of god. As we will see in what follows, unlike the story of the Tower of Babel, which tells of a disintegration into incoherence and chaos, the dream of the one and the many is a movement outward and into the world, the experience of various and multiple iterations that partake of a whole.

WOMB AND TOMB: OPENING AND CLOSING

In the dream of the one and the many, the depictions of totality tend to be "bigger than big, and smaller than small"—very large and also very small worlds—a motif hidden in our contemporary conceptions of an infinitely expanding universe and in the tiny little microcosms that have been opened up by electron microscopy and subatomic particle physics. The iconic image of Indra's net mentioned in the introduction—an infinite web of nested mirroring jewels—finds an echo in our huge modern communications networks and also in the large and tiny worlds of fractal geometry. Figure 14 is a high-resolution image of broccoli, a vegetable that has a fractal structure. Fractals are shapes that can be split up indefinitely, each part of which is a smaller-sized copy of the whole—a property called self-similarity. Many natural systems display the self-similarity and scale-free properties of fractals—snowflakes, coastlines, mountain ranges, clouds, and blood vessels approximate fractals in their structure and in their behavior. Fractals reproduce by a form of feedback known as iteration, and scale-free networks like these appear to be self-organizing.

It seems that the totality of the one and the many is often expressed poetically in both directions: as the many from the one, and the one from

Figure 14: Romanesco broccoli fractals (photograph taken with a Canon D60 camera and 28-135 mm lenses).

the many. In the first direction, the same substance or idea manifests in a variety of ways that are similar to and yet different from the original unity. Figure 15 shows a contemporary Mexican Huichol yarn painting by Jose Benitez Sanchez depicting the myth of the dismemberment of Watakame. According to interpreter Juan Negrin, Watakame was the prototypical survivor of the Flood, the primordial male ancestor, and the first cultivator. Following the guidelines set by the oracular Great-Grandmother, when Watakame died the various parts of his body were scattered over the land. They grew into different plants and vegetables, thus laying the basis for human life.

Figure 15: *Dismemberment of Watakame*, by Jose Benitez Sanchez (1973), yarn painting with wood, beeswax, and wool yarn, Juan Negrin and Wixarika Research Center, Mexico.

In a stunning juxtaposition to this mythologem, we find the motif of one and the many mirrored by the discovery of stem cell processes— so vigorously championed as a panacea and so strongly resisted as malevolent—in which the many literally arise from the one. Figure 16 is a fluorescent microscopy image of hundreds of human embryonic stem cells in various stages of differentiation into neurons. Stem cells are capable of regenerating tissue over a lifetime. Some are self-renewing and unipotent; they can undergo numerous cycles of cell division but remain undifferentiated, like magic circles. Some stem cells are pluripotent; they can differentiate into specialized cell types like neurons. A human embryonic stem cell (from an embryo that is four to five days old) is pluripotent—it can develop into any of the more than two hundred cell types in the human body. The red cells in the photograph have become neurons, while the green ones are still precursors of nerve cells (the yellow is an imaging artifact that results when cells in both stages overlap).

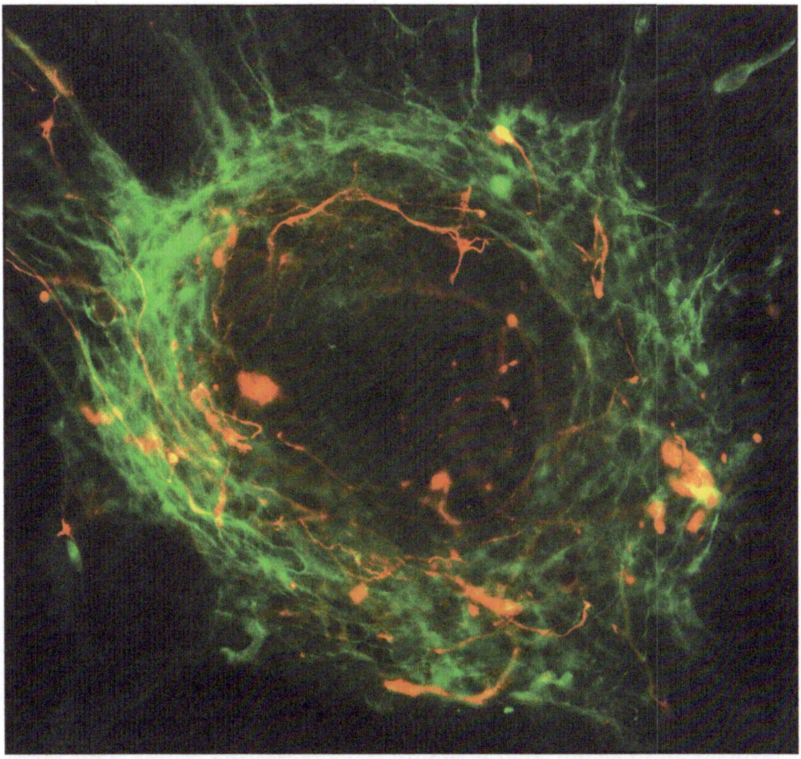

Figure 16: Human embryonic stem cells, from the laboratory of Guoping Fan, California Institute of Regenerative Medicine, University of California, Los Angeles.

It's worth pausing for a moment to note that both Watakame and Kronos (figure 5) are ancestor figures, both are fertility gods (Kronos's sickle is also a harvesting scythe), and agriculture falls under both their domains. Yet the underlying attitudes toward death and composting—how what's new does or doesn't get built from the bones of the old—are quite different. In comparing the two, we can see the motif of the one and the many expressed in different directions: as the many into the one, and the one from the many. Kronos dismembers new life and tries to stuff it into what already exists, or, viewed more benignly, death and time really do conquer all. Creation mythology is portrayed here as a fight for life against stagnation. In the second version of the one and the many, the ancestor figure gives birth to the many possibilities of the future. With Watakame, the stress is on the new beginning, on the dismembering of the ancestor in service to new life, and on the composting process. This is ancestry as part of creation mythology via inheritance. The first start dies, and new forms of life sprout from its bones.

We also find the motif of the one and the many in modern sociopolitical guises, expressed, for example, in *E pluribus unum* ("out of many, one"), which in 1776 was included on the seal of the United States and functioned as America's unofficial motto until it was replaced in 1956 by "In God We Trust." America's ancestors, the founding fathers, appeared to have thought that a democracy of freedoms and equality such as they imagined required a reciprocal relationship between the many and the one: one nation of many communities and faiths making for a workable and sufficiently loose community. In opting for religious freedom and secular democracy, the founders chose the motif of the one and the many as America's dream of totality and made this motif the signature creation myth of the United States of America.

However, as we are beginning to know all too well, America's dream of totality, secular democracy, did not protect completely against the dangers of totalizing systems. One of the first signs of trouble came in the form of the doctrine of manifest destiny—the idea that the United States should continue expanding its territory on the North American continent and beyond, that it should stake increasing claims. This sense of destiny was fueled by a religious fervor—perhaps as a consequence of the Puritans having been previously disenfranchised in England—and by the seduction of seemingly boundless open land. This coupling produced a psychological blindness enabling negation and disenfranchisement of the indigenous people who already lived on what Americans saw as a frontier. By 1956, the one God in which we trusted had become not many, but money—a system called free-market capitalism. Anything but free nowadays, market capitalism in contemporary life often seems more like Kronos gobbling up his children in a nasty form of integration, that is, corporate globalization.

The threat of new developments and disenfranchised elements of society being devoured remains quite active, even though the American system of market capitalism and a democracy comprised of individuals with equal rights under the law began as a corrective to the exclusionary effects of rigid deity- and monarchy-centered systems. We are now experiencing the malignant aspect of a conflation between capitalism and democracy in the destructive effects of the cult of the individual and its kissing cousin, the spread of unlimited corporate power. The economic breakdowns that took place at the beginning of the twenty-first century were in large part a result of unregulated economic markets, a move that had exclusionary tendencies. What was left out, or pushed out, were ethical considerations of community and social welfare. The collective (however perversely) entered through the back door with the mama grizzly bears—in the form of an oxymoronic corporate personhood. It may be that experiencing the devouring perfection of our most cherished dreams—being squeezed by the shadow of free market economics—will create the necessary tension to begin a systemwide breakdown. This may be hastened by an information culture that gives social concerns a voice and brings people into connection—attempts at takeover by corporate and media infotainment notwithstanding.

This brings us to the last aspect of totality that we need to acknowledge and to which images of globalization may be a response. This is a kind of Humpty Dumpty totality, in which the one comes undone and the parts do not come back together. This has been imagined in the collective psyche as coming about either because of intractable malignancy or because of an outright desire for incompleteness. Although this seems a particularly modern story and contemporary quandary, and I explore it with respect to contemporary systems like virtuality and globalization in part III, we can glimpse its beginnings long ago, in the story of Yahweh's destruction of the mighty tower and city of Babel, for example. In this tale of woe, the people spoke in one language and imagined themselves as mighty creators. The Lord was not happy with this and caused them to fall into a fragmented state, babbling in different tongues. As the King James Bible tells it:

> And the whole earth was of one language, and of one speech. And they said, Go to, let us build us a city and a tower, whose top may reach unto heaven; and let us make us a name, lest we be scattered abroad upon the face of the whole earth. And the Lord came down to see the city and the tower, which the children built. And the Lord said, Behold, the people is one, and they have all one language; and this they begin to do; and now nothing will be restrained from them, which they have imagined to do. Go to, let us go down, and there confound their language, that they may not understand one another's speech. So the Lord scattered them abroad from thence upon the face of all the earth: and they left off to build the city. (Genesis 11:1–9)

Fast-forwarding in time, this theme was heard again in another octave as a response to industrialization and the machine age, in great stories like Herman Melville's *Moby-Dick,* where an overreaching and righteous attempt to conquer what is beyond our grasp ends in extreme disintegration and defeat, and in Mary Shelley's *Frankenstein,* where the creator and his creation became irreparably and tragically alienated from one another.

The dynamic works the other way too. When our dreams of totality become dreams of perfection they become malignant, and we take action and revolt. We take down our dreams of totality as surely as we create them, despite totalitarian or romantic attempts to bind them forever. In the Hollywood film series *Matrix,* humanity mutinies and slips through the cracks of a fully architected digital machine world. The film *Avatar,* perhaps despite its intentions, succinctly portrays a world a lot like Aldous Huxley's *Brave New World;* the quasi-religion, drugs, and stupefying sex of Huxley's nightmare are cleaned up and replaced with the quasi-religious green high of plugging one's hair into a totem animal and going for a mystical ride. It is no wonder that this eye-candy dream world invited destruction. It was perfect.

Reality, of course, is much grittier and more bleak. Commenting on this state of affairs as reflected once again in literature, Christopher Booker noted that in the last two hundred years many stories have tended to "go wrong" or "lose the plot."[44] Elements of disintegration, alienation, uprootedness, and fragmentation abound, as what were reliable centers of gravity shift—and even disappear. Literary scholars disagree about whether this landscape of no exit, dead ends, and floating signifiers is something aberrant, whether it provides clues to what is going awry in the collective psyche that should be righted, or whether it represents something entirely new. In any event, attempts to resuscitate romantic dreams of oneness with nature ring Hollywood hollow when juxtaposed with the reality of the world's developing societies struggling to make their way into the twenty-first century before it's too late. Furthermore, as Jeffrey Sachs persuasively argued in *The Price of Civilization*, any ideas about organic farming and the like being a panacea for the global population and climate crises are utterly unrealistic. The solutions will be as yet unknown twenty-first-century solutions informed and implemented by twenty-first-century technology.

Summing Up

From a psychological point of view we can take note of several things. Our imagination's propensity to create totalities has a particularly mutable character; it disappears from view as we live within its bounds, then suddenly becomes visible in startling new guises when times call for new adaptation. Nevertheless, the back-and-forth compensatory relationship between fragmentation and wholeness, the call and response dynamic of dreaming of totality still holds, even in contemporary living—fragmentation and loss of centers call forth images of unification in the imagination. It's not an accident of history that grand archetypal gestures of unity, like globalization and the Web, enter the collective imagination at this juncture, responding to the postmodern mindset of deconstruction and ambiguity and to the fact that we have entered a landscape in which the plurality of political life and the multiplicity of social roles and identities dominate and cannot be denied.

Under the umbrella of globalization and its modus operandi, the World Wide Web, a new variation on a familiar move seems to be afoot in the collective imagination. A migration outward is taking place, a migration housed not in spirits or a transcendent deity but in an externalization of imagination. Logging on and surfing the Internet are increasingly replacing introspection and reflection, the subjective and private activities that used to be a sine qua non for experiencing a sense of wholeness. We "find ourselves" more and more not within, but rather without, in something that seems both objective and collective—the Web. This development is having the interesting effect of once again relativizing the individual—as the gods who presided over older dreams of totality once did. This development is hailed as salutary and decried as dangerous. It's hailed as an opening up into a full communion with others, even a release from grandiosity and from the painful limits and bondage of subjectivity. It's damned as being a disconnection from embodied reality, a final engulfment in a detached uncaring medium, in a world of free-floating mental simulacra.

Sound familiar? Magic circle or mandala? The one and the many, or the many forced into a one? The potential for both is present, and that is the point. In order not to devolve into polarized ideologies, we need to look at our contemporary dreams of totality both ways. If we don't, we miss the symbolic truth: that globalization and the Web carry our projections of totality. Information superhighways and global marketplaces, unbounded possibilities and egalitarian societies in the blogosphere, outer space and cyberspace—in the imagination these all share and communicate the emotional essentials of our time. They answer a call for space and freedom in response to a crowded planet with diminishing resources. Whether our regnant dreams will lead to a better world, whether Microsoft's promise, "a computer on every desk and in every home," signals expansion and a leveling of the playing field, or a colonization of it, remains to be seen.

There is an enduring relationship between totalitarian control and cataclysmic upheaval that holds true for both individuals and societies. We can infer from this that the more incomplete our dreams of totality are allowed to be—the more tension and flow we can bear with—the less the inevitability of change needs to take apocalyptic form. If dreams of totality express messages about the psyche's emerging relationship with itself in the world, then the contemporary forms they are taking seem to be tending in the direction of transparency, toward loose and proliferating associations between societies and between people, and toward shifting centers of gravity. What we don't like to acknowledge though is that the Web and the global marketplace are, in fact, bounded and monitored. Legitimate and illegitimate claims and rights are being staked out, attempts to control social undesirables like al-Qaeda and pornographers are in full swing, and regulation is just around the corner. The possibility exists that the many will disappear into the one once again, that the robber barons of the Gilded Age have returned in the form of dot-com corporate cyber barons, that a malignant form of unity still lurks in the background.

We can take heart from knowing this. In the same way that the alchemical "gold is not gold," or that Rilke's perfect rose is sleeping yet full of desire, we may be in a position that allows for dreams of totality to be seen through to their symbolic ground, if for no other reason than that the rapidity of events does not allow for their enshrinement. If real culture is dependent on symbolization, then the more we know about imagination and how it shares essentials, the more we can actually connect with different cultures and their unique elaborations on our common essentials—and not only by religious or economic conversion. Deeply ambiguous and contradictory as they are, as revelatory and as deceptive, dreams of totality communicate those essentials in ways that express the particularities of a moment in time, of place, and of heart. For good and ill. They answer a call, and in responding to what is wrong, in responding to what ails us, dreams of totality have curative and noxious effects. It is to this point that we now turn, to how dreaming of totality functions as one of the most potent medicines for both individuals and societies.

Notes

[1] Thomas Friedman, *The Lexus and the Olive Tree* (New York: Random House Anchor Books, 2000), p. 9.

[2] For those interested in a view of globalization different from Friedman's, Manfred Steger explores it from a less sanguine and more multidimensional perspective in *Globalization: A Very Short Introduction* (Oxford, UK: Oxford University Press, 2009).

[3] Andrew Samuels, *The Political Psyche* (London: Routledge, 1993), p. 61.

[4] Mark Johnson, *The Body in the Mind* (Chicago: University of Chicago Press, 1987).

[5] This may be analogous to the complex adaptive systems observed in biological and chemical systems, as described by Murray Gell-Mann in *The Quark and the Jaguar: Adventures in the Simple and the Complex* (San Francisco: W. H. Freeman, 1994). Complex adaptive systems such as ant colonies, the immune system, the biosphere, the brain, and cities seem to learn to self-organize at ever more complex levels of function. Thought to have what are called emergent properties, interactions between systems result in behavior and functioning that goes beyond

the sum of the various functions, and results in higher levels of functioning and more comprehensive systems of order. The way in which emergence occurs when systems are undergoing self-organization has been described by Joseph Cambray in *Synchronicity: Nature and Psyche in an Interconnected Universe* (College Station, TX: Texas A&M University Press, 2009). From these perspectives we can also think about our imagination as a complex adaptive system with emergent properties.

[6] Gilles Fauconnier and Mark Turner, *The Way We Think: Conceptual Blending and the Mind's Hidden Complexities* (New York: Basic Books, 2002), p. 396.

[7] C. G. Jung, *Psychological Types*, vol. 6, *The Collected Works of C. G. Jung* (Princeton, NJ: Princeton University Press, 1923), §745.

[8] Ariana Huffington, "Sarah Palin, 'Mama Grizzlies,' Carl Jung, and the Power of Archetypes," August 1, 2010, accessed at http://www.huffingtonpost.com/arianna-huffington/sarah-palin-mama-grizzlie_b_666642.html.

[9] Paul Radin, *The Road of Life and Death: A Ritual Drama of the American Indians* (Princeton, NJ: Princeton University Press, 1991), p. 4.

[10] Vilayanur S. Ramachandran, *A Brief Tour of Human Consciousness* (New York: Pi Press, 2004); Giacomo Rizzolatti and Corrado Sinigaglia, *Mirrors in the Brain: How Our Minds Share Actions, Emotions, and Experience* (Oxford, UK: Oxford University Press, 2008).

[11] Sigmund Freud and C. G. Jung, *The Freud/Jung Letters*, edited by William McGuire (Princeton, NJ: Princeton University Press, 1974), p. 540.

[12] C. G. Jung, *Memories, Dreams, Reflections* (New York: Vintage, 1963), p. 175.

[13] C. G. Jung, *The Red Book: Liber Novus*, edited and introduction by Sonu Shamdasani (New York: W. W. Norton, 2009), p. 199.

[14] *Ibid.*, pp. 198, 201.

[15] *Ibid.*, p. 229.

[16] Jung, *Memories, Dreams, Reflections*, p. 193.

[17] Jung, *The Red Book*, p. 241.

[18] Jung, *Memories, Dreams, Reflections*, p. 221.

[19] See also Sherry Salman, "The Creative Psyche: Jung's Major Contributions," in *The Cambridge Companion to Jung*, 2nd ed., Polly

Young-Eisendrath and Terence Dawson, eds. (New York: Cambridge University Press, 2008).

[20] Jung, *The Red Book*, p. 308.

[21] *Ibid.*, p. 241.

[22] In 1919 British Orientalist Sir John Woodroffe published *The Serpent Power* (under his pseudonym Arthur Avalon), a book that brought transformation of energy symbolism and the practice of Kundalini yoga to the West. Jung had a well-annotated first edition.

[23] Wolfgang Giegerich, *Technology and the Soul: From the Nuclear Bomb to the World Wide Web* (New Orleans: Spring Journal Books, 2007), p. 336.

[24] For a discussion about how Jung was affected by the scientists of his day, especially theoretical physicist Wolfgang Pauli, whose dreams Jung analyzed and with whom he worked on the theory of synchronicity, see Beverley Zabriskie's introduction to C. G. Jung and Wolfgang Pauli, *Atom and Archetype: The Pauli-Jung Letters 1932–1958*, edited by C. A. Meier (Princeton, NJ: Princeton University Press, 2001).

[25] Jung collected and analyzed Pauli's dreams without treating him; they are discussed in C. G. Jung, *Psychology and Alchemy*, vol. 12, *The Collected Works of C. G. Jung* (Princeton, NJ: Princeton University Press, 1953, 1968), in the chapter "Individual Dream Symbolism in Alchemy."

[26] Jung, *Psychology and Alchemy*, §§308, 310.

[27] C. G. Jung, "Psychology and Religion" (1938), in *Psychology and Religion*, vol. 11, *The Collected Works of C. G. Jung* (Princeton, NJ: Princeton University Press, 1958, 1969), §110.

[28] *Ibid.*, §138.

[29] Jung, *Psychology and Alchemy*, §325.

[30] For a discussion of Jung's relationship with National Socialism and anti-Semitism, see Stephen Martin and Aryeh Maidenbaum, eds., *Lingering Shadows: Jungians, Freudians, and Anti-Semitism* (Boston: Shambhala, 1991).

[31] Phyllis Grosskurth, *The Secret Ring: Freud's Inner Circle and the Politics of Psychoanalysis* (New York: Addison-Wesley Publishing, 1991), p. 47.

[32] *Ibid.*, p. 52.

[33] Mircea Eliade, *The Myth of the Eternal Return* (Princeton, NJ: Princeton University Press, 1954, 2005), p. 113.

[34] Alisa LaGamma, *Art and Oracle: African Art and Rituals of Divination* (New York: Harry Abrams, 2000), p. 23.

[35] Bruce Bynum, *The African Unconscious: Roots of Ancient Mysticism and Modern Psychology* (New York: Teachers College Press, 1999), p. 306.

[36] Robert Lifton, *The Protean Self: Human Resilience in an Age of Fragmentation* (New York: Basic Books, 1993), p. 225.

[37] *Ibid.*, pp. 231, 230.

[38] On March 26, 1997, during the period that comet Hale-Bopp was at its brightest, police discovered the bodies of thirty-nine members of the group Heaven's Gate who had committed mass suicide. The group believed that Earth was about to be "recycled" and that the only chance to survive was to leave immediately. Combining Christian doctrine (particularly the ideas of salvation and apocalypse) with elements of science fiction and evolutionary fantasies, the group "left their physical vehicles" to travel to other worlds.

[39] Eliade, *The Myth of the Eternal Return*, p. 74.

[40] See Mario Jacoby, *Longing for Paradise: Psychological Perspectives on an Archetype* (Toronto: Inner City Books, 1985, 2006), for a discussion of the relationship between this archetypal image and issues of separation and individuation.

[41] See Christopher Booker, *The Seven Basic Plots: Why We Tell Stories* (London: Continuum, 2004), for an extended discussion of numbers and storytelling.

[42] Jung discusses the symbolism of the square, the circle, the one becoming the fourth, and the mandala as these pertain to psychological development, differentiation, and wholeness. See Jung, *Psychology and Alchemy*; "Commentary on 'The Secret of the Golden Flower'" (1957) and "The Visions of Zosimos" (1954), both in *Alchemical Studies*, vol. 13, *The Collected Works of C. G. Jung* (Princeton, NJ: Princeton University Press, 1967); and *Mysterium Coniunctionis*, vol. 14, *The Collected Works of C. G. Jung* (Princeton, NJ: Princeton University Press, 1955).

[43] Booker, *The Seven Basic Plots*, p. 253.

[44] *Ibid.*, p. 700.

CHAPTER TWO

POISON AND PANACEA:
A UNIVERSAL MEDICINE

Why seek ye the living among the dead. He is not here.
(Luke 24:5)

Religion, whatever it is, is a man's total reaction upon life.
—William James, *The Varieties of Religious Experience*

You will hardly know who I am or what I mean,
But I shall be good health to you nevertheless,
And filter and fibre your blood.
Failing to fetch me at first keep encouraged,
Missing me one place search another,
I stop somewhere waiting for you.
—Walt Whitman, *Song of Myself*

One pill makes you larger, and one pill makes you small.
—Grace Slick, "White Rabbit"

Medicines

In 2008, a team of research scientists at Johns Hopkins reported a similarity between the state of oneness and unity described throughout history by mystics and their own experimental findings that "mystical-type" experiences of wholeness induced by ingesting psilocybin continued to facilitate "the attribution of personal meaning and spiritual significance" over a year after the drug was taken.[1] Following on this, the authors suggested that drugs like psilocybin might be useful in treating depression, obsessive-compulsive disorder, post-traumatic stress disorder, and the like. This is not news to those familiar with the exploration of psychedelic substances that characterized the 1960s. The search for a prescription for wholeness goes way back and appears to be rediscovered periodically. In the ancient world, the blood from Medusa was considered to be a *pharmakon*, a drug used by the Greek gods of medicine both to spread the plague and to heal; it was said that the blood from the right side of her body could save lives while the blood from her left side killed. In Aeschylus's *Prometheus Bound*, medicines appeared among the dangerous gifts from the gods that Prometheus gave to humanity. In the Bible, the flesh of the devouring monsters Leviathan and Behemoth was depicted as also being an antidote to poisons. In most ancient mythologies, there is no getting away from the ambivalent "just so" of the *pharmakon* of healing.

These stories illustrate the connections between our desire to feel whole, the art of medicating, and the poisonous dangers of hubris. That we continue to struggle with this in contemporary life is witnessed by our widespread addiction to mood-altering drugs—prescription and otherwise—and the constant war on drugs that we wage. Unlike the ancients and many traditional cultures, for whom the ties between the dangers and the boon of wholeness were perhaps an accepted fact of psychological life, this creates a tense and conflicted state of mind in us. As we saw in the preceding chapter, the intense polarization over stem cell research and applications, for example, reveals how we split the *pharmakon* of healing. Hailed as a panacea promising the regeneration of life, damned as an evil usurping the provenance of a divine creator, stem cells easily absorb the projection of a universal medicine, of a path to both heaven and hell. And we have trouble coming to terms with that.

Imagine yourself in ancient Greece however. There, upon becoming ill, you might be taken to the temple sanctuary of the divine physician, Asclepius, son of the god Apollo. In his temple (provided you were neither a coward or a drunk) you were admitted into rites of purification. First came a soothing, cleansing bath, then you were swaddled in white linen like a baby and taken to the innermost sanctuary of the temple. There you would drink a sleeping potion and be left to sleep and, most of all, to dream. You might remain there for several days, sleeping and dreaming, a virtual prisoner of the god, incubating in a chrysalis, waiting for what the ancients called "the healing dream."[2]

The healing dream was no ordinary dream; the divine healer Asclepius had to appear in all his terror and glory. Asclepius was the son of Apollo, and Apollo could send a plague on humanity or bestow wisdom. If you had the healing dream, it meant that you received either a gracious blessing from Asclepius's touch or a nasty, painful bite from his animal companion, a serpent or a dog. However it occurred, it was the god's touch that was important. The ancients envisioned sickness as the effect of a divine action, which could only be cured by another divine action: like cures like; what wounds also heals. Sickness and health were imagined in symmetry, as two parts of a whole. What seemed most terrifying was also what cured; in fact the illness was often a distorted form of the cure. After the healing dream, you would rise from the incubation couch whole again, give an offering to the god, tell your dream to the priests who wrote it down, and pay your fees to the temple. It was a tried and true ritual, and many were cured in the ancient world after a visitation from the god.

There is an interesting echo of the Greek incubation ritual in the biblical story of Job's suffering, in which the well-meaning Job suffered from disease, tribulations, and indignities that he couldn't understand and did not seem to deserve. While struggling with his belief that a virtuous man does not suffer from a just and all-good God, suddenly, from "the heart of the tempest" as the Bible puts it (Job 38:4–21), Yahweh the Leviathan appears, proclaiming, "Where were you when I created Earth and the Sea? Can you control Dawn, Darkness, and the Netherworld?" (Job 41:1–34)—revealing himself as encompassing both good and evil, as being both healing and deadly. After this encounter with Yahweh, Job's own storm begins to pass. The story seems to place suffering and meaninglessness within a larger sensibility, an advance that is healing. This same motif about the healing power of suffering is carried forward in the image of the bloody body of Christ suspended on the cross, being transformed into bread by the Christian mass, becoming a *medicina*, a prescription for resurrection sprung from an appreciation that suffering heals the soul and transforms the body. It appeared again in Western medieval alchemy, a tradition in which *medicine* was another name for the elixir of life and the philosopher's stone, an image of the reformation process, of turning the suffering of lead into the "gold that isn't gold."

This sensibility of symmetry between illness and healing is ubiquitous. Figure 17 shows a sibyl with a medicine bowl from Sierra Leone. This figure was placed as a guardian in front of a treatment center for mental disorders. It contained an entire society's spirit medicine and functioned as both the medium providing insight into illnesses and the medicine with which to resolve them. The offerings placed in the bowl on behalf of the illness, the medicine contained in the figure, and the spirit embodied by the sibyl are personified by a single form, expressing a sensibility about sickness, medicine, and healing that keeps illness and cure bound together in a whole picture. In a similar fashion to the way sins and sorrows are given up to Mother Mary in the Christian tradition, the sensibility portrayed by the sibyl and medicine bowl is of a spirit ample enough to contain both the distress and the balm.

Proscribed and collective as they were (it was the god or the society's spirit medicine that cured), what is notable for us about the healing rituals of ancient and traditional cultures is that there was no sign of the modern-day sentimentality about being responsible for one's own illness. Quite the opposite: illness was a divine and dignified mystery, with is own healing potential already within it, beyond an individual's responsibility. What was required was adopting the correct attitudes: submitting to the mystery, leaving the matter to the divine physician, and making the sacrifices necessary to reinstate wholeness and right order.

Anyone who has been gravely ill will recognize this deep need to mobilize factors beyond the margins of ego identity, as well as the necessity of withdrawing the divine or demonic projection of healing and illness from medical professionals and deconstructing our fractured dream of perfect health. This latter is not easy; the World Health Organization, for example, still defines health as " a state of complete physical, mental, and social well-being and not merely the absence of disease or infirmity."[3] Our contemporary culture has made instant makeovers, prescription and recreational drugs, and perfect health conferred on us by those in the know our unattainable gods. This makes death and disease the terrifying enemy, and we have forgotten that healing takes place because of being sick or wounded, not in spite of it.

As we will see in part II, aspects of the old incubation rituals would be carried forward again by psychoanalysis into the various rituals and

Figure 17: *Sibyl and Medicine Bowl* or *Yassi Society Figure*, Sherbro, Sierra Leone (19th-20th century), wood, University of Pennsylvania Museum of Archaeology and Anthropology, Philadelphia.

healing practices of that craft, such as the regression induced by both the illness and the treatment that yields up an influx of memory and new libido, providing for reconstruction that contains ambivalence and possibilities. The idea that symptoms are somehow related to cure, which was inherent in older healing traditions, rests in large measure on the sensibility of the one and the many. These traditions share this sensibility with the art of divination—or, in psychological language, the projection of possibilities. The underlying idea was that the multiplicity of events and experience, including illness, is a manifestation or reflection of the one—if it's a transpersonal signifier—or we might express it in contemporary terms as a unified field or particle/wave identity or in images such as synchronicity, wherein the many and the one stay close together in the imagination. In the older art of divination, for example, it is unlocking the patterns of experience in this world that is key to unlocking the door to the unity of the one. It is finding this mirrored relationship that both promotes healing and allows predictions to be made.

An example of this is shown in figure 18, a Yoruban divination tray from the Republic of Benin used in a type of divination oracle called "casting Ifa." The diviner and questioner sit with the tray between them. The images on the border of the tray represent the diversity of interdependent archetypal patterns that are crowned by the three sacred world calabashes on the diviner's side of the tray. There is an open channel between the divine and earthly worlds at the bottom of the tray; this is the questioner's side. When casting Ifa (who was the god of time and destiny), sixteen nuts are thrown onto the empty circular area of the tray. The patterns formed by the nuts correspond to one of 256 octograms, which correspond to written verses. These verses provide answers and direction for the questioner. The Ifa verses form a complete literary corpus of myths, folktales, incantations, songs, proverbs, and riddles, known as Odu Ifa, which, in 2005, was added to UNESCO's list of "Masterpieces of the Oral and Intangible Heritage of Humanity." Odu Ifa is the most systematized and largest literary tradition in Africa, a social and spiritual system that both structures and reflects the mythologems of human experience within that particular culture. Very similar to the method of consulting the *I Ching*, the core of Ifa divination rests in the meaning of the pattern made by the nuts, in the correspondence between the meaning

Figure 18: *Ifa Divination Tray*, Aja-Fon region, Benin (early 17th century), wood, Ulmer Museum—Weickmann Collection, Ulm, Germany.

of the moment during which the nuts are thrown and the larger whole of human experience, represented by the verses.

The object of the divination ritual is to determine what sort of sacrifice is necessary in order to resolve the questioner's problem, receive blessings, or mitigate the effects of a bad destiny. The correct sacrifices are contained in the verses. They are specified either by the diviner, who describes the sacrifice made by a mythological character under circumstances similar to those of the questioner's, or they are specified by the questioner, who finds his or her own answer by choosing the section in the verse that seems most related to the situation. In either case, although this world and a transpersonal world are assumed to be inextricably linked together, it is also assumed that they have separated from one another—this being, in essence, the problem—and the questioner has to make a sacrifice in order to find his or her way back to the totality and harmony of experience. The Ifa system contains two familiar warnings about respecting the psyche's deep ecology. First, mythological characters who did not comply by making the appropriate sacrifices courted misfortune—a full one-third of the Odu Ifa tells these sad stories. Second, the laws of Ifa, guardian of time and destiny, must always be respected. Playing with memory, as disrespect is called, is an act that afflicts the whole world, and playing with memory for self-serving reasons is particularly odious, a kind of black magic and sorcery that always courts fatal retribution.

Accidents happen though, and the laws of Eshu—the god of accident and chance—must be equally respected. In the mythology of Yoruban culture, destiny and chance, Ifa and Eshu, are best friends, one rarely found without the other. This is also true in the mythopoetic mind of all people and cultures that acknowledge, as Lewis Hyde wrote, "that contingency is prophecy, at least to those who have ears to hear."[4] The stories and incantations of Odu Ifa resonate in the mythopoetic imagination like poetry and music do, forming a bridge between the many idiosyncratic worlds of personal experience and the sensibility of those worlds being part and parcel of a larger field of awareness and action. This sensibility of participating in dynamic and interconnected worlds is the key to the healing properties of the *pharmakon* of totality as it has been imagined in so many cultures. And as we will see more deeply in what follows, if it is lacking the dynamism and unpredictability of real life, or if an individual does not find his or her appropriate and full emotional relationship to destiny, power, and time, the *pharmakon* of totality falls under the provenance of manipulation and black magic.

It was Plato who first took up the issue of the *pharmakon*'s ambivalence from a surprisingly explicit and modern perspective, couched this time as the activity of writing. In the *Phaedrus*, Plato has Socrates compare written texts to a drug, a *pharmakon* that acts as both a remedy and a poison.[5] Socrates tells his pupils an Egyptian myth about the origin of writing in which the god Theuth, already in charge of numbers and astronomy, invents writing and takes his new creation to the king of Egypt, offering it as a gift for the people. It was a move not unlike the gift of medicines that Prometheus gave to humanity. After Socrates tells his pupils this tale, an impassioned dialogue ensues about whether writing is a beneficent recipe and technique—on the one hand it could improve memory and make humanity wiser—or whether writing is really a malignant charm because it distorts truth and diminishes the creative art of memory, reducing it to mere reminding, in effect encouraging forgetting. As we've seen, for the Greeks the word *pharmakon* already referred to both beneficial and harmful prescriptions. A subtextual distinction develops in the *Phaedrus*, a distinction between something like reified logos (writing) and a more feeling-toned logos—a kind of inspired mythologizing. If this more erotic logos—the art of memory and mythologizing—is missing from the logos of the written word, the *pharmakon* of writing becomes a killer disguised as a clever magician.[6]

Socrates comes down on the side of living speech, which, he claimed, has truth and knowledge as its goal (Socrates had a daimon, a *genius* or inner guide, to which he listened with utmost fidelity and who apparently never steered him wrong) and against written simulacra. These latter have probabilities and persuasion as their end game and, he adds, are favored by politicians and lawyers! Living speech is inherently fertile and alive, the other sterile and dead. But the very undecidability of the question, the essential ambivalence of the *pharmakon*, is already implicit and at play in the *Phaedrus*. Plato alludes to the ambiguity by contrasting literality and fixity with process and imagination. And at the end of the dialogue, Socrates shifts position himself, introducing the idea that perhaps writing can sow seeds that will sprout in the soil of suitable souls, thus becoming, in effect, a beneficent *pharmakon*. And in a later dialogue, the *Phaedo*, the *pharmakon* reverses itself completely: the hemlock given to Socrates to drink is a poison, the citizenry having found him guilty of failing to adequately acknowledge the gods of Athens—he followed the daimon—but the poisonous drug he drinks is transformed by his mind and his method into a cure for the soul of the Republic.

This quality of the *pharmakon,* its reversibility and oscillation, the very undecidability of its value, was taken up in depth again many years later by Jacques Derrida in his essay "Plato's Pharmacy." Drawing out the nuances of the word *pharmakon*, Derrida deconstructed it further. He begins by pointing out that a remedy often already contains its own opposite—while scratching relieves itching, it is harmful in itself. There are no harmless remedies—their benefits do not prevent them from hurting. The *pharmakon* moves back and forth between positive and negative values; it crosses over our habitual mental boundaries between good and bad, inside and out, true and false. It induces a play of opposites without being negated by them. As Derrida expresses it:

> The essence of the *pharmakon* lies in the way in which, having no stable essence, no proper characteristics, it is not, in any sense (metaphysical, chemical, alchemical) of the word, a *substance* . . . It is rather the prior medium in which differentiation in general is produced.[7]

This definition of *pharmakon* brings the discussion squarely into the psychological domain. If the *pharmakon* isn't a substance, it refers more properly to a process (the prior medium) wherein thoughts, feelings, and images interact in a way that can be healing and destructive, always eluding complete interpretation. We personify this process in images and project it, especially onto all fields in which remedies play a role: medicine, the arts, psychology, music, myth, and religion. The power of the image lies in its ability to penetrate deeply into the psyche and also to evoke the opposite of what it appears to be. Its hiddenness and mutability give it a shape-shifting quality—which is why the *pharmakon* is beloved not only by philosophers, healers, and the masked occult arts, but also by quacks and charlatans, by black magicians, and by manipulators. However, in a kind of in-between place, in another of its guises—the perfumes and paints of art and artifice—the *pharmakon* can leave a living trace, a scent and a sign of something real and essential.

Some may remember the iconic, even prophetic TV commercials of the 1970s for Memorex tape that featured the great American jazz vocalist Ella Fitzgerald hitting a high note and shattering a wineglass. The ad showed a replay of Ella's recorded voice also shattering a glass, while a voice-over delivered the tagline, "Is it live, or is it Memorex?" In this case, rather than being merely degrading, imitation seemed to offer access to something entirely new. We can say the same, and much more, about the countless ways available to us now for reproducing what used to be uniquely human and singular events. But to the extent that a *pharmakon* is completely artificial, it runs the risk of disturbing the natural course of things by the cleverness of its imitation, of going against life, of masking what's dead by simulating the living. The *pharmakon* being close kin to sorcery and sleight of hand means that contrived images—particularly when they are clever imitations of the real thing—can be deeply manipulative, disturbing the imagination and the psyche's deep ecology. We certainly don't have to cast a wide net to find clearly pernicious *pharmakons*. They are rampant in the form of feel-good prescription and recreational drugs, immersive entertainment experiences that substitute for active engagement, and patriotic fervor that masks feelings of despair and impotence.

Sometimes, though, telling the difference between what's living and what's dead is not so easy, being as immersed as we are in the images and virtual experiences manufactured by the image industry. Derrida was referencing the ambivalent nature of the *pharmakon* (as writing) to buttress his attack on the boundaries between inside/outside and center/periphery and thus argue that there is no possibility of closure in regard to texts, even that the end of the book and the logocentric mind were at hand. This has proved to be true to the extent that reading words is losing ground to looking at images in contemporary culture. On the other hand, the threat of reification lurks in the background here as well—in the form of Web archiving. Everything is saved just as it was, our words, our pictures and stories, our deeds and destinations, all frozen in place. The art of memory—of putting ourselves together afresh as needed, of reflecting on experience rather than just recording it—could be in jeopardy. Just as Socrates feared might be the case with writing, being online may support forgetting precisely because the Internet remembers everything for us— what we did, with whom, why, and where. And the extent to which we are in denial about this is astounding. We imagine we have privacy when we don't. We act as if we are invulnerable and as if our communications are inviolate in the face of the terrifying fact that the electronic traces we leave are real and can be distorted and manipulated.

To make matters even more complicated, the images and ideas that contain us are now subject to all the instantaneous engagement that our technology allows for and fosters—mixing, mashing, clipping, sharing, looping, sampling, editing, and appropriating. It now seems irrelevant to ask, "Is it live, or is it Memorex?" Our situation may be a harbinger of psychological chaos and a loss of personal freedom from which it will be hard to recover, or, conversely, the breakup of fixity may allow for a sense of wholeness and connection to be derived from easy movement between multiple images. As the play and inclination of unseen factors are alternately revealed and concealed, the enigmatic nature of our dreams of totality may force our engagement in genuinely creative events, events that stand against the baleful eye of fate and the manipulative aspects of the *pharmakon*.

However it comes about, our active engagement with the *pharmakon* of totality is crucial. In "Plato's Pharmacy" Derrida noted that in classical Greek society the *pharmakon* played a particular role in ritual drama in the form of a *pharmakos*—a human scapegoat who was sacrificed or expelled from the community in a ritual of purification during times of disaster or crisis. Implicit in the word *pharmakon*—"in the back room" to use Derrida's idiom—are traces of the sacrificial *pharmakos*. This refers directly to our propensity to try and preserve social order and coherence by excluding whatever is disturbing to that order. Derrida notes the remarkable fact that although Plato never states it, Socrates became a *pharmakos* himself: he was outcast and sacrificed by Athenian society because his words acted like a *pharmakon*, changing the minds of his listeners, both curing and poisoning the Republic. Standing at the boundary between what is sacred and what is cursed, the *pharmakos*—like the illness that cures and the wound that heals—embodies the ambivalence that we try to split in two by ejecting what's unwanted.

In our individual lives and in the history of cultures, there is a profound connection between the healing and poisonous actions of the *pharmakon* and sacrificial acts. Sacrifice in the form of expulsion or exclusion has been the traditional means by which dreams of totality have remained intact and protected. In less violent ways, sacrifices are made, things are given up, behavior is changed, all in order to heal what's been fractured, to reestablish the perception of integrity in a field of experience, or sometimes to open a way for what's new to enter the field. Sacrificing our attachments to particular dreams of totality is what allows psychological and social creation to go forward. We might even say that in addition to its unpredictability, what keeps the *pharmakon* of totality honest is the quality of the sacrifices we make in relation to it. This is a subject I take up in depth in chapter 5; for now, it is enough to take note that it matters a great deal whether we accept emerging dreams and make the necessary sacrifices, or whether we push them out of our magic circles with prejudice, taboo, or manipulation. Just as the potential for sorcery and manipulation is implicit in the character of the *pharmakon*—*pharmakos* also meant magician, sorcerer, even poisoner—the associations between the medicinal aspects of dreams of totality, illusions, and scapegoating are also ever-present.

Our dreams of totality emerge from inner and outer needs, moving between the two and with the currents of psychic life, growing with the situation, not merely displacing it with a quick fix. Drawing on the pharmacy of the creative imagination, this is a living process in constant adjustment, and only if the process becomes static or co-opted, manufacturing a one-size-fits-all drug, will our dreams of totality fail to respond and adjust to the needs of the moment with nuance and flexibility. The rub comes because the dreams we cook up are usually very enchanting, in both the redemptive and manipulative senses of the *pharmakon*. They can even act like a vaccine that indoctrinates (and protects) an entire population. Most important, the sense of salvation and closure that we feel when a dream of totality comes into focus often prompts a messianic impulse, an urge to make it real and permanent. We fall in love and want to hold on to our creations.

Religion

Some time after he broke with Freud, C. G. Jung made the point that

> the *genius religiosus* is a wind that bloweth where it listeth. There is no Archimedean point from which to judge, since the psyche is indistinguishable from its manifestations. The psyche is the object of psychology, and—fatally enough—also its subject. There is no getting away from this fact.[8]

Although many stories and symbols in religious imagery beautifully narrate the sensibility of entire cultures, unfortunately, most of the world's great religions *do* judge, and often very unkindly. The great cultural *pharmakon* of religion illustrates perhaps as nothing else can the ambivalent nature of a dream of totality. Like the old incubation stories, the dreams of totality that power religions can be a medicine that is containing, inclusive, sometimes even revolutionary. But when codified into systems, dogma, and ritual, these world visions often become coercive and, as Freud rightly noted in *The Future of an Illusion*, "the universal obsessional neurosis of humanity."[9]

On the other hand, the critiques of religion begun by Freud and continued in contemporary style by Richard Dawkins and Christopher Hitchens, often fail to find their footing in the reality of psychological experience.[10] If the converse of rationality is merely irrationality, then religious belief will appear to be a delusion, no doubt about it—a blindness, a destructive distortion of instinct, at best an illusion. If one views the mythopoetic mind as merely a repository of repressed longings and childish wishes, infantile fears and needs, or as generating prescientific explanations of nature, then religion can be handily reduced to a recapitulation of the longings of humanity or the necessary—if dour and unfortunate—means by which social organization trumps instinct, the "Big Daddy" motif. This view was put forth most succinctly by Freud, in his description of religion as society's great superego, the defensive arm of civilization which functions to coerce and compel the renunciation of instinct so as to quell the antisocial trends always threatening to destroy what little civilization there exists. As he famously opined, "The 'fiction' of religion is important for the maintenance of human society."[11]

As we've seen, though, it's precisely this fictionalizing and narration, all the moves that the psyche makes as it creates its own containing images and structures, that do provide an Archimedean point, not from which to judge, but from which to understand a psychological process. Without this perspective, without finding our footing in the mythopoetic imagination, we can't approach the question of why religious imagery and belief continue to appear in an enlightened world, other than by scorning it as a vestigial organ or patronizing it as primitive—a consequence of poor education and the like.

This belittling attitude and ultimate condemnation is the tack taken—perhaps disingenuously—by both Richard Dawkins and Christopher Hitchens, representatives of what has been dubbed the New Atheism.[12] Regrettably, what the New Atheism seems to have in common with its archenemy fundamentalism is its one-eyed claim on truth. Both the New Atheism and fundamentalisms adopt the position that god is something anthropomorphic and literal. Neither group pays much attention to other traditions about god, such as mysticism, which move toward the experiential and psychological dimensions of the god image, or to the philosophical conceptions of, for example, Buddhism—all of which tilts the religious rhetoric toward a less literalized perspective. Had Dawkins and Hitchens taken those traditions into account they might have quickly bumped up against—heaven forbid—the problem of psychological experience as it pertains to religion. This is something that William James put squarely on the table over a century ago in *The Varieties of Religious Experience*, his comprehensive study of religious experience as a psychological phenomenon. Many others have followed suit in a long line of inquiry about the psychological underpinnings of the religious impulse and experience, something the New Atheists are doubtless aware of but seem to have chosen to ignore.[13]

Instead, New Atheists try to invalidate religious belief using evolutionary theory, brandishing that sword with an almost biblical fervor. Both Dawkins and Hitchens have come up with odd concoctions of scientific ideas that claim to explain the ubiquity and tenacity of religious belief. Dawkins, for example, posited "simulation software" in the brain, software that makes us invent visionary experiences and religious beliefs, going so far as to suggest that the different religions might be alternative "memeplexes."[14] Like genes in a gene pool, memeplexes are supposed bundles of hard-wired genes that somehow align themselves with other cultural memes for primo survival odds and propagate by "unconscious evolution."[15] Dawkins likens Islam, for example, to a carnivorous gene complex and Buddhism to an herbivorous one (!).

While Dawkins concedes that neuroscience may eventually find a "god centre" in the brain and that the brain is very good indeed at making models—even likening this model making to dreaming and imagination—he consistently skirts the implications of this. Rather than acknowledging that the imagination is essential and terrific at organizing information and emotions, he downgrades both model making and imagination to hallucination, children's imaginary friends, ghosts, or "especially if we happen to be young, female and Catholic—the Virgin Mary."[16] "What," Dawkins asks, "is the primitively advantageous trait that sometimes misfires to generate religion?"[17] He reverts to a patronizing vestigial-organ hypothesis: the misfiring of a "module" that had the evolutionary advantage of "trusting your elders without question."[18] We might as well be back in imperialist Victorian Europe with Freud, who claimed, "Comparative research has been struck by the fatal resemblance between the religious ideas which we revere and the mental products of primitive people and times."[19] From this point of view, the fatality and primitivity of the resemblance is not a compliment to anyone, and the implications of the resemblance fail to be drawn out.

This kind of analysis is partly an artifact of projecting backward onto history for explanations. Dawkins does acknowledge that "it is possible that a form of natural selection, coupled with the fundamental uniformity of human psychology, sees to it that the diverse religions share significant features in common" and that "religions probably are, at least in part, intelligently designed, as are schools and fashions in art"—although, again, this may not be meant as a compliment to schools and fashions in art.[20] The focus of the New Atheists' unilateral gaze stays fixed on the past, on the notion that religious imagery is irrational—by definition delusional, misguided, hence prejudiced as primitive—while the adaptive function of mythopoetic and symbolic thinking is ignored or scorned as dualism, a mind/body split, or, finally, attributed to the notion that children and primitives are native teleologists and creationists, just going around benightedly attributing purpose to everything.

It's a view from above and outside the psyche that resembles—perversely—the fundamentalist's signature symbol of totality, the motif of the eye of God. Figure 19 is an image of the Helix Nebula (in the constellation Aquarius), known colloquially as the Eye of God. This is actually a dying star, one of the planetary nebulae nearest to the Earth, but in the imagination it resonates with the Eye of God, a cross-cultural motif of illumination that resembles a mandala, in this case projected onto a contemporary cosmic representation. The Eye of God is all seeing and all knowing as it searches our hearts for truth, and in its absolute omnipresence it is utterly containing in its vision, a panacea expressing the unity of being. By virtue of these same qualities, the Eye of God is also unbearably scorching, unable to see nuances of meaning, shadows, or shades of grey, and deadly if one is caught and exposed under the high noon of its implacable gaze. Many have burned or been indelibly altered in the face of the lone Eye of God—both disfigured and transformed in the furnace of intense emotion or riveting revelation. The singularity of

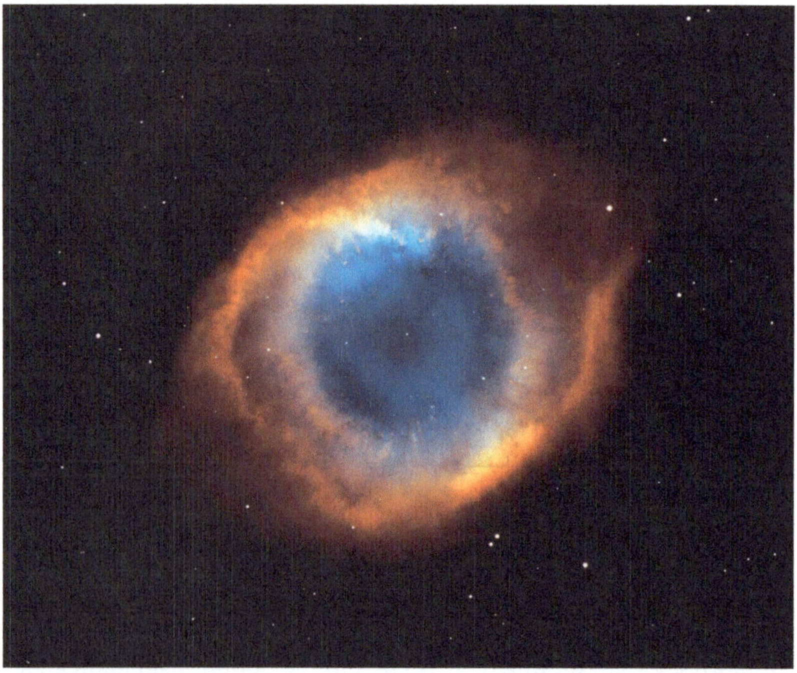

Figure 19: Helix Nebula, photographed by the Hubble Helix Nebula Team, NASA.

the eye of God also expresses the feelings of paranoia and persecution that arise when totality is projected so completely "out there" that it is felt to be looking back at us with overwhelming and inescapable fixation. This persecutory dynamic is disturbingly evident in the relationship between fundamentalist believers and the New Atheists, both of whose totalizing visions obscure what is being looked at and how it is being seen—and always requiring annihilation of the "blind" enemy.

The ambivalence and mutability of the *pharmakon* of totality is consistently co-opted by neat rhetorical maneuvers on the part of both fundamentalists and New Atheists. Idolatry (fundamentalism) and iconoclastic idol smashing (New Atheism) are familiar ritual behaviors that have gone hand in hand throughout the history of religious movements, usually with devastating consequences, and this masked attack against the mythopoetic imagination by contemporary New Atheists and fundamentalists alike is no exception. What's actually new in contemporary life is that contributions from psychology, neuroscience, comparative anthropology, and cognitive science have situated essential questions about dreams of totality, such as God, within the larger formulations of symbol formation and cultural narrative, which are unbiased with regard to primitivity. Even within the religious tradition itself, especially the mystical traditions, there is a well-developed trajectory that points straight inward to psychological experience.[21] While not panaceas in themselves, these contributions should render certain forms of the religion question moot.

For example, the assertion that Jesus was born of a virgin is something vehemently avowed by believers and gleefully dissected by Christopher Hitchens in *God Is Not Great*. From a literal perspective it's about as likely as Athena springing full-blown from the head of Zeus. From a symbolic perspective, though, the ubiquitous motif of virgin birth conveys something important about humanity's psychological and emotional experience. One of the signal characteristics of a savior or cultural hero in most mythologies is having divine ancestry of some sort, one or the other parent being immortal or divine. Being the child of such mixed parentage symbolizes the advent of something new or important, something special and different—the ability to bring something essential from outside the status quo onto the scene. Following in this tradition of saviors and heroes, what is created from the virgin birth (the child)—whether it is Christ embodying the willingness to suffer and be sacrificed or Athena embodying the androgynous ethos of classical Greece—is envisioned as an unusual, even special, type of consciousness that blends the eternals of the big picture with the new demands of life in the present moment. A contemporary inversion of the virgin birth story illustrates the point: the birther movement in the United States that took hold during President Obama's campaign and first term in office. The birthers filed numerous lawsuits questioning the legitimacy of Obama's U.S. citizenship and hence his eligibility to be president, claiming that he was born somewhere offshore (with a missing and foreign father to boot) or that his birth certificate (from Hawaii) was actually a forgery.

If one of the constructive contributions of postmodernism has been to deconstruct totality, then the New Atheists have provided a mighty broom and dustpan to clean out the totality called God, at least the god-image that is a "Big Daddy" or misfiring module. They have done a service by exposing the poisonous and coercive nature of many religious organizations and beliefs. And on a lighter note, it is also patently true that, as Emerson quipped, "the religion of one age is the literary entertainment of the next,"[22] and as Jung remarked more seriously,

> The gods have become diseases; Zeus no longer rules Olympus, but the solar plexus, and produces curious specimens for the doctor's consulting room, or disorders of the brains of politicians and journalists who unwittingly let loose psychic epidemics on the world.[23]

Dreams of totality respond to the calls of particular times and places, and when they have done the job, if allowed to change form and function, they do.

Where the New Atheists go wrong is in failing to keep open the aperture they created. Instead, they fill it with quasi-scientific explanations the like of which would have horrified poor Socrates and proved his point about the tricky and pernicious *pharmakon*. Both the New Atheists and religious fundamentalists miss the significance of the mythopoetic mind, one aspect of which is the *genius religiosus* that creates symbols which express our experience of living. This is a function of the psyche, not an entity, not a mindless illusion, and not a secondary artifact of evolution.

My second quarrel with the New Atheists concerns their participation in a kind of intellectual scapegoating—the attempted slaughter and gutting of the *genius religiosus*. In its attempts at unveiling and disclosure, the rhetoric resembles, even if unintentionally, that most seminal religious dream of totality—Judgment Day. If part of what keeps the *pharmakon* honest is the quality of the sacrifice made in relation to it, then the prescription offered by the New Atheists for the abolition of religion is not exactly honest. Taking recourse in conjuring up scenarios that reduce religion to an artifact of evolution and in the scapegoating that seems to always accompany such conjuring rises to the level of a serious intellectual and ethical problem in our times. Instead of crediting the symbolization process that drives it, the sometimes righteous glee evinced by the New Atheists as the religious enemy falls often seems like a contemptuous identification with destruction. We might also ask whether the creation stories and dreams of totality such as were projected onto the Human Genome Project, for example, serve us better than God or more poorly? The answer can be yes and no.

What I urge instead is that a shift toward an appreciation of dreams of totality—religious and otherwise—as being symbolic creations will find a parallel in a shift from the warrants of blood sacrifice like scapegoating and taboos toward a more gentle abandonment of literalism. This sacrifice is also painful, but it draws a different kind of blood. Understanding that dreaming of totality works like a *pharmakon* powering religious belief and imagery doesn't require belief in the God of fundamentalists or the New Atheists, nor in an abstract philosophical or theological entity. Neither do the power of dreams of totality have to be explained with conjuring tricks of evolutionary magic or reductive fantasies projected backward onto our primitive ancestry. The resemblance of these maneuvers to the poisonous *pharmakon* that Socrates deplored is clear: while they hypnotize us with their affective and rhetorical vehemence, the living symbol is sucked out while we're not looking. This tendency to take refuge in misappropriated statements about evolution fails everyone. As the 1960s song of dissolution proclaimed, "One pill makes you larger, and one pill makes you small." Arguments and explanations for and against religion that fall short in taking account of the symbolization process don't help us remember or create anything new, but rather they make us forget who we are: symbol-making creatures.

One is tempted to agree with Jesus when he said that unless we are born again in spirit, the doors to the kingdom of heaven on earth are shut.

I want to emphasize that as we come right up against ourselves as both dreamer and dream interpreter, we face new ethical issues. As philosopher Martha Nussbaum wrote in *The Fragility of Goodness*, in relation to ethics and social concerns, when faced with ourselves we tend to move in two directions:

> Suspended between beast and god . . . the human being is defined against both of these self-sufficient creatures by its open and vulnerable nature, and the relational character of its concerns. But if being human is a matter of the character of one's trust and commitment, not just a natural fact, then the human being is also the being that can most easily cease to be itself—either by moving upwards towards the self-sufficiency of the divine, or slipping downwards into the self-sufficiency of doggishness. And the difference between the two is not altogether obvious . . . both involve a closing off of human things.[24]

One of the most human things we face into now is our relational responsibility for our imaginary creations. This means taking them on their own terms, not reducing them to genetic determinants or upgrading them to metaphysical entities in an effort to distance ourselves from them but adopting a psychological ethic instead. Carrying the currents of collective imagination as they do, dreams of totality provide more than an enhanced high-definition transpersonal environment or a repository of old vestigial genetic combinations. They open up new grooves in the psyche, creating new riverbeds for the flow of imagination that can compete effectively—like a medicine—with those etched by trauma or manipulation. Or they can poison those riverbeds. This becomes especially pertinent during our most vulnerable altered states, during emotional and psychological upheaval. These are the times when we can participate most fully in the destruction and creation of old paths and new possibilities or be most effectively manipulated. Dreaming of totality is one of the ways that we treat, dose, and manage our moves into and out of dissolution, making, as the alchemists would have said, what's fixed unfixed, and what's unfixed fixed. And when they go bad or are manipulated, dreams of totality send us into a hyperreality of fixation and dissociation that loses touch with the human concerns that created them.[25]

Notes

[1] R. Griffiths, W. Richards, M. Johnson, U. McCann, and R. Jesse, "Mystical-type experiences occasioned by psilocybin mediate the attribution of personal meaning and spiritual significance 14 months later," *Journal of Psychopharmacology* (2008): 1.

[2] For a thorough discussion of Asclepian healing rituals and psychotherapy, see C. A. Meier, *Healing Dream and Ritual: Ancient Incubation and Modern Psychotherapy* (Einsiedeln, Switzerland: Daimon Verlag, 2003).

[3] Preamble to the constitution of the World Health Organization as adopted by the International Health Conference, New York, signed on July 22, 1946, by the representatives of sixty-one states and entered into force on April 7, 1948; Official Records of the World Health Organization, no. 2, p. 100, accessed at http://www.who.int/en/. The definition has not been amended since 1948.

[4] Lewis Hyde, *Trickster Makes This World: How Disruptive Imagination Creates Culture* (New York: Canongate, 1998), p. 135.

[5] Edith Hamilton, Huntington Cairns, and Lane Cooper, eds., *The Collected Dialogues of Plato: Including the Letters* (Princeton, NJ: Princeton University Press, 2005).

[6] Francis Yates, *The Art of Memory* (Chicago: University of Chicago Press, 1966) is a classic study of how people retained vast stores of knowledge before the invention of printing.

[7] Jacques Derrida, *Dissemination,* trans. Barbara Johnson (Chicago: University of Chicago Press, 1983), pp. 125–126.

[8] C. G. Jung, *Psychology and Religion*, vol. 11, *The Collected Works of C. G. Jung* (Princeton, NJ: Princeton University Press, 1958, 1969), § 87.

[9] Sigmund Freud, *The Future of an Illusion*, ed. James Strachey (New York: Doubleday Anchor Books, 1927, 1964), p. 71.

[10] See Richard Dawkins, *The God Delusion* (New York: Houghton Mifflin, 2006); and Christopher Hitchens, *God Is Not Great: How Religion Poisons Everything* (New York: Twelve, Hachette Book Group, 2007).

[11] Freud, *The Future of an Illusion*, p. 43.

[12] James Wood, "God in the Quad," *The New Yorker*, August 31, 2009.

[13] To make matters worse, when Dawkins claimed that Jung was a "strong theist," insisting that Jung held to "100% probability of God"

because he had stated "I do not believe, I *know*," Dawkins missed the point entirely. Jung was actually drawing a sharp distinction between belief and knowledge. What he said to John Freeman in the BBC interview series *Face to Face* (broadcast on October 2, 1989 and available on YouTube) was, "I do not need to believe, I know! I have had the experience of being gripped by something that is stronger than myself, something that people call God." The knowing that Jung refers to is based on a subjective psychological experience, an experience that may be called God but could easily be called something else, that is, awe or grace. This knowing is not dependent on or derivative of belief. Jung made no claims whatsoever on any knowledge of divine or metaphysical entities. He insisted on this distinction. He was, in fact, suspicious of blind belief and preferred to confine himself to psychological experiences alone, hence the distinction between knowing, as a product of experience, and believing.

[14] Dawkins, *The God Delusion*, p. 232.
[15] *Ibid.*, p. 233.
[16] *Ibid.*, p. 116.
[17] *Ibid.*, p. 202.
[18] *Ibid.*, p. 207.
[19] Freud, *The Future of an Illusion*, p. 63.
[20] Dawkins, *The God Delusion*, pp. 220, 233.
[21] Connie Zweig, *The Holy Longing: Spiritual Yearning and Its Shadow Side* (Bloomington, IN: iUniverse, 2008).
[22] Ralph Waldo Emerson, *The Complete Works of Ralph Waldo Emerson* (New York: Houghton Mifflin, 2004), vol. 7, p. 443.
[23] C. G. Jung, "Commentary of 'The Secret of the Golden Flower'" (1957), in *Alchemical Studies*, vol. 13, *The Collected Works of C. G. Jung* (Princeton, NJ: Princeton University Press, 1967), § 54.
[24] Martha Nussbaum, *The Fragility of Goodness* (Cambridge, England: Cambridge University Press, 1986), p. 417.
[25] *Hyperreality* is a term first used in semiotics and postmodern philosophy to describe a state of consciousness unable to distinguish reality from a simulation, especially in technologically advanced postmodern societies where a multitude of media can radically alter an original event or experience. Some influential theorists of hyperreality include Jean Baudrillard, Albert Borgmann, Umberto Eco, and Daniel Boorstin.

Part II

Of Human Things

Chapter Three

Psychology's Dreams

So far I have found no stable or definite center in the unconscious, and I don't believe such a center exists. I believe that the thing I call the self is a dream of totality.
—C. G. Jung, 1957 interview with Miguel Serrano

You shall listen to all sides and filter them from your self.
. . . .
And these tend inward to me, and I tend outward to them,
And such as it is to be of these more or less I am,
And of these one and all I weave the song of myself.
. . . .
Walt Whitman, a kosmos, of Manhattan the son,
. . . .
Do I contradict myself?
Very well then I contradict myself,
(I am large, I contain multitudes.)
—Walt Whitman, *Song of Myself*

And how could I endure to be a man, if man were not also poet and reader of riddles and . . . a way to new dawns.
—Nietzsche, *Thus Spake Zarathustra*

Migration Inward

Our sensibility of totality was first experienced through the mysterious actions of spirits and gods, who drew their protective magic circles around humanity from the depths and heights with terror and beauty, providing coherence and finality, "just so" and complete. Later the many gods were drawn together into the monotheistic gods of Judaism, Christianity, and Islam—and dreams of totality were experienced as coming from a single transcendent other. Figure 20 shows the front panels of Hieronymus Bosch's famous triptych *The Garden of Earthly Delights*. It's the god's-eye view seen when the triptych is folded closed, and it's called *The Creation of the World*. Figure 21 is a photo of Earth from space, "The Blue Marble," in which humanity has assumed the god's-eye view. In the West, as the one God was incarnated as a man, the dream of totality in which we still live—although shakily—the image of humankind as the exalted microcosm of the universe dominated the modern imagination, for good and ill. Figure 22 shows a twenty-first-century advertisement that captures the quality of our modern inversion of the creation theme.

With the advent of psychology, humanity's presumed projections were once again recast, this time as psychological projects: the gods and God became conscious—or better said, became the unconscious. As the source of humanity's dreams and dreamers migrated firmly inward, dreaming of totality fell further under psychology's umbrella, becoming imbued not only with the scent of gnosis that had always enveloped the process, but also with a more scientific visage—much to the chagrin and furor of religious systems. With these developments, the dreams of totality that were previously experienced as originating outside ourselves now seemed to come entirely from within, a move that mirrored the ever-increasing turn toward the subjective me, and our imagination's increasing fascination with itself as an object. But vestiges of the gods remained.

Freud began his landmark *Interpretation of Dreams* with Virgil's famous epigraph from Dante's *Inferno*: "If I cannot bend the gods above, then I will move the infernal regions." Figure 23 is a photograph of Freud's desk in his London consulting room, replete with the many statuettes he kept of the gods and goddesses of antiquity. We might even say that the unconscious was discovered to a significant degree by the notion that the whole pantheon of the gods was alive in the psyches of contemporary

Figure 20: *The Creation of the World* (closed front panels of *The Garden of Earthly Delights*), by Hieronymus Bosch (1504), wood, Museo del Prado, Madrid.

people, that the emotional and psychological processes personified as the gods caused disturbance and also pointed a way toward healing, as we explored in the last chapter in relation to the incubation mysteries. Many contemporary ideals of psychological health are still driven by this particular dream of totality: that of interiority, of "me and my unconscious." Reconnecting an alienated and afflicted ego to its instinctual roots, to the archaic wisdom of the unconscious, is presumed to restore a sense of wholeness. This wisdom, like that attributed to animals and the gods—both of whom live absolutely true to their natures and are

Figure 21: "The Blue Marble, East," NASA (2002).

unable to do otherwise—entailed a regrounding in mythopoetic awareness, an awareness that was considered sacred in all tribal cultures but which modern man had turned his back on. Jung in particular, was an avid proponent of the idea that the archaic psyche with its attendant instinctive wisdom was a key to psychological health for moderns who were suffering from a loss of soul.[1]

All of early psychoanalytic theory involved the idea that there were emotional and unconscious factors that were separated from conscious identity but ran the show in powerful and unexpected ways. This idea held sway regardless of whether the unconscious was imagined in the form of a monomythic sexual instinct (Freud) or as a wider assembly of hardwired archetypal patterns (Jung). The psychological dream of

Figure 22: Advertisement on the *Hindu Business Line* website (2005).

interiority is one in which the microcosm of the unconscious contained everything, being in effect, as Jung put it, a collective unconscious. Metaphors and correspondences from the pantheon and mythologies of the gods and from studies of animal behavior were deployed to explain the potency and ubiquity of unconscious, that is, deep, psychodynamic processes. Charles Darwin had set the stage for this migration inward in his last book, *The Expression of the Emotions in Man and Animals*.[2] In addition to his own research, Darwin drew inferences from his observations of children, psychotics, and the emerging science of ethnography, which suggested that if emotions are basically grounded in instinct, it followed that they should be relatively consistent and recognizable across cultures and populations and over time. That has turned out to be the case, confirmed, for example, by psychologist Paul Ekman's comprehensive work on emotion, facial expression, and empathy.[3]

Figure 23: Freud's Consulting Room, Freud Museum, London.

From our contemporary perspective we can understand the initial idea of the unconscious to be a projection of the imagination onto an imagined entity "out there," namely, as something separate from ego identity, which in the case of the unconscious was then relocated "in here." Later on, the prelinguistic and translinguistic experience of emotion would come to be recognized by psychology as being part and parcel of the symbolization process, not separate from it. As Jung wrote, in the style of his time, "There can be no transforming of darkness into light and of apathy into movement without emotion."[4] As we will see in what follows, this move toward radical interiority contributed—correctly, and also mistakenly— to the criticism that much of psychotherapy is merely self-serving and self-referential and thus essentially immature and clueless.

In addition to asking who is the dreamer who dreams the dream, the early psychologists began asking where is the dream dreamed. Another way to follow the great migration inward is to follow the story of the head. To begin with, it is only relatively recently that the head was recognized as the locus of consciousness. For the ancients, the abode of thought and feeling was imagined to be either in the heart, chest, or the liver, even though the head and the brain were imagined to be extremely potent, at the very least home to the divine genius.[5] Because the genius resided there, the head was often believed to be immortal, thus associated with resurrection and oracular power, even able to speak after being severed from the body, as did the heads of Orpheus, John the Baptist, and many other cephalophoric Christian and Islamic saints. Athena, goddess of wisdom and warfare, born from her father Zeus's head, placed Medusa's frightful severed head on her war shield to petrify her enemies. In many other cultures as well, the head of one's enemy was a prized possession and a sure sign of strength. Many of our ancestors ate the brains of their enemies in order to assimilate powerful mana and assume dominance. In another variation on the motif, Irish warriors mixed the brains of a fallen comrade with earth, fashioning a ball that was then used as a deadly projectile weapon. And along these lines, it's possible that during the French Revolution the obsessive use of the guillotine and the display of severed heads may have been a ritual attempt to redistribute power and resources from the aristocracy to the populace.

On a different note, the cult of the head also included the use of skulls as sacred drinking cups. The Holy Grail was one such transmogrified skull, and the Knights Templar—who are associated with the Grail of Christendom—were reputed to have taken their orders from a disembodied head with three faces named Baphomet. For others, the head and the brain were simply holy. In Minoan Crete, horns were thought to grow from the head as a sign of procreative life force. In the Christian tradition Christ was imagined to be the Head of the Church, his community of followers the Body; and in Jewish Kabbalistic lore each hair on the head is a "breaking of the divine fountains" issuing from the hidden brain.

But when Shakespeare's confused and unhappy Prince Hamlet tried to consult the skull of his ghostly father's jester, he found that poor Yorick was silent. The old magic was gone, and Hamlet had to live within the confines of his own mind and heart, a place fraught with uneasy contradictions. By the seventeenth century, the phrase "racking the brain" became associated with the alembic—an alchemical vessel for cooking—suggesting that the imaginary source of transformation had now migrated firmly into the brain. We can fast-forward to the drug imbibing psychedelic heads of the 1960s, who opined their signature recipe for cosmic consciousness, "feed your head." But even as the genius of psyche first became localized in the mind, and the mind then became localized in the brain—taking on its most respectable scientific countenance to date—we can still observe the telling fact that we nevertheless continue to "consult the head"—now in the form of the brain—as the latest in a series of dark *rotundums* of totality.[6]

The brain, a soft jellylike mass with its billions of synaptic connections, weighs in at only 2¼ to 3¼ pounds. It provides us with an internal representation of reality at the same time that it carries our projections of wholeness and of the alchemical alembic, the vessel in which everything important takes place. In the brainstem and limbic system we experience our commonality with animal ancestors, and our fantasies about higher order cortical brain functions connect to those about a universal Mind, as the image of a crown chakra illustrates (see figure 12). A dark *rotundum,* the brain quickly became the quintessential black box, which we feel compelled to open in pursuit of the ancient imperative "Know thyself." A proliferation of neuro disciplines like neuroscience, neuroepistemology, neuroethology, and psychoneuroimmunology now hold the promise of unlocking the X factor (by neuroimaging) and providing access to the mysteries of being.

Our unending fascination with the brain speaks to the way it functions as a symbolic container, a dream of totality in the contemporary psyche. We can get a sense of this by looking closely at our ideas about the brain, many of which reveal echoes of nineteenth- and twentieth-century tendencies toward specialization, like geography and brain maps, discrete centers of emotion and memory, types of intelligence, localizations, right brain/left brain splits, and the like. We can also hear recent, more holistic, metaphors, such as brain networks and fields, neural ecosystems, plasticity, and neuronal mirroring. These two themes—specialization and holistic functioning, fragmentation and wholeness—come together in the sensibility portrayed in figure 24, a painting titled *Brain Story*, by contemporary Aboriginal artist Rachel Napaljarri Jurra. It depicts four fields of brain function that together comprise the whole story of human experience within the Aboriginal cosmos. In order from top to bottom, the first field depicts the interconnectedness of cultural intelligence—the myths and thoughts of "story brain." Next down are the relationships and emotions of "family brain," depicted as people sitting around a fire or hearth. A field of flowers, hills, and water sites—the territory and geography/environment of "country brain"—follows. And at the base lies the area of somatic vitality—the physical and molecular domains of "body brain."

Figure 24: *Brain Story*, by Rachel Napaljarri Jurra (1994), acrylic on linen, Alice Springs, Australia.

Subject to both brainwashing and brainstorming, our ideas about the brain are informed as much by our fantasies about ourselves as by scientific and technological innovation. As the terra incognita of the brain continues to open up, it is worth noting that as we look at images and scans of brain functioning, what we are also seeing is the psyche imagining itself. And like any good dream of totality, our fantasies about the brain can open up or close off imagination, encompass reality and distort it. This may be part of what Emily Dickinson was implying—perhaps cheekily—in her poem, ca. 1862, "The Brain Is Wider Than the Sky":

> The Brain—is wider than the Sky—
> For—put them side by side—
> The one the other will contain—
> With ease—and You—beside—
>
> The Brain is deeper than the sea—
> For—hold them—Blue to Blue—
> The One the other will absorb—
> As Sponges—Buckets—do—
>
> The Brain is just the weight of God—
> For—Heft them—Pound for Pound—
> And they will differ—if they do—
> As Syllable from Sound—[7]

One of the more startling conjectures about interiority, the brain, and the migration into the head was proposed by psychologist Julian Jaynes in *The Origin of Consciousness in the Breakdown of the Bicameral Mind*.[8] I discuss it here not because it grasps the paradox of parts and wholes, as Dickinson's poem does, but because it provides another compelling illustration of the way in which our imagination projects the fluctuations in its experience of totality and disintegration backward into the mists of time and linguistic ancestry. Jaynes's thesis was that our ancestors had a split-hemispheric (bicameral) brain organization that was more rigid than ours and that, as a consequence of this, they heard what appeared to be commands coming from the gods via what we would now call auditory hallucinations originating from the right brain hemisphere. According to Jaynes, emotional stress was the trigger for the release of the hallucinations, and the "archaic mind" experienced the hallucinations as something separate, the gods. A deviation from the norm—a stressor that required a decision or a change in behavior—would cause the gods to "speak" in the bicameral mind, offering instruction and a reconstitution of wholeness.

Although he rescued auditory hallucinations from the dumpster of pathology, Jaynes, like Freud and the New Atheists, looked backward for explanations, conjecturing that bicamerality evolved as a form of social control, a stage in the evolution of civilization and its discontents. Simply put, the voices of the gods kept people in line by providing guidance and direction. Jaynes also suggested that there might have been a periodicity to the ancient bicameral theocracies that explained the mystery of why some ancient cities seemed to have been vacated relatively quickly: when a society became so complex that the gods could no longer be heard through the din—or perhaps when they could not handle the stress—whole societies deserted their cities. The people returned only after a rest period of tribal living, a presumably simpler, quieter lifestyle, during which the gods could be heard again. Jaynes cites an ancient Sumerian text that lamented in an uncanny and familiar way,

> The people became numerous . . .
> The god was depressed by their uproar
> Enlil [Lord of the Open, the Wind] heard their noise,
> He exclaimed to the great gods
> The noise of mankind has become burdensome.[9]

Jaynes speculates that as humanity evolved the hallucinatory voices stopped, replaced first by oracles and divination, then by the great prophets, and finally by the thoughts of moral and wise people. As social systems continued to develop, the bicameral mind broke down even further, and unitary consciousness as we know it became predominant. We became, in effect, more conscious of our consciousness. According to Jaynes, all forms of isms and systems still active today, from astrology to communism, embody a "fervent search for archaic authorization . . . umbilical cords reaching back into the sustaining unsubjective past."[10] Truth itself, wrote Jaynes,

> is a part of the pervasive nostalgia for an earlier certainty. The very idea of a universal stability, an eternal firmness of principle *out there* that can be sought for through the world as might an Arthurian knight for the Grail, is, in the morphology of history, a direct outgrowth of the search for

lost gods in the first two millennia after the decline of the bicameral mind. What was then an augury for direction of action among the ruins of an archaic mentality is now the search for an innocence of certainty among the mythologies of facts.[11]

According to Jaynes's schema, the thirst and yearning for living gods remains with us even now, heard in the voices of muses, poets, and artists. As we saw in the preceding chapter, this reductive approach has a bias in primitivity, and as we will see in what follows, the whole scenario is not unlike the one taken up by many of the early psychoanalysts as they searched for their own forms of "archaic authorization," trying to "open the mouths of the gods" and listen to their wisdom in pursuit of psychology's dream of interiority.[12]

Taking a reductive approach, looking backward for evidence of archaic authorization or living gods, may be more an identification with a fantasy of lost innocence, with a dream of paradise, than anything else. It seems much simpler, and less biased toward primitivity, to take the mythopoetic mind at face value as an enduring type of consciousness and awareness that often has projection as its modus operandi. There are always times when the dreams of totality spun by the mythopoetic mind no longer hold; it's in the very nature of the process that they break down and reform. There is no compelling reason to conclude that poetry, art, and all forms of mythopoetic expression are actually a longing or nostalgia for archaic authorization from the gods or a throwback of evolutionary history. If that were so, we would expect these forms of experience and expression to just dry up—which they don't. Although sometimes, as the Sumerians divined, the voice of the mythopoetic mind is hard to hear through the din and uproar. That's when psychopomps materialize.

Psychopomps

Psychology has always had a colorful array of psychopomps, images, fantasies, and actual persons that have guided us into the terra incognita of the mythopoetic mind. Fascination and fantasies about the brain—bicameral or otherwise—are only the most recent. Experiencing a renewed sense of wholeness often requires the intervention of a psychopomp—a word deriving from the Greek for "soul conductor," meaning a guide for souls on their way to the underworld. In psychological language, a psychopomp is a psychological process, usually personified, which acts as a bridge to what's unknown—to what has been variously imagined as the land of the ancestors and the dead, the underworld, the otherworld, the chaos before creation, heaven and hell, terra incognita, and later the unconscious. A psychopomp, or someone who carries that projection, opens a doorway and takes us toward a renewed sense of totality in which prior ambivalence is resolved, the scales are balanced, life is rightly measured, or simply where what was out of reach may be finally found. In the ancient world, for example, jackal-headed Anubis of Egypt led the dead to the otherworld, and the magician Hermes Trismegistus opened the portal of hermetic and occult wisdom. In the Middle Ages, Virgil led Dante through the inferno to paradise.

Psychopomps are personifications of the ways by which individuals and cultures negotiate their way into new territory. They represent our sense of going somewhere, they symbolize how we move through the ambiguity of living into a sense of wholeness, of how we move across the boundaries from the known to the unknown, the seen to the unseen, often from the here and now to a sensibility of the eternal. Psychopomps usually appear at the boundary zone of a prevailing dream of totality, at the point of weak connection, where things no longer hold together, personifying the psychological and cultural dynamics that are pressing for entry or rearrangement into a new story. These emotional elements that disrupt dreams of totality are often portrayed in mythology as trickster figures or disenfranchised persons, figures that transgress boundaries—motivated by need, by hunger or greed, or by unabashed gleeful perversity and the love of boundary busting.

For example, there were several psychopomps that led the way into psychology's dreams of wholeness, and these were clearly figures that carried disenfranchised, even "dirty" elements of individual and collective life. At the turn of the twentieth century, mediums and hysterics (usually women) and their male counterparts, the shell-shocked soldiers who fought in World War I, opened the doors into the territory of psychoanalysis. They led the way into the taboo territory of sexuality, into the mysteries of trauma and dissociation, into the unconscious, the family romance, and the creative imagination. For Freud and Jung, dreams and dissociated complexes became the "royal road to the unconscious." After the founding fathers departed the scene, the psychology of the child appeared, with a coincident emphasis on infant development and the primacy of the mother/infant dyad, that is, attachment theory. With this development, the "inner child" movement and the related issues of incest and child abuse moved to center stage. More recently, attention has moved once again to dissociative states of mind, to the psychology of multiple selves, and to mood disorders. The fact that these are the psychopomps de jour reflects how we are experiencing dimensions of psychological experience that feel new—our ability to multiply social roles and identities and to seemingly rise above embodiment.

Spirit mediums, hysterics, the traumatized, the unconscious, mothers, children, multiples, and even neuroscience have all functioned as the mediums—in both senses of the word—that beckoned to us and still promise to lead somewhere more inclusive, somewhere more real than our experience on this side of the divide. Psychopomps appear from the mythopoetic mind during the interregnum, at the portal, at twilight and at dawn, in all the in-between places between here and there. The birth of psychology itself took place at the gates to the world of gods and ancestors, in a soup of mediumistic flair, divination, and communication with the unseen world. At the turn of the twentieth century, spiritualism was the vehicle through which the psychoanalytic dream of interiority first entered the collective imagination. Mediums in trances were all the rage, and conducting séances and consulting Ouija boards to seek wisdom from the departed in the land of the dead was de rigueur for many seekers after truth. Many of the founding fathers of modern depth psychology took part in this *fascinosum*; nearly everyone was under the influence. The more important players were William James, whose *Varieties of Religious Experience* would appear in 1902, Theodore Flournoy, whose book about a popular medium served as the model for C. G. Jung's dissertation, and a friend of James's, the unsung F. W. H. Myers, an English psychologist and psychic researcher who coined the terms *clairvoyance, precognition,* and *subliminal imagination*. Myers and James were both presidents of the influential London Society for Psychical Research, a group that had a fascination with the Delphic oracle. Members of the London Society, which had also included Freud and Jung, devoted themselves to assessing scholarship about the oracle as it pertained to spiritualism and the clairvoyant powers of imagination. Such was the climate, the medium, and the message that nurtured early psychological theories.

When the pioneers of psychology entered the spiritualist arena, the gates to the beyond closed, and the material that surfaced from the mythopoetic mind during an altered state was moved firmly into the psychological field. It was conceived of as being mediated by unconscious personalities in the form of, for example, a spirit medium's guide. This irrevocable shift was depicted vividly in Flournoy's *From India to the Planet Mars*, a book about the popular medium Helene Smith and her spirit guide Leopold, which was published in the same watershed year of 1900 that Freud's *Interpretation of Dreams* first made its appearance. In the introduction to a recent edition of Flournoy's study, historian Sonu Shamdasani makes a compelling case for Flournoy's formulation of unconscious multiple selves having been the true discovery of the unconscious, that in altered states of consciousness the creative imagination is hard at work.[13] It was Frederic Myers who first suggested a model of the unconscious based on subliminal selves with creative capacities and, as he termed it, a "mythopoetic" function.[14] Jung would take this idea and run with it. Freud would come to adopt an ambivalent posture toward this "black mud-tide of occultism," as he put it, and with that, eventually, a skeptical stance toward the prospective, creative aspect of the mythopoetic mind.

The Early Days

At this juncture, it's worth pausing to summarize what had been discovered and reformulated in those early days. From within their particular dream of wholeness—the conscious/unconscious dyad—the founding fathers took over the function of spirit mediums as psychopomps. Leaning very heavily on their female patients—hysterics and ordinary neurotic dreamers—they both drew from them and attributed to them many of the ideas specific to the psychological enterprise of the twentieth century: symptom conversion, the importance of sexuality and the forbidden, fantasies about women, mothers, children, the feminine, trauma, repression, creativity, and reconstruction. The overarching theme was that healing came about via a descent into the unconscious, a regression that in one way or another restored emotional and psychological wholeness.

What had been discovered, or rediscovered, was that just as the reality of relationships and objects can't be reduced to intrapsychic phenomena, there is a reality to psychological phenomena that can't be reduced to relationships and objects. Psychological experience is related to, but not reducible to, other registers of experience, for example, to spirits, the biochemistry of the brain, or the givens of one's family of origin. The psychological and emotional experiences that we personify as images should be taken as they are experienced, as substantial in their own domain as physical objects appear to be in theirs.

Extending this idea further, for many of the early psychologists the unconscious could never be entirely repressed, exhausted, or even emptied out. In fact, such a situation would be disastrous for psychic health, because the unconscious was the source—in the parlance of that day—of the creative imagination. Consequently, the danger of being flooded by or identified with imaginal processes (engulfment or possession) was always present, and a kind of madness was always possible. Jung's solution to this was a happier one than Freud's: he conceived the relationship between the ego (the domain of conscious identity) and the rest of the psyche (the unknown, unconscious domain) as being in continuous dialogue, a dialogue that was by definition a never-ending process. What changes over time is the nature of the conversation. There is no end to the relationship, but rather, as the alchemists imagined it, "the goal is the art"—meaning the art of back-and-forth exchange between the two domains, between rational thinking and fluid mythopoetic process. But the early psychologists differed a great deal with respect to their postures toward the vast unknown of their newly discovered unconscious, fearing being overwhelmed by it or desiring an experience of unity with it. And their reactions mirrored the ambivalent medicine of the *pharmakon*.

For many, like Jung, this newly discovered unconscious was considered to have a more vital, useful, or higher intelligence than one's usual consciousness. Key here was the idea that dissociative states of mind like hysteria, or any other symptom complex for that matter, could be the carrier of new possibilities—the old idea that the illness contains the cure. There was no need to invoke the dead, spiritual entities, extraterrestrials, sexual repression, or even childhood traumata to explain altered states. The psyche was just inherently multidimensional and also working toward integration, and the vehicle of mythopoetic thinking and expression was key to understanding both. As Jung would state later on, in relation to the appearance of mandala symbolism in his patients' dreams as an instance of the creative capacity of the psyche to bring together dissociated states, "all so-called causes become mere occasions."[15]

Strange and remarkable things had been observed and experienced during those early days—things not immediately available to the conscious mind. The early psychoanalysts had experimented with automatic writing, hypnosis, spirits and séances, free association, and word association in their efforts to get beyond the margins of ego identity. And they faithfully followed the fascinating mythopoetic trails of imagination found in dreams and visions, firmly believing that all culture, including the culture of an individual psyche, originated from welcome and unwelcome incursions of imagination. These incursions, these altered states of imaginal process, were the portals through which the founders passed and were what defined the craft of depth psychology at its beginnings. What had been rediscovered was the mythopoetic mind and its capacity to spin healing fictions, to retranscribe and rewrite memory and experience into new stories.[16] As we will see in what follows, these healing fictions were imagined as being movements toward an ever larger field of experience, toward a more inclusive identity, both of self and in relation to community.

This idea that the mythopoetic mind contributes to integration is enjoying resurgence in light of what we now know—in the parlance of our day—about memory and narrative reconstruction. For example, the psyche creates key metaphors and narrative points of origin for itself, including for the seemingly inviolate memories of personal trauma.[17] Recent work on the emergent properties of memory suggests that what constitutes memory is a continuous process of neuronal recategorization, a rewriting and retranscription of events, rather than a simple process of retrieval. There is no fixed library of memories, no stored replicas, only potential categories that are formed in relationship to other categories, so that when new experience takes place, the mapping of similar past experience is remembered in the light of the new data. Memory is always emerging and created afresh in the light of new experience.

This activity was imagined in the ancient Greek mind by delegating the goddess of memory, Mnemosyne, as the mother of all the Muses—making memory, imagination, and creativity one big family. Fact and fiction, remembering and fictionalizing, may not be as different as we like to think they are; we dream and daydream ourselves into new awareness every day. Memories are just one story line in the play of consciousness. They can be moved around, spliced together, or edited to tell a different story or the same story with different feelings about it. They can be omitted from the narrative altogether. Memory is filed with gaps and holes; it's selective and it's temperamental. Dreaming of totality fills in those holes and gaps, creating stories that contain current experience as much as—maybe more than—the actual past. It may be most accurate to say that we use memories to create new images and narratives, to recreate our sense of wholeness and integrity.

This may be why accessing memories in therapy works—not because unearthing traumata presumed to have caused a malady is curative in itself, but because remembering in a new emotional and cognitive context is a creative activity—a way that new riverbeds for processing experience are carved out instead of just flowing through the same ruts. Consider this phenomenon, familiar to therapists and patients alike: the parent who was remembered as being good is suddenly remembered as being harmful, or the bad parent unexpectedly comes into view as having been good. Heretofore unseen qualities and effects of these parents and their actions seem to appear with unsettling and often liberating consequences in present time. The actual facts of the past have, of course, not changed. What seems to happen is that other stories appear, constituting a different emotional narrative about childhood, and one becomes, in that sense, a different child. Or, in a related phenomenon, one becomes aware of having been a player oneself all along, not just a passive recipient of others' actions. Following this shift in memories, there's often a sense of being one's own person, born—to continue the metaphor—out of one's own story. This plays out the same way in literary genres, for example, the narratives of literary memoirs which don't represent the facts of experience (boring), but rather tell us about the author's active engagement with his or her memories. That is what makes them compelling. The "lure and blur of the real" takes place at the boundary between fiction and nonfiction.[18] This is just how imagination operates—fictionalizing narratives about experience, experiences that will in turn alter their shape and meaning in accord with emerging narratives. We only recognize the authenticity of both memory and narrative when they arrive at a (mytho)poetic truth that captures the integrity of the present moment.

At the same time that the early psychologists recognized the mutability of psychological process—its shape-shifting and creative aspects as well as its propensity to organize experience into wholes—some of the early theories were becoming, not surprisingly, cohesive to the point of rigidity in their sweep and scope, resembling monomyths or magic circles in the totality of their visions. Whatever they were, they purported to understand everything, to give ultimate and definitive direction and meaning to life. This gave the enterprise a cultlike cast, with a tenor and tone that was fervent, almost religious. The theories often presumed a condition of lost innocence and wholeness a la Plato or Rousseau, a "fall" of humanity into the modern alienated state of being conscious, social, and technocratic beings. Jung, especially, initially romanticized the wholeness of natural man—what he called the "archaic psyche" and the "wisdom of the unconscious." Freud also placed natural man center stage, but in Freud's vision, the aura cast around him was less a romantic glow and more of a despondent gloom.

Interestingly, as the unconscious became increasingly elevated, another dream of totality came into play, one that was directly compensatory to the story about the archaic, natural wisdom of the newly discovered unconscious. And it was equally sweeping. It was a monomyth about the primacy of consciousness, about human consciousness even completing the creation of the world. For example, in his autobiography *Memories, Dreams, Reflections,* Jung wrote about a formative experience he had in Africa, which had occurred at the same time that he was being most impressed by the wisdom of the archaic mind that he imagined resided undisturbed in Africa. As he surveyed the Athi Plains of Kenya, Jung thought,

> Now I knew what it was, and knew even more: that man is indispensable for the completion of creation; that, in fact, he himself is the second creator of the world, who alone has given to the world its objective existence—without which, unheard, unseen, silently eating, giving birth, dying, heads nodding through hundreds of millions of years, it would have gone on in the profoundest night of non-being down to its unknown end. Human consciousness created objective existence and meaning, and man found his indispensable place in the great process of being.[19]

Many people today would be aghast at this politically incorrect privileging of humanity and the many shadows that follow in its wake. We are painfully aware of the perverse interiority and the destructive narcissism or overt imperialism that can flow from considering human consciousness indispensable. There's been a shift in our certainty about what consciousness is and who, or even what, possesses it. Our field of engagement has opened up, both relativizing and focusing our position in the great process of being. But the founders of psychology had totalizing visions and theories, especially about consciousness, and were also often correspondingly totalitarian in their execution and exclusivity, demanding total commitment and fidelity from disciples and a sacred reverence for seminal texts, as we saw in chapter 1. Even today, professional psychoanalytic groups are notorious for infighting and bitter scapegoating of those who do not sign on wholeheartedly to the program at hand. Although the rift between Freud and Jung is the most well known of these stories, it is by no means the only one. As psychoanalyst Julia Kristeva wrote, "Infinite are the metamorphoses of the dead father," and the story of psychology is in many ways a story of progressively narrowing splits or increasingly fine-tuned differentiations—depending on one's attitude.[20]

Even at psychology's beginnings the motif of the one and the many hovered in the background. How were the phenomena of altered states and dissociation that the founders observed to be squared with the fact that experience also feels unified, somehow also all of a piece? The solution in those days, in the form of an image, was that the sum total of secondary selves was linked up with a timeless, mythic big Self. William James expressed it first, suggesting that consciousness is split up into parts that are dissociated from one another, nevertheless playing complementary roles. The sum of these complementarities he considered to be the sense of self.[21] This idea of a fragmented and yet unified personality being the penultimate model of emotional and mental health would not leave the field of psychology for a long time. The entire sensibility was in line with the older, magical Hermetic pattern, in which the one thing give birth to all dualities and contradictions, these many in turn seeking to return to the one. Jung took this notion all the way, expressing it poignantly:

> The ancient and long obsolete idea of man as a microcosm contains a supreme psychological truth that has yet to be discovered. In former times this truth was projected upon the body, just as alchemy projected the psyche upon chemical substances. But it is altogether different when the microcosm is understood as that interior world whose inward nature is fleetingly glimpsed in the unconscious . . . And just as the cosmos is not a dissolving mass of particles, but rests in the unity of God's embrace, so man must not

> dissolve into a whirl of warring possibilities and tendencies imposed on him by the unconscious, but must become the unity that embraces them all.²²

Although Jung was very concerned with unity, he was also keenly interested in "warring possibilities," which was one reason he was initially taken with Freud's notion of dissociated traumatic memories. But Jung never believed that warring possibilities were necessarily caused by sexual trauma or by any trauma at all. For Jung the psyche was inherently dissociative, with complexes and archetypal tendencies functioning autonomously as multiple fields of experience. Following William James, the dream of totality that emerged for Jung was one of multiple complexes and personalities working to create wholeness, in the same sense in which mysterious or distressing symptoms are usually both a wound and the beginning of the cure, because they are expressing what is pushing to be integrated into the personality. Shades of the ancient incubation mysteries. Fits of vengeful rage, for example, bouts of depression, eating disorders, and compulsive behavior of all sorts were approached as subpersonalities as it were, as behavior and emotions that were admittedly stuck in their form of expression, nevertheless revealing something essential, often in mythic and dramatic ways. The situation might be mirrored in a familiar dream: of ugly, threatening, or mysterious persons or animals breaking into the house or transgressing a boundary. What is outside the margins of ego identity appears alien and often dangerous but also presses to be included, which, if it occurs, enlarges one's scope of emotion and possibilities.

Another way to get a handle on this is to ask the *pharmakon* question: How are fluctuating states of mind or distressing symptoms of whatever sort both poison and panacea? A reductive perspective usually takes the poison approach. This predominantly archaeological method delves into the ruins of the past in order to understand the present and considers dissociative states to be what interferes with integration and emergent processes, what is not complementary but rather opposed to the big Self. Dissociative states might initially be engineered to defend the integrity of identity—like magic circles—but they become entrenched and block emergent processes. In this view, the destructive aspects of dissociation are the reason narratives get stuck. The synthetic perspective, on the other hand, is concerned with the present as it gives rise to future developments and considers dissociative states to have an integrating function as a generator of new emotional and psychological meanings, the panacea perspective. In this view, the purpose or aim of a symptom or dissociative state is as important, if not more so, than its initial cause. A symptom develops not because of prior history, but in order to express what's otherwise inexpressible but pressing to be integrated into identity. The clinical question is not reductive, but synthetic: What is this symptom doing, and what is it for?

Putting the reductive and synthetic approaches together in regard to dissociative states—which is actually what happens in good depth psychotherapy—holds the poison and panacea paradox of the *pharmakon* together. At this juncture I am only going to note the interesting parallel this poses in relation to contemporary discussions about the fragmentation that is characteristic of postmodern culture—as to whether the dissociative states of mind that seem to abound in collective life are blocking integrative processes, enhancing them, or both at once? This issue will be taken up in detail in chapter 6. At this point, we can simply appreciate that the most serious form of emotional and mental disease—whether individual or cultural—is probably not the existence of dissociated states per se, but the breakdown of the psyche's ability to rectify its emotional landscape by bringing dissociated material into awareness and to rewrite its own stories with the new material.

The early psychoanalysts faced several questions that we still engage in contemporary theory. How are the various aspects of psychological process organized or not organized? How is it that the dream of totality called the self seems to encompass both a stable sense of identity and an ever changing, fluctuating consciousness, even a sensibility of multiple selves? In modern discourse, Erik Erikson thought that maturation through the stages of life resulted in something stable, even though that something was embedded in changing relationships and contexts. His student Robert Lifton took the other view, emphasizing changing narratives and multiple identities, suggesting that the self was more protean and resists fixity. So the dance goes on: from the point of view of solidity and stability, the protean self is immature and marginal, and from the protean self's perspective, the stable self is stuck and rigid, even Kronos-like in its predilection to swallow up what is new. In many ways, the story of psychology itself is one of searching for a rapprochement between the sense of wholeness we experience and the fragmentation and mutability of many selves and many narratives that we also experience. A myth about the one and the many, about fragmentation and wholeness.

Resolving this dilemma is also a never-ending story. Jung, for example, tried to resolve it by positing a dynamic factor in the psyche that he termed the Self, by which he meant the psyche's image of its own potential wholeness and its movements toward that cohesion. The Self was imagined as much more inclusive than the little self of ego awareness, and under optimal conditions ego identity functions as a kind of executor or vehicle for expression of the Self. The Self was a symbol for the condition of wholeness because it encompassed conflicting and multiple tendencies in the mind and emotions—love, hate, envy, hope, vulnerability, and the like—and as such was different from the image of perfection. Perfection is, in fact, a state of *in*completeness because it lacks a living acknowledgment of suffering and malignancy.

If, for example, someone suffered abuse as a child, the work of healing (imaged as Self) would probably include experiencing fear, rage, recrimination, and victimization. This is necessary not only as an end in itself (catharsis) but as movement toward an acceptance of the effects of the abuse as part of one's own particular life givens. Distressing and destructive as it was, the abuse has to be included into identity and then disidentified from (again, part of the remembering process), rewritten into other emotional and mental narratives of self and identity. This is its meaning; it becomes one's own story. This brokers a different relationship with suffering, and the new narratives usually include empathy with the suffering of others, the sharing of essentials, and a movement out of encapsulated subjectivity into a more objective awareness of our human condition. The marriage of lighter and brighter elements with darker factors yields the Self experience and allows a mature wisdom to shine through one's particular experiences and identity. Or, put another way, what was given as fate is reclaimed as destiny. Compulsive behavior grows into a more conscious life, a life that both rests in the containment of its boundaries and givens and cuts across them by the moves of disidentification and empathy. If most psychological processes are reconstructive, we can even hazard to say that all history, even the most traumatic, seeks another story.

Jung's initial idea was that the Self was present at the beginning of life, a potential totality of the personality made up of capacities, attributes, and genetic determinants, all there in concealed form waiting to unfold like a seed or genetic blueprint, acting as an organizing function throughout development. As he matured, Jung elaborated the goal of totality using the alchemical imagery of the stone (the seed) that begins its journey as a chaotic *massa confusa,* passes through innumerable alchemical tortures—heating, cooling, vaporizing—in the alembic of living until it becomes the *pharmakon,* the philosopher's stone, the elixir of immortality. Some of this torture just happened naturally in the course of living but some required hard-won awareness and an ethical sensibility, as described above. Jung imaged this latter part as an *opus contra naturam,* a singular work against nature. At the end of development (a condition never fully realized), the Self was no longer a seed but a mandala, which by encompassing contradictions in the manner we discussed before symbolized wholeness and health. What was there at the beginning *in potentia* is still there at the end, but the stone is no longer just a stone.

In his later work, Jung came to feel that symbols of the Self were expressing an essential mystery of being and identity formation that was fundamentally unknowable. It was unknowable not because of epistemological issues, not because the Self is both the subject speaking and the object of its contemplation, nor because it had not yet unfolded. It was unknowable because it didn't really exist; it was a "dream of totality," simply a symbol of process, part and parcel of the psyche's acts of creation.[23] This conception of wholeness pointed toward a postmodern perspective, a central metaphor of which is the dynamic interchange among subject, object, the intrapsychic, the interpersonal, the transpersonal, and the world—with images of the Self symbolizing integrative events, markers of the moments when the imagination creates new psychological ground.

For example, a woman who had suffered abuse as a child dreamed she was at a mixed-breed dog show. Each of the dogs sat excitedly on its own staging platform, all of which were arranged in a circle. As the dreamer went around from dog to dog, she saw that one of them was wagging a braid made from ribbons that had been attached to his rear, like a prosthetic, in place of the tail that had been cut off as a pup. The dreamer was impressed by how well the braid worked and moved that the dog show included a wounded contestant. The dream seemed to mark a particular moment and tell a story about how the abuse was being woven into a bigger picture of identity—how issues of wounds, perfection ("best in show"), and judgment were being reassessed as part of that process. The magic circle of the abuse dynamics that had excluded conflicting and even dissociated self-identifications was opening into a mandala of more differentiated experience. Her psyche imaged this as a Self event.

However, as much as someone like Jung was adamant about imagination's provision to fashion dreams of totality like the Self, he was also adamant about not becoming identified with these:

> What is troubling you in the head is, though you may not know it, like a rare jewel. It is like an animal that is strange to you, forming symbolically the centre of many concentric circles, reminiscent of the centre of a large or small world, like the eye of God in medieval pictures of the universe. Confronted with this a healthy mind would fight against identification with the centre, because of the danger of paranoiac God-likeness. Anyone who gets into this spider's net is wrapped round like a cocoon and robbed of his own life. He is isolated from his fellows, so that they cannot reach him, nor he them. He lives in the loneliness of the world-creator, who is everything and has nothing outside himself.[24]

Jung went on to add, "If, on top of all this, you have had an insane father, there is the danger that you will begin to 'spin' yourself."[25]

I will return to the theme of the insane father and the ways in which we spin ourselves collectively in part III. At this juncture we can simply note that in many ways, we in the West have had an insane father for quite some time and have been spinning a grandiose cocoon of totality around ourselves accordingly. The early psychoanalysts were, in a way, trying to hedge against this identification, although they also imagined that the many voices of mind and emotion that they observed were crying out for integration and union. They held fast to the idea of multiple fields of conscious and unconscious identity that were (or pathologically were not) in relationship and dialogue with one another. It was the dialogue that was presumed to yield an experience of totality and an enhanced appreciation of our shared reality. Their model was something like King Arthur's round table in a "Camelot of the psyche": multiple voices integrated into a unified experience, with ego identity having a special place at the table, so to speak. Like the once and future king, this never-ending story still lies at the heart of most systems of psychotherapy. Suffering with the multiplicity of one's psyche is thought to generate a kind of ferment—like the yeast that causes bread to rise or juice to turn into wine. This ferment of dialogue, in the sense of "bearing with," is the medicine, the process by which a sense of wholeness and integrity is built up. But this vision began to give way in psychology's dream to looser and more unruly groupings.

Fugitives

As a postmodern sensibility entered the field of psychology, it left imprints of some of its central ideas: pluralism (multiculturalism, diversity), reversals, uncertainty, the social construction of identity (feminism), the relational quality of meaning (ecology), the collapse of subject/object distinctions, and the appearance of "fugitive selves," selves in flight and in hiding from any essentialist meaning whatsoever.[26] While we have been able to inhabit many social selves for quite awhile now—for example, psychologist, wife, mother—it is fast becoming possible for identity and roles to be loosened from body identity—in vitro fertilization, gender bending, even transgendering. No longer purely metaphoric, the "man in the woman," the "woman in the man," cloned creatures and new hybridized species, shifting and multiple identities are real. As Malcolm Bull points out in *Seeing Things Hidden*,

> We already have little difficulty dealing with holders of dual or even multiple nationality, so there seems no intrinsic reason why individuals of dual or multiple races, genders, sexualities, ages or species should not also be satisfactorily accommodated within our conceptual and legal systems.[27]

In contemporary discourse, the unity of the self has been thoroughly decentered. Psychologists like James Hillman emphasized an image of psychological process as peopled by multiple and separate centers of consciousness—the ego being only one among many centers—each having its own integrity and mandates, complete in itself, none being particularly privileged. These many selves are their own mediums, containing their own messages and their own meanings, and they tilt away from the one and toward the many. This move became mirrored by the observation that there is no center of activity in the brain where the self resides or even a definite location where oneself is felt to be; this center migrates, in fact, between the head, the heart, the throat, and, for blind people, the fingertips. As was discussed before, the self has no permanent memories or even an accurate recall of events that happened. Even personality, grounded as it is in physiological temperament, is being understood as having aspects that are always being synthesized. Memory, emotions, events, and even the givens of our lives are scripted into new neural schemas that are themselves continuously emerging and being updated, a process heavily biased toward what has subjective value and meaning for the individual at a particular time and within a particular culture. In *Private Myths*, analyst Anthony Stevens suggests that this emergent process we call self is part of what is going on during REM dreaming.[28] So it's tempting to conjecture that when Jung remarked that "the thing I call the self is a dream of totality," he may have been more precise than he knew.

While contemporary discourse about the self is about emergent consciousness, a kind of streaming experience, it also includes a very persistent story about a self who does things and remembers. The popularity of blogging seems to be one way in which that self is finding its way into the multiplicity of possibilities and the flow of images and information. People shape their own stories with an urgency to tell all, in a kind of open-ended research on the self, at the same time that we inhabit many—even masked—online selves. These personae, in a reversal worthy of the *pharmakon*, are in turn exposed to reification and manipulation via digital archiving. And who or what will categorize them as real or illusory? A tension remains between inhabiting the multiple identities that contemporary living offers, and increasingly demands, and a sensibility of unity. New terms like *politics of recognition,* the *multicultural soul,* and *cosmopolitan citizenship* have come into language, bringing with them recognition of a unifying sense of sameness and a sense of multiplicity and differences—belonging to the globalized world and belonging to distinct cultural communities, for instance. But many are worried about confusion and manipulation and about how identity will be recognized in the future. For example, Malcolm Bull pointed out that,

> in the politics of recognition, the unity of the self is preserved, and difference is accommodated through single selves inhabiting multiple spaces rather than multiple selves inhabiting a single social space. But the two are in no sense equivalent, for unless multicultural politics also allows for a multiplication of the self, it is hard to see how it constitutes a giving rather than a denial of recognition.[29]

Psychology's identity crisis carries many of the same tensions. The assumption that psychological process and imagination are the ground of psychology still persists—although some would say barely—but there is also a proliferation of many psychologies: gender psychology, organizational psychology, cognitive behavioral psychology, neuropsychology, and the like that further specify psychology but also lose the connection with psyche. The burgeoning of different psychotherapies, psychotropic medications, spiritual disciplines, and twelve-step programs—particularly in America—may be part of a targeted approach to psychological process, or it may be one more way in which specificity moves away from the imagination and the access to reconstruction that imagination provides. Added to this mix is the further decentering of the self due to the incorporation of Eastern dreams of totality that emphasize no-self, or at least a radical disidentification from ego identity. From a Buddhist point of view, for example, actions and their consequences (karma) are real, but the self that acts is a temporary construction. To put the case even more forcefully, the self is an illusion that is the root of all suffering when it seeks to make itself permanent.

Of course, there is a paradox here, another *pharmakon*. We tell ourselves a story about the self that is both true and false. The fiction of the self is a very effective illusion that nevertheless seems to contribute to psychological health, as well as a delusion that can make us sick when fixed and grandiose. Our contemporary experience of totality seems to be compensating for this grandiosity—our sense of self is often floating and arbitrary, dictated by the ebb and flow of media images and sometimes held together by magical thinking. As analyst Toshio Kawai described it, "self-reflection is formal and without content and character."[30] It was described poignantly by Douglas Coupland in the novel *Generation X: Tales for an Accelerated Culture*. One of the post–baby boom characters complains (with typical offhand flippancy):

> But my crisis wasn't just the failure of youth but also a failure of class and of sex and the future and I *still* don't know what. I began to see this world as one where citizens stare, say, at the armless Venus de Milo and fantasize about amputee sex or self-righteously apply a fig leaf to the statue of David, but not before breaking off his dick as a souvenir. All events

became omens; I lost the ability to take anything literally . . .
My life had become a series of scary incidents that simply
weren't stringing together to make for an interesting book.[31]

Even the most together among us are not unfamiliar with these feelings.

In summary, then, the dreams of totality presided over by spirits, ancestors, and the hereafter gave way first to a migration inward, landing in psychology's dreams of interiority and the self, subsequently taking form as an equally dark *rotundum*, the brain. We are leaving behind the dream that one's unconscious seeks to become conscious—and thus whole and redeemed—and we can also recognize that the black box of the brain that we are compelled to open is, from a symbolic perspective, also a psychopomp, a creature of imagination, another redemptive dream of totality. The totality of selfhood is becoming increasingly relativized by a sensibility of multiple fields of identity and of multiple selves, a development reflected in social and political movements and buttressed by developments in neuroscience and psychology that highlight the narrative nature of the self. With these shifts in the collective psyche from the one to the many, images of meaninglessness and fragmentation also abound, as we see ourselves reflected in shards and fragments of what used to feel like an integrated self.

At the same time that we struggle with selfhood and fragmentation within our particular spheres of experience, we are also confronted with the fact that there are multiple modes of social organization in the contemporary world. Tribal, feudal, modern, postmodern—all these societies and psyches sit side by side, giving living forms to their collective dreams of totality. These forms are colliding with one another—also making us sick—at the same time that we are reorganizing our self-image of human society. We try and pull together in images like globalization and the cybervillage, but glaring differences remain. The consciousness of modernity, for example, continues on. People still feel an angst-ridden separation and alienation from nature and community and a desired reunion, the *Avatar* dream, for example, harboring fantasies about organic farming that will save the world population from starvation and degradation. In some cultures modernity is just developing or, alternatively, is being actively resisted. There are also many community-based societies in the world, religious and otherwise, in which the primary identification is with the group—here or in the hereafter. In Japan, for example, at the same time that Western capitalist economies, with their lack of social safety nets, have become ubiquitous, the dominant mode of consciousness is collective, asking, What does the social group want and need? And as we saw before, in fundamentalist communities of all stripes, the kingdom of heaven is always somewhere else. What goes on down here on planet Earth is significant only to the extent that it aids the coming of a distant paradise—a radical dissociation and projection of consciousness.

Nevertheless, there seems to be a sacrifice of symbolic forms of wholeness being exacted as we experience breakdowns and splits in every area of personal and social life. If fragmentation is itself a psychopomp, a prelude to another dream of wholeness, we are well on our way. Updating psychology's dream of totality seems to necessitate widening out the dream of self into what used to be called psyche, a move that connects self more firmly with other selves and with the world. In that respect it is not a coincidence that digital and communications technology allows us to make ourselves up out of recognizable fragments of culture, to shape ourselves and to distort ourselves, to blog and Tweet ourselves into being, to make a self that everyone can see and share in. To the extent that these new sensibilities of self enhance the flow of connection and awareness of imagination, they will be a panacea. On the other side lies the *pharmakon*'s sleight of hand, the dissociative draw to archive and upload ourselves for all to see and manipulate. The mythopoetic mind and the dreams of totality it spins always provides for a sharing of essentials—for both the panacea of mirroring and mutual recognition and the poisonous contagion of projections and exploitation. The dialogue with the other, with what lies outside the boundaries of identity, is also just that: the forging of an empathic or destructive connection with actual others. It is to society's dreams that we now turn.

Notes

[1] Chapter 7 in C. G. Jung, *Modern Man in Search of a Soul* (Orlando, FL: Harcourt, 1933, 1955), provides a discussion of the wisdom of the archaic psyche, as do many of the fantasies and commentaries in C. G. Jung, *The Red Book* (New York: W. W. Norton, 2009).

[2] E. O. Wilson, *From So Simple a Beginning: The Four Great Books of Charles Darwin* (New York: W.W. Norton, 2005).

[3] Deemed by *Time* magazine to be one of the one hundred most influential people of 2009, Paul Ekman also studied the relationship between emotional expression, truth, and deceit. His work was the basis for the popular television crime drama *Lie to Me*. See Paul Ekman, *Emotions Revealed: Recognizing Faces and Feelings to Improve Communication and Emotional Life* (New York: Holt Paperbacks, 2007).

[4] C. G. Jung, "Psychological Aspects of the Mother Archetype" (1954), in *The Archetypes and the Collective Unconscious,* vol. 9i, *The Collected Works of C. G. Jung* (Princeton, NJ: Princeton University Press, 1959), § 179.

[5] Richard Onians, *The Origins of European Thought* (New York: Cambridge University Press, 1991).

[6] For a discussion of the head and brain as archetypal images, see the respective entries in *The Book of Symbols: Reflections on Archetypal Images*, Archive for Research in Archetypal Symbolism, Ami Ronnberg and Kathleen Martin, eds. (New York: Taschen, 2010), pp. 340–345.

[7] Emily Dickinson, *The Collected Poems of Emily Dickinson* (New York: Barnes and Noble Classics, 2003), p. 70.

[8] Julian Jaynes, *The Origin of Consciousness in the Breakdown of the Bicameral Mind* (New York: Houghton Mifflin, 1976, 1990).

[9] Jaynes, citing W. F. Saggs, *The Greatness That Was Babylon* (London: Sidgwick and Jackson, 1991), p. 384.

[10] Jaynes, *The Origin of Consciousness,* pp. 320–321.

[11] *Ibid.*, p. 446.

[12] The ancient Egyptian ritual of the washing and opening of the mouth was performed to reanimate the living soul of the deceased. After being washed and purified, images of the gods, the mummified statues of rulers, or even favored animals had their mouths ceremonially opened by a sacred blade. This allowed the dead to see, hear, breathe, and eat—in short, to enjoy the offerings of food and drink made to them, thereby sustaining their living *ka*, their spirit. Once the rejuvenation had been accomplished, the images or mummified statues could reciprocate, speaking and helping out the living. See R. T. Rundle-Clark, *Myth and Symbol in Ancient Egypt* (London: Thames and Hudson, 1959, 1978).

[13] Sonu Shamdasani, introduction, Theodore Flournoy, *From India to the Planet Mars: A Case of Multiple Personality and Imaginary Languages* (Princeton, NJ: Princeton University Press, 1900, 1994).

[14] Henri Ellenberger, *The Discovery of the Unconscious: The History and Evolution of Dynamic Psychiatry* (New York: Basic Books, 1970).

¹⁵ C. G. Jung, *Psychology and Alchemy*, vol. 12, *The Collected Works of C. G. Jung* (Princeton, NJ: Princeton University Press, 1968), §249.

¹⁶ For the classic exposition of how contemporary archetypal psychology understands the notion of healing fictions, see James Hillman, *Re-visioning Psychology* (New York: Harper, 1977), and James Hillman, *Healing Fiction* (Woodstock, CT: Spring Publications, 1998).

¹⁷ Daniel Stern, *The Interpersonal World of the Infant* (New York: Basic Books, 1985), p. 258.

¹⁸ David Shields, *Reality Hunger* (New York: Alfred A. Knopf, 2010).

¹⁹ C. G. Jung, *Memories, Dreams, Reflections* (New York: Random House, 1963), p. 256.

²⁰ See Ellenberger, *The Discovery of the Unconscious*; Phyliss Grosskurth, *The Secret Ring: Freud's Inner Circle and the Politics of Psychoanalysis* (New York: Addison-Wesley Publishing, 1991); and Julia Kristeva, *This Incredible Need to Believe* (New York: Columbia University Press, 2009), p. 63.

²¹ William James, *The Principles of Psychology*, vol. 1 (New York: Cosimo Classics, 1890, 2007).

²² C. G. Jung, "The Psychology of the Transference" (1946), in *The Practice of Psychotherapy*, vol. 12, *The Collected Works of C. G. Jung* (Princeton, NJ: Princeton University Press, 1954), §397.

²³ Miguel Serrano, *C. G. Jung and Herman Hesse: A Record of Two Friendships* (New York: Schocken Books, 1966), p. 50.

²⁴ C. G. Jung, "Flying Saucers: A Modern Myth of Things Seen in the Skies" (1958), in *Civilization in Transition*, vol. 10, *The Collected Works of C. G. Jung* (Princeton, NJ: Princeton University Press, 1964), §672.

²⁵ *Ibid*.

²⁶ Malcolm Bull, *Seeing Things Hidden: Apocalypse, Vision, and Totality* (New York: Verso, 1999), p. 282.

²⁷ *Ibid.*, p. 283.

²⁸ Anthony Stevens, *Private Myths: Dreams and Dreaming* (Cambridge, MA: Harvard University Press, 1997).

²⁹ Bull, *Seeing Things Hidden*, p. 274.

³⁰ Toshio Kawai, "Postmodern Consciousness in Psychotherapy," *Journal of Analytical Psychology* 51 (2006): 447.

³¹ Douglas Coupland, *Generation X: Tales for an Accelerated Culture* (New York: St. Martin's Griffon, 1991), pp. 30–31.

Chapter Four

Society's Dreams

> Ideologies are never interested in the miracle of being.
> —Hannah Arendt, *The Origins of Totalitarianism*

> To put it in a few words, the true malice of man appears only in the state and in the church, as institutions of gathering together, of recapitulation, of totalization.
> —Paul Ricoeur

> Society seems to be a process rather than a thing.
> —Victor Turner, *Structure and Anti-Structure*

Our dreams of totality move through the margins of individual identity into the larger domain of humanity's imagination and out into the world—into the heart of darkness of lived experience, into the shock of both internal recognition and recognition of the ever-present other. Akin to what Henry Corbin called the *mundus imaginalis*, dreams of totality are not simply bridges between subjectivity and objectivity but become wrapped around both, and like exceptional works of art they express the passions that shape our worldviews, giving image and voice to historical epochs and transitions, as well as to everyday social and cultural life.[1]

Dreaming of totality is a response to signals of tension and distress in our social systems, as well as in ourselves. We are well aware of the poisonous contagion that can reach from a dream of totality into the world and back. War, genocide, and terrorizing ideologies weave their way throughout history in dark counterpoint to every dream that opens up new possibilities. They are, as Stalin proudly proclaimed in regard to the incontrovertible logic of his ideas, "like a mighty tentacle that seizes you on all sides as in a vise and from whose grip you are powerless to tear yourself away; you must either surrender or make up your mind to utter defeat."[2] And the spread of ideologies is not a phenomenon isolated to long-gone and explicitly totalitarian governments. Western doctrines like manifest destiny, and its latest incarnation as free-market capitalism, are being deployed in various attempts to dominate the global economy. The long-standing refusal of Middle East governments to encompass the possibility of Israel and Palestine as two states instead of one still holds the contemporary world hostage to the threat of nuclear warfare. If this apocalyptic explosion brings on the heavenly city of New Jerusalem, so much the better for those who are banking on that dream of totality. As Jung warned, any identification with the spider's net of totality should indeed be very "troubling in the head."[3]

However, as Jung also remarked, it is like a rare jewel as well. We tend to dwell less on the more gracious side, the empathic connections forged by imagination and shared emotions. The fluidity of dreaming of totality and the urgency of the call and response dynamic opens us up to the subjectivity and objectivity of other selves and other realities. Dreaming of totality permits sympathy for the devil and empathy for the other, as what was foreign, disenfranchised, disfigured, or simply new is allowed entry. Every new dream of totality, whether of a culture or an individual, creates psychological and collective narratives that have thematic resonance with what came before. But dreaming of totality doesn't just re-create old stories and paradigms. It pulls them apart, crunches them up, and creates new narratives, new variations on universal themes which point the way toward future possibilities. Dynamic and under construction, these new dreams and variations are often at odds with prevailing collective mores and structures. This gives dreaming of totality its subversive cast, understanding *subvert* as "to turn from below."

In this chapter I explore dreaming of totality as a social *pharmakon*—how it functions as collective panacea and poison. By looking at several interrelated aspects of collective life—sacred cities and digital communities, sexuality and the beloved, utopias and dystopias, totalitarianism and transgression—we will see how the cycles and progressions of emancipation and eventual oppression that characterize many sociopolitical movements resemble the opening and closing that characterizes dreaming of totality.

Sacred Systems and the Sharing of Essentials

We start with cities, which provide social order and arenas for new life dramas to unfold, allowing great numbers of people to benefit from cooperation with one another in a multitude of ways and also housing and breeding the great social ills of poverty, disease, and overpopulation. Cities magnify, as Lewis Mumford wrote, "all the dimensions of life, through emotional communication, rational communication, technological mastery, and above all, dramatic representation."[4] In this sense, keeping cities alive and keeping watch for the ills that plague them from within is essential for collective health. The rise and fall of cities have also reflected the rise and fall of collective dreams of totality and the corresponding body politic and historical epochs with which we identify particular cities.

As we saw in chapter 1, many cities are structured and arranged around a symbolic center. In ancient cities, the god-presence was always at the center, whether it was Machu Picchu in Peru, Jericho in ancient Palestine, Teotihuacán in Mayan Mexico, Babylon, Delphi, the mythical Himalayan city of Shangri-La, or a European cathedral, a house of God. City centers formed nodal points with both vertical and horizontal components orienting collective life. A vertical axis connected earth, the underworld, and heaven, while the horizontal plane radiating from the center signified the everyday domain of community life. The sacred place where the two met was the point and moment of creation, and geomantic theories and construction rites governing the structure of cities attest to the symbolic significance of the center of creation; like the breaking of ground we still practice, they animate the area by repeating the original cosmic gesture of creation. Real time and eternal time come together at a city's center, imparting a sense of starting over, a return to the "once upon a time" of the first creation.

The rebirth motif imaged at the center of a city also mirrors spiritual and healing traditions in which the ritual of circumambulating or reaching the center is a profound symbolic repetition of the creation of the world.

This return to the center persists even in secular traditions. New York City, for example, still boasts a Central Park, with its *Angel of the Waters* statue keeping watch from her perch in Bethesda Fountain at the re-creational heart of Manhattan. New York seems to function as a healthy contemporary city in part because the hub of city life is organized around lively civic interests, human relationships, nature, and culture. We can also grasp the ongoing importance of the city center as seen in figure 25, an aerial photograph of Moscow at night. In this great ancient city with its mandala-like construction, inhabited since the second century, everything radiates around the Kremlin, a fortified complex at its heart. Enclosed by high, forbidding walls and only recently opened to the public, the Kremlin in Red Square contains the entirety of Russia's defining social structures: ancient cathedrals, imperialist tsarist palaces, Soviet government buildings, and now, festooned like a ring around Red Square, ultra upscale retail stores.

Figure 25: *Moscow at Night*, photograph by Alexey Kochemasov.

In the classical ancient world, it was probably the city of Delphi that had it all, and like all great cities it was much more than the sum of its parts. At that time Delphi was the center of the known universe, and by virtue of its signature navel-stone—the omphalos (the same one, by the way, that Kronos mistakenly swallowed)—it was reputed to stand at the very center of the earth. The east side of the temple of Delphi was dedicated to Apollo, the westward side to Dionysus, and this dual sensibility embodied the spirit of classical Greece, a sensibility both prophetic and ecstatic. The gods and oracles of the temple at Delphi were the great medicines of the ancient world, speaking their famous riddles in mythopoetic tongues that provided universally trusted guidance, making Delphi a religious and social institution that reigned supreme over the ancient world for many centuries.

The story of the Delphic oracle portrays a collective *pharmakon* that held sway for centuries. It began with the god Apollo killing a great primordial serpent—the Python. Apollo threw the Python's carcass into a volcanic fissure, where it putrefied in the depths, emerging in changed form as hallucinogenic vapors. Apollo set his temple over the fissure, and in the inner sanctum of the temple the hallucinogenic fumes entered the body of Apollo's priestess—the Pythia—as she sat on a sacred stool set over the hole. When thus fully altered and possessed, the priestess would sing, speak, or even shriek the divine prophecies of Apollo. This mythopoetic sequence, in which the great power of instinct develops into prophecy when it's expressed through the human psyche, is a variation on the ubiquitous mythology of the serpent power mentioned in chapter 1 in connection with Jung's painting (p. 31). The same motif is also found, for example, in African voodoo, wherein a priestess is symbolically penetrated by a god in the form of a snake, after which she can prophesize. It's also found in the Eastern tradition of Kundalini yoga, in which psychic energy is depicted as a serpent rising from the base of the spine, making its way up the body, winding around the spinal cord until it reaches the crown of the head—a symbol of total awakening (see figure 12). In all these traditions, energy is imagined as forming an arc or circle, traveling between instinct and some form of conscious realization.

The eventual demise of the Delphic oracle seems to have been the result of both overinstitutionalization and competition from another collective *pharmakon*, Christianity. When the emperor Diocletian came to Delphi in 303 AD to ask why the quality of oracular utterances had deteriorated, the oracle stated (perhaps defensively and apologetically) that it was because of the Christians. This pronouncement set off a persecution of the Christians living in Delphi, followed by retaliatory attacks by the Christians against the oracle. These battles came to a head in 389 AD, when the temple was finally shut down. Four years later, when the last Roman emperor Julian attempted to consult the last Delphic oracle, she is reputed to have declared:

> Tell the king; the fair wrought house has fallen.
> No shelter has Apollo, nor sacred laurel leaves;
> The fountains are now silent; the voice is stilled.
> It is finished.

After a run of eight hundred years, no further oracular statements were given.

The end of Delphi as the center of the ancient world and the succeeding rise of Christianity is an example of a large cultural transition in which one dream of totality, and one form of *pharmakon*, seems to replace another. It is not my intent here to survey historical epochs—that is beyond the scope of this book and beyond my expertise. That there *are* such large transitions, however, is something that most scholars seem in agreement about, or at least inclined to use as a hermeneutic device. Karen Armstrong, for example, makes the case in *The Great Transformation* that something extraordinary happened all over the world during the ninth century BCE, that violent events in four distinct regions of the world—China, Israel, Greece, and India—led to the development of the religious traditions that we recognize today as monotheism, philosophical rationalism, and Buddhism.[5] We can also understand these shifts in the regnant systems as having had their corresponding psychopomps—Confucius, Socrates, Buddha, the prophets, and so on.

But like one city built into the bones of another, a variety of dreams and paradigms of totality coexist in the psyche and in our institutions; we structure and perceive the world through many images simultaneously. While historical narrative divides time and ideas into chronological sequence, into phases and transitions, in our imagination dreams of totality similarly develop from one to the next but also coexist. This creates a lot of confusion. For example, in the afterword to *From So Simple a Beginning: The Four Great Books of Charles Darwin*, sociobiologist Edward O. Wilson waxed incredulous about the continuing disjunction between religious and scientific views about creation. "Why," he asked,

> does such intense and pervasive resistance to evolution continue 150 years after the publication of *The Origins of Species*, and in the teeth of the overwhelming accumulated

evidence favoring it? The answer is simply that the Darwinian revolution, even more than the Copernican revolution, challenges the prehistoric and still-regnant self-image of humanity.[6]

He goes on to identify several "schizophrenic" aspects of the global world—"opposing" images of the human condition: God-centered religions, sociopolitical behaviorism, and naturalistic scientific humanism. And for Wilson and many others, rapprochement is neither possible nor desirable.

> In the early part of this century, the toxic mix of religion and tribalism has become so dangerous as to justify taking seriously the alternative view, that humanism based on science is the effective antidote, *the light and the way at last placed before us.*[7]

These sorts of images—of light, toxicity, and antidotes—propels us firmly into the psychological domain of the *pharmakon* and into the imagination's propensity to dream of totalities. There is nothing intrinsically pathological about that. Any dream of totality can go bad, become rigid and coercive or just too limiting. This is no less true of scientific paradigms, as the history of eugenics, psychological testing, and the current fad for reductive pseudo-evolutionary explanations have shown. The multiplicities of humanity's creation myths are not merely the beginnings of science; they express essential concerns and discoveries about the human experience in their own domain. It's no doubt true, however, that the fight to the finish professed by some religious believers is infinitely more destructive than disputes between different schools of artistic expression or competing scientific theories. And it's also the case that science contains the explicit provision to test hypotheses and to discard them, while religious dreams of totality, for example, are notoriously conservative. But all these paradigms, even humanisms based on science, are informed by underlying mental processes by which we share the essentials that form and inform our world. Until we understand the value of the mythopoetic mind as the ground of symbol formation—not something archaic that will be outgrown—we will continue to identify with various dreams of totality in a way that misses their meaning as symbolic process. Another way of saying this is that it's not the dream of totality that is primitive; what's primitive is identifying with it. And although it may have always been so, it is becoming more transparent than ever that the only thing at the center of collective life is psyche.

In his classic study, *The Ritual Process: Structure and Anti-Structure*, cultural anthropologist Victor Turner identified the sharing of essentials within social groups as occurring in a liminal altered state he called "communitas," a mode of experience common to all humans.

> Communitas breaks in through the interstices of structure, in Liminality; at the edges of structure, in marginality; and from beneath structure, in inferiority. It is almost everywhere held to be sacred or "holy," possibly because it transgresses or dissolves the norms that govern structured and institutionalized relationships . . . Liminality, marginality, and structural inferiority are conditions in which are frequently generated myths, symbols, rituals, philosophical systems, and works of art. These cultural forms provide men with a set of templates or models which are, at one level, periodical reclassifications of reality and man's relationship to society, nature, and culture. But they are more than classifications, since they incite men to action as well as to thought . . . moving people at many psychobiological levels simultaneously.[8]

From his extensive study of the Ndembu tribe of Zambia, Turner inferred what he understood to be two forms of interrelationship that human social systems oscillate between: structure and anti-structure. The first form was a structured, differentiated, and hierarchical system of social ranking, a system that tends to become fixed. The other form of social relationship was something looser and undifferentiated but equally strong, held together not by structure but by the feeling and experiences of communitas. This anti-structure phase of social life seemed to emerge most prominently during periods of breakdown and change and was usually initiated by liminal personae that Turner called "threshold people" or "edgemen," people who slipped through the network of social classifications that locate positions in cultural space.[9]

Ambiguous and indeterminate, threshold people are neither here nor there. They are usually associated with death, the womb, the wilderness, bisexuality, and so on, and they have no rank and no accepted social status other than that of initiating social transitions. From a psychological perspective they play the role of psychopomp, personifying the determining factors in social change as seen through the eyes of the mythopoetic mind. While identifying this subversive element of the "savage mind," as it was often called, Turner also related it to the politics of the present in that turning the world and its structures upside down is always basic to the growth of cultures. "Nor is it accurate," wrote Turner, "to speak of the 'structure of a mind different from our own.' It is not a matter of different cognitive structures, but of an identical cognitive structure articulating wide diversities of cultural experience."[10]

I will explore more fully in the latter part of this chapter the transgressive and trickster elements inherent in this view of social change and its relation to dreams of totality, as well as the observation that these liminal states are characteristic of open societies or of pivotal ritual moments in more closed societies. For now, I simply want to point out that Turner's thesis suggests that social pressures that would reify into totalizing fixed systems get re-scripted by the experience of shared essentials and, most importantly, by transgressions. Following in Turner's tradition, Lewis Hyde wrote that "cultures take their shape from distinctions such as 'gift and theft,' 'the clean and dirty,' 'the modest and the shameful,' 'essence and accident.' These exactly are the joints of the cultural web and therefore the potential site's of trickster's play."[11] Identifying either with structure or with the kinship feeling of communitas—in other words, when the oscillation ceases—will result in a pathological manifestation of what gets repressed. The ways in which social systems deal with their own dirt, ethnic cleansing, or tolerance, for example, determines the resilience of a given society. Healthy societies participate in the relatively smooth alteration between structure and communitas, between institutionalizing dreams of totality and allowing for their breakdown and reformation.

So it follows that one of the first things that any totalitarian system tries to shut down or manipulate is the kinship feeling of communitas and especially its expression in the gift, the dirty, the shameful, and most especially the experience of human sexuality and love, which is then one of the first things that inevitably transgresses and breaks down systemic or hierarchical boundaries. Enter the great *daimon* Eros, whereby essentials are shared, total surrender is claimed, individuality is born, and new culture is created. For, as Rilke wrote, "we close a circle by means of our gazes, and in it the tangled tension fuses white."[12]

Sexuality, Love, and the Beloved Other

During adolescence, bathed and awash in a hormonal elixir, the mind's ability to dream of totality develops very strongly, not only with belief in a romantic or spiritual love that will make us complete but with extreme convictions of idealism and nihilism, with a lust for absolute isms of all sorts, with a longing for communion, or as a fervent wish to take one's place in the larger community of adult life. Whether it be Romeo and Juliet's duet to the death, an ardent passion for god, hopes for a new society, or even degraded forms like the fascination with celebrity hookups that characterizes so much of contemporary Western culture, adolescent dreams of totality express the experience of separation and reformation that signify the *rite de passage*, the interregnum of adolescence, in both individuals and cultures.

Another way to look at this developmental passage is through the metaphor of the breakdown of the imagined paradisiacal unity of the mother-child couple. The Madonna and child fantasy, often symbolizing the longing for undisturbed well-being, comes apart during adolescence, changing form into a longing for one's beloved (or disturbing) other half. Or, we can say that the narcissism of the child is likewise transfigured into a search for the missing other, into an engaged relationship with others and the world, and into developing aspects of personality that are starting to emerge. If this process gets stuck, as analyst Mario Jacoby described,

> it is in keeping with psychological experience that the longing for Paradise, for unitary reality, often includes the yearning for a predestined partner who, as a narcissistic object, is always there for the purpose of serving one's own needs. In other words, the regressive form of the mother complex becomes acute, and it becomes difficult to affirm the conflicts and demands of reality.[13]

If things go well—whatever the object of the projection is—paradise is lost and something else is found at another register of experience. From a symbolic perspective—one in which the psychological dynamics aren't reduced to family dynamics—we can say that earlier projections of unity and completeness dissolve, reform at another level of awareness, dissolve again and reform, in an ongoing generative process that finds its most compelling expression as desire.

Figure 26: *The Wheel of Time, Kalachakra* (17th century, Tibet), mineral pigments on cloth, Rubin Museum of Art, New York.

This is beautifully illustrated in figure 26, a seventeenth-century Tibetan Kalachakra mandala known as the Wheel of Time. *Kalachakra* is a Sanskrit term in the Tantric Buddhist tradition that signifies time cycles or a wheel of time. I mentioned one type of Kalachakra mandala in chapter 1—the Buddhist sand paintings that are meticulously created, then swept away and sprinkled into a river, signaling the relationship between creation and destruction, that is, impermanence. In the Wheel of Time, it's the generative coupling with the beloved that tells the story of time. Here, Kalachakra refers to the deity with black skin at the center of the image representing everything under the influence of time. Kalachakra's consort, the Kalachakri goddess, represents what is outside of time, the timeless and unbounded. The completeness of the couple comprises its own whole, which is held within the circle of a larger mandala. Their coupling suggests a differentiation between body-bound time and a sensibility of timelessness and the all-important desire to unite them, an intimation that generativity comes from a passionate coupling of the now with a sensibility of the eternal.

We can also see this dynamic at work by looking at other images of time. As we saw in chapter 1, with respect to magic circles, time is often experienced as cyclical, repeating and renewing itself in endless cycles of creation and destruction, narrated in the myth of eternal return. Everything comes back to a beginning or to a center, and there is nothing new under the sun. Time is also imagined as unfolding in a linear way, as finite, body-bound history, a history that will come to a definite end, an end that is the product of development. This dream of progress is particularly characteristic of Western cultures, underlying, for example, dialectic materialism, which rested on the image of an innocent humanity subsequently corrupted by class and money, a humanity whose innocence will only be regained when class struggle finally ceases, corresponding with the end of history. But even the great escape from the cyclic time of Buddhism, the breaking of endless reincarnations by attaining nirvana, is a developmental fantasy. What the linear image usually shares with the cyclical one is a vision of a golden age at the beginning or at the end of time—of paradise or extinction. At this final juncture, time and suffering, as we know them, cease.

These great images of time and history inform our thinking about social structures and the efficacy of social action. They interact with one another, coexist and complement one another, as the Kalachakra mandala implies. From a psychological point of view, what's really interesting is that when we ask and answer questions about the viability of social systems and the need for social action most ardently, we usually seem to be locating ourselves and our relationship with time in a period of darkness, at an end or a beginning of a cycle or at the precipice of release. We associate this twilight state with becoming self-aware; we "wake up" between the end and the new beginning.

It is no accident that the whole struggle of embodied existence catches hold most firmly in adolescence, in images of love forever lasting or flaming out into the eternity of death. The twilight period, the momentary break from cycles and history, is often categorized in a pejorative way as "adolescent" and deemed dangerous by those resisting it. Evil seems on the rise or in full flower at twilight. We become hyper aware of, for example, the apparently youth-obsessed sex and technocratic nature of our culture or of al-Qaeda-like networks of terror powered by young people willing to die for a cause. Twilight is when the call and response for a new way of living goes out, when childhood dreams of totality break apart, when on the cusp of new identity everything seems to be going to hell—sometimes in a good way. The immensely popular *Twilight* vampire books and the subsequent films, which appealed to budding adolescent girls coming of age on the cusp of the twenty-first century, played with a powerful mix of sexual awakening, the immortal animal, and identity formation in response to passion and disintegration. In a hubristic twist characteristic of our culture (avoiding the problem of embodiment and limitation), rather than feeling pity toward or fearing the undead, or getting rescued from the hell of a disembodied life by a flesh-and-blood hero—as in the *Dracula* tales of an earlier time—the languid existential heroine of *Twilight* chooses vampiric power so that she can remain with her diffident but endearing demon lover (who is not really, like, *that bad*) and give birth to a half-divine (albeit vampire) child.

The ongoing press to couple and uncouple that is an aspect of dreaming of totality—to merge and to separate, to create and to destroy, to live an individual and embodied life within the context of a larger vision—either fails at critical junctures, gets stuck in endless projections, or builds up one's resilience and creativity. Powered by hormonal sea changes, the ability to weather this process is a psychological and emotional development of major significance. Not being able to dream the dream of the beloved—in whatever cultural form it takes—is an impasse with far-reaching consequences, usually portending an early limit to further psychological and emotional development. And at the next step, when the dream of the beloved inevitably frays or comes apart altogether, the feelings of despair, hopelessness, even apocalyptic rage that arise threaten the integrity of identity—to put it mildly. Many don't make it through these waters. Negotiating and metabolizing this poisonous aspect of the *pharmakon* of love and sexuality is the great and perilous threshold of adolescent development. This may be the case for societies as well, witnessed in the ways in which a given society acts toward sexuality and particularly girls and women.

In terms of the romance with the beloved, the realities of disenfranchised, ignored, or unwanted elements eventually (hopefully) find their way in, creating tension and friction. As we saw in chapter 1, images of totality are usually organized quite symmetrically, in numerical formations or as round or square. Even at the most basic physical level, we know that symmetry of facial features and proportion in body form play a significant role in erotic preferences and desire. Men the world over find women attractive when their waist-to-hip ratio is .7, and women find men universally attractive if their facial features or body build are symmetrical. It is also an astonishing fact that phantom limb pain—the often excruciating sensations that are felt to be emanating from a missing limb—is relieved by using mirrors to restore the missing visual symmetry. Symmetric patterns feel calming, orderly, and harmonious; that may be their particular power. But breaks in mirroring and symmetry are the necessary preconditions for more-complex adaptive systems to build up, for more inclusive dreams of totality to emerge.[14] The trade-off for loss of symmetry is gain in complexity. When weak links rupture at points of asymmetry, when the beloved no longer appears to be one's other half or does not become one's ideology of salvation—a symmetrical mirror of oneself—there is a further loosening of symmetry. What ensues is dissolution (even suicide), controlling or delusional fixation (abusive dynamics), or a reorganization that includes disparity and unconformity; an image of wholeness opens to include more than a mirror of self.

We need to pause here and take stock of something that has been alluded to throughout but needs to be made explicit, and nowhere is this more evident than in matters of love. Although the great danger inherent in dreaming of totality is being too literal, it's in the nature of the process that it takes concrete form. When gripped by the dream of the beloved other, for example, not just any old beloved will do. He or she is specific in the extreme: her hair, his voice, his body, her smile—all the personal perfections and imperfections are cherished, and nothing can substitute

SOCIETY'S DREAMS 137

for the uniqueness of the beloved at that moment in time. In fact, when any old beloved does suffice, we often recognize something undeveloped in the relationship between mirroring, empathy, and imagination—and rightly call it narcissism. Figure 27, *Narcissus*, attributed to Caravaggio, illustrates many of these dynamics in an exquisite and sophisticated way. The young Narcissus is poised on a cusp. We can see the absolute, even

Figure 27: *Narcissus*, attributed to Michelangelo Caravaggio (c. 1597–99), oil on canvas, Gallery Nazionale d'Arte Antica, Rome.

magic circle–like, mirroring of the self and the absence of another. The painter also alludes to the possibility of dissolution—by drowning or by the breakup of mirroring. Especially poignant are the links in the painting, the delicate places where the tips of Narcissus's fingers and the palms of his hands just meet the water's edge; he could put them in further and break the projection or withdraw them completely and preserve it.

The pain and the dangers of love are as legendary as the ecstasy. Sometimes when the weak links are exposed, when mirroring fails and the dream begins to falter, rather than suffering a complete collapse or accomplishing reformation in a more inclusive experience, there is fixation and addiction instead. Rather than projections loosening, they get even tighter. Either violence or rebellion ensues, because the other does not conform or, in the narcissistic response, the dream is held in place by rigid, repetitive, that is, addictive behavior. And the points of weak linkage are not just subject to foreclosure, they are easily manipulated. Totalitarian control can take hold not just from within but from without.

The classic example is the way that German fascism—which arose from the wreckage of World War I in a dream of nationalistic authority that defended traditional values—gave way first to National Socialism and finally to Nazism (all of which were characterized by anti-Semitism). The obsession with racial purity and the annihilation of whatever did not mirror the ideal became increasingly urgent and rigidified. At the zenith of Nazism, even anti-Semitic Catholicism became suspect, since it too didn't conform to the racial mythology that undergirded Nazism. By the time it was all over, a horrendous brew of isms had destroyed seventy million people, and along with the apocalyptic pièce de résistance of the atomic bomb, modern consciousness had been traumatized. This kind of genocide—that most revolting product of isms—continues into the twenty-first century in areas like Darfur in Africa, which are undergoing their own chaotic twilight period of reorganization.

Among the first things that any totalitarian regime (utopian or dystopian) tries to control are women (rape), children (starvation, brainwashing), and the sexual mores and behavior of its citizens. This is because desire and love are among the most powerful ways that individuals experience not only pleasure, but generativity, empathy, imagination, and creativity of all kinds. In love and desire we become conscious of ourselves, and we are (usually) moved by close contact with another. In addition to becoming aware of our own desires and particular feelings, sexuality and love connect us to one another in bonds of relationship that are particularly human, and through experiencing the particularity of those desires and bonds, we share the essentials of being a human animal. Totalitarian systems (be they internal ones like narcissism or sociopolitical systems) thus have to either enforce strict prohibitions and regulations around sexuality and desire or encourage the soporific and addictive aspects of sexuality. Both of these mechanisms distort and pervert the *pharmakon* of sexuality and love and foreclose on dreaming the dream of the beloved other, thereby stunting imagination, freedom, and growth.

Aldous Huxley's *Brave New World*, first published in 1932, was the seminal novel about the manipulation of sexuality and love being made to serve a utopian dream of social cohesion that cast a long dystopian shadow. In this new world of Huxley's imagination, government had outlawed biological birth in favor of controlled test-tube gestations that produced genetically precise human beings who were slotted into corresponding intellectual, social, and economic castes. No one had an actual mother anymore—it was much too personal and emotional a relationship—and the word itself was an obscenity. Instead, society took care of everyone's material needs and proscribed the direction and course of almost everyone's life. Constant sexual activity was encouraged and facilitated—as long as it took place with multiple and changing partners, since no personal or enduring relationships were permitted.

In one memorable scene from the book, after an early dinner at the Aphroditæum, Bernard Marx, Huxley's resentful and haltingly transgressive hero, takes a taxi to the Community Singery (formerly London's Westminster Abbey). He's hurrying to attend the obligatory Solidarity Service, a ceremony in which a pod of twelve new world citizens fuse together in a quasi-religious sexual orgy. A loving cup of strawberry ice cream laced with hallucinogenic *soma*—the perfect happiness drug that confers a "holiday from reality" with all the advantages of religion and alcohol and none of their side effects—gets passed around. With the formula "I drink to my annihilation" being duly recited, everyone imbibes. As the drug takes effect, Bernard and his fellow pod mates begin to dance and chant,

> Feel how the Greater Being comes!
> Rejoice, and in rejoicing, die!
> Melt in the music of the drums!
> For I am you and you are I.[15]

"And," wrote Huxley,

> all at once a great synthetic bass boomed out the words which announced the approaching atonement and final consummation of solidarity, the coming of the Twelve-in-One, the incarnation of the Greater Being. "Orgy-porgy," it sang, while the tom-toms continued to beat their feverish tattoo:
>
> > Orgy-porgy, Ford and fun,
> > Kiss the girls and make them One.
> > Boys at one with girls at peace;
> > Orgy-porgy gives release.
>
> And as they sang, the lights began slowly to fade—to fade and at the same time to grow warmer, richer, redder, until at last they were dancing in the crimson twilight of an Embryo Store. Then the circle wavered, broke, fell in partial disintegration on the ring of couches which surrounded—circle enclosing circle—"Orgy-porgy" the deep Voice crooned and cooed.[16]

Huxley may have been inspired, or better put, dispirited by the nascent social movements of the 1920s, which in their own pseudoscientific way had been attempting to control sexuality in the service of social cohesion. For example, Paul Popenoe, the father of marriage counseling, best remembered for his contributions to the preservation of "masculinity" and "fit" families in the iconic *Ladies Home Journal* column, "Can This Marriage Be Saved?" was also the author of the 1918 volume *Applied Eugenics* and a leader in the campaign to sterilize the mentally disabled and the "weak of mind."[17] In our own society, which also encourages uninspired sexuality, we should be just as wary as Huxley was—of both the soft porn being sold by the infotainment industry and also of the harder brand of pornography that is readily accessible to everyone on the Web. We should be suspicious not out of moral outrage or misplaced modesty or from a fearful clinging to rigid forms of sexual expression. We should be leery because we are in thrall. Ubiquitous pornography may herald a movement that renders the imagination out of commission and under control. As Huxley portended, with a citizenry under hypnosis and fully addicted, a spreading corporate consumerism can move in and take over very easily, co-opting our ability to create new culture. Much the same can be said—in the other direction—about the spread of fundamentalisms, whether Middle Eastern or Western, with their controlling rituals around sexuality that also destroy the integrity of sexuality and imagination, along with the freedom those bring to compete with prevailing religious traditions. Both of these developments, the bloated and addicted sex and consumer culture and its fundamentalist shadow, cross one another and meet at the point of control and manipulation. And young people are, by design, the hardest hit.

The consuming passions and absolute truths that power the adolescent psyches of both individuals and cultures, with their dual claims of ecstatic union paired with breakdown and disappointments, need to be negotiated. They are the rocks on which many founder. Oscillating between wholeness and fragmentation, adolescent passions are fatal—sometimes literally—if dreaming of totality becomes irrevocably stuck or remains in an on/off, "all or nothing" binary position, which is evident, for example, in the typical adolescent pairing of perfect love with grisly death. The fragile individuality and idealism that reflects the perfect oneness of adolescent psychology makes it fundamentalist in its absoluteness and easy to manipulate, easy to send up in the flames of religious martyrdom or snuff out in a deluge of consumption. The shadow of totalitarianism can fall fast during twilight.

Utopias and Dystopias: From Totality to Totalitarianism

As we have seen, totalitarian dystopias and utopias are often the children of fundamentalist psychology. In *The Origins of Totalitarianism*, political theorist Hannah Arendt argued that the source of the mass appeal of totalitarian regimes is a simple ideology, which provides a comforting, single answer to the mysteries of the past, present, and future. For Nazism, all history was the history of racial struggle; for Marxism, all history was the history of class struggle. Once those sorts of premises are accepted, argued Arendt, all actions of the state could be justified by appeal to nature or the law of history and the like, along with the establishment of authoritarian state apparatus. As she wrote,

> When the Nazis talked about the law of nature or when the Bolsheviks talk about the law of history, neither nature nor history is any longer the stabilizing source of authority for the actions of mortal men; they are movements in themselves. Underlying the Nazis' belief in race laws as the expression of the law of nature in man, is Darwin's idea of man as the product of a natural development which does not necessarily stop with the present species of human beings, just as under the Bolsheviks' belief in class-struggle as the expression of the law of history lies Marx's notion of society as the product of a gigantic historical movement which races accordingly to its own law of motion to the end of historical times when it will abolish itself.[18]

Collective dreams of totality overlap and intersect, and as isms they have a nasty way of becoming conflated. In this case, Darwinism, which is actually an open-ended process, was manipulated in service to a dominant ideology and became a law of development with an endpoint. Isms tend to clump together, mixing and melding according to both mythopoetic likeness and political manipulation. As Arendt wryly noted, Friedrich Engels couldn't think of a greater compliment to pay Karl Marx than to declare him the "Darwin of History," opining at Marx's funeral that "just as Darwin discovered the law of development of organic life, so Marx discovered the law of development of human history."[19]

Totalitarian systems are absolutist, demanding complete surrender and containment in a magic circle; many are intimately bound up with scapegoating, and all make claims on fragile morality and simplistic beliefs, as well as on money, power, and sexuality. Anything outside the system is profane by definition and dealt with by punishment or damnation. Ideological thinking becomes independent of experience and sensory reality, providing complete explanations not just about what is but about what was and what will be, proceeding with a consistency that doesn't exist in the reality of living. A dominant ideology can defy legality and apply itself to an abstract humanity without bothering with the rights of actual individuals. In fact, ideological thinking usually seeks to produce a very specific vision of universal humanity as its end product, excluding whatever doesn't conform to the idealization. Even the sweet, high, hippie dream of free love and peace that flowered in the 1960s—with its nostalgic longing for a natural and peaceful life presumed to exist before the infamous military-industrial complex took over—had its darker ideology: "Don't trust anyone over thirty."

Following the path of the *pharmakon,* most collective dreams of totality answer the call for solutions to social ills and end up having coercive effects, usually as a result of emotional or political terrorism by agencies that seek to stabilize, that is, enforce it. In trying to understand totalitarianism, Christopher Hitchens, for one, concluded: "all that the totalitarians have demonstrated is that the religious impulse—the need to worship—can take even more monstrous form if repressed."[20] It's not, however, just about a need to worship or repression of the religious impulse. The push for consistency and stabilization that characterizes the reification phase of dreaming of totality requires that the fringe elements that are constantly appearing (Jews, the poor, etc.) be done away with, and once totalitarian thinking seizes hold, the sacrifices exacted become more and more severe as less and less is felt to belong inside the purity of the magic circle. Privacy, sexual freedom, and individuality are driven underground, giving rise to the bizarre adaptations and compartmentalization that also characterize totalitarian systems—like the pairing of extreme moralism with sentimentality, abusive sexuality, or exhibitionism.

The magic circle character of totalitarianism is not limited to the obviously horrendous. The insidious intertwining of democracy with corporate capitalism that reigns supreme in the global marketplace of contemporary culture is a subtler example. There is no intrinsic reason that democracy should be driven by corporate capitalism; they are discrete systems. But capitalism has colonized democracy, and there is an increasingly monocular focus on the profit motive disguised as the unbridled free market. Under the umbrella of capitalism, universal human rights tend to be sacrificed and the social dimensions of life find limited expression only as an interconnected telecommunications network, its users floating freely through shopping malls in a "sea of denim."[21]

Corporate culture has become its own ideology—housing and restricting the flow of money and power, trying to stabilize and control it, convincing people that the dream of capitalism will make them happy and that the dream of socialism will destroy them—and all the while curtailing the rights of individuals. In service to the gods of commerce, individual needs are subsumed for the sake of the whole system. As a result of the 2010 United States Supreme Court decision, *Citizens United v.*

Federal Election Commission, for example, corporations have the right to contribute unlimited amounts of money from their general treasuries in order to finance the elections of public officials, these being, of course, the ones who are sympathetic to corporate interests. The majority Court decision argued that corporate personhood is a legitimate, nonmetaphorical entity entitled to the protection of its political and civil rights—just like a person—including the First Amendment right to free speech.

Although Hannah Arendt, in *The Origins of Totalitarianism*, was referring to the terror implemented by explicitly totalitarian regimes, we can substitute any dream of totality—including corporate capitalism—in her chilling analysis of the power of "the One":

> It substitutes for the boundaries and channels of communication between individual men a band of iron which holds them so tightly together that it is as though their plurality had disappeared into One Man of gigantic dimensions. To abolish the fences of laws between men—as tyranny does—means to take away man's liberties and destroy freedom as a living political reality; for the space between men as it is hedged in by laws, is the living space of freedom . . . . Terror destroys the one essential prerequisite of all freedom which is simply the capacity of motion which cannot exist without space.[22]

The capitalist dream is wound so tightly around contemporary culture that Americans, for example, are terrified to step out of the rags to riches myth, even voting against their own self-interest—against, for example, significant funding of health care and public education. The fear of the malignant aspect of the One is projected onto universal health care, with a consequent fear of mythical death panels that would pass judgment over the dying and the unfit to live—something which, of course, has in fact happened under past totalitarian regimes. But the poor are already dying, de facto, as a result of the corporate monopolization of health care in the United States; *E pluribus unum* has hardened up into a corporate ideology that denies the many and varied needs of the citizenry.

We should be terrified, because this is how most social systems go bad; lack of empathy is why most social systems collapse. While images of cohesion provide many of the templates for governance, commerce, and conceptual systems, it is empathy and imagination that play the definitive roles in anchoring the relationships between the players and their dreams in an open and resilient way. We can grasp the implications of this more clearly by taking note of the fact that psychopathic and sociopathic behavior is held together by rigid intellectual and behavioral repertoires and also characterized by a lack of empathy, with a coincident lack of imagination. We also know that the presence, or absence, of connections between various sectors of any individual's psyche is often the determining factor in character, fate, and resilience. Compartmentalization as a defense against conflict works only up to a point. This applies equally well to the fate of nations, cultures, and conceptual systems.

Rather than a reciprocal relationship between the many and the one, sociopathic terror usually destroys relationships between the many. This creates splinter groups that flee from totalitarian societies, just as monomythic notions of ideal health or identity create fugitive selves. These two developments come together poignantly in, for example, cyberpunk, a postmodern genre of science fiction set in a lawless subculture of an oppressive dystopian society dominated by artificial intelligence and computer technology. The good news is that utopias and dystopias often collapse when the marginalized or fugitive facts of experience prove too much for the system. Like the fragments and multiple selves formed by the individual's liberation from monomythic identity, social conceptions also multiply as a product of emancipation. There's a resemblance between the destruction and reformation process that characterizes dreaming of totality and the movements of oppression and emancipation that characterize sociopolitical developments. While on the one hand, this is a chaotic situation if splintered political groups harden up or opt out, but it can also allow space for the movement and reflection that generate genuinely creative gestures.

The Digital Community and the Sharing of Essentials

While I was writing this chapter, hundreds of thousands of protesters were thronging the cities of Cairo and Alexandria, demanding an end to decades of tyrannical government. The entire world held its breath as different dreams of totality collided. Police thugs on camels thundered into the squares of Cairo, brandishing their weapons like something out of a demented Arabian nights, and in response thousands of citizens raised their cell phones high into the air, recording the assaults for all to see on YouTube. It was as though the sacred lotus flower that was once Egypt was rising from the mud, as the call from the disenfranchised for democracy turned everything upside down.

It did not escape anyone's attention that satellite communication and social media had been important in facilitating the Arab Spring protest. The government shut down the Internet for several days in an attempt to disrupt the opposition, but the country couldn't survive unplugged—it was inextricably wired in to the twenty-first century. This lent credence to the fantasy that the network of the Web was indeed a better place and that there was, in fact, an enlightened global village on the horizon.

Which brings us back to the beginning of this chapter, with a contemporary twist. Like the all-knowing city of Delphi, fantasies about the global village and the Web "have it all," and there is a feeling of "knowing it all" via open access to streaming information. There is a sense that the twenty-first-century technological revolution has sparked an unprecedented social revolution, even that we are on the brink of a new utopia, riding on a wave of freely flowing information that will democratize the flow of power. Many people favorably disposed to this idea now imagine themselves in possession of something like cosmopolitan citizenship, granted by communications technology or, even more extreme, that being plugged into the Web will rewire our brains in a way that encourages connection and mutuality over isolation and self-interest.

As befits the *pharmakon*, others feel otherwise. Many have a visceral antipathy to being inextricably connected to a hive mind, constantly buzzing, addictively entangled with one another, in an overwhelming complexity that discourages depth of feeling and individual considerations of meaning. And not only that: worried, fully alarmed, or just plain skeptical, we also suspect that rather than the flow of information portending freedom and democracy, the Web can spread disinformation and confusion or become a cacophony of rumors and propagandas. In other words, it can be used equally well by totalitarians and conspiracy theorists to enforce conformity and falsity, as by freethinkers to encourage multiplicity and truth. As I was editing this chapter, the situation in Egypt changed; political realities and an unwillingness to democratize power resurfaced, threatening to marginalize revolutionary and progressive forces. Social media had not been a panacea.

Jumpy nerves and joyful hearts trade places rapidly as we experience what was once hidden inside us finding a place out there in the digital world—both our human craziness and our humane sanity—as we take in what until very recently seemed clearly foreign. Stepping across boundaries as we are doing is a creative transgression, if we can bear with it and sacrifice security. If not, it calls forth the retaliatory retrenchment that often comes on the heels of revolution. In the next chapter we explore how sacrifice is the *sine qua non* and the primary means by which we construct our dreams of totality and destroy them—the way that we sort out experience and then disrupt that order.

Notes

1 Henry Corbin, *Creative Imagination in the Sufism of Ibn'Arabi* (London: Routledge, 2007).

2 Stalin's speech of January 28, 1924, quoted in Hannah Arendt, *The Origins of Totalitarianism* (New York: Harcourt Books, 1966), p. 472.

3 C. G. Jung, "Flying Saucers: A Modern Myth of Things Seen in the Skies" (1958), in *Civilization in Transition*, vol. 10, *The Collected Works of C. G. Jung* (Princeton, NJ: Princeton University Press, 1964), § 672.

4 Lewis Mumford, *The City in History* (New York: Harcourt, Brace and World, 1961), p. 576.

5 Karen Armstrong, *The Great Transformation* (New York: Random House, 2006).

6 E. O. Wilson, *From So Simple a Beginning: The Four Great Books of Charles Darwin* (New York: W. W. Norton, 2005), p. 1481.

7 *Ibid.*, p. 1483; italics added.

8 Victor Turner, *The Ritual Process: Structure and Anti-Structure* (New Brunswick, NJ: Aldine Transaction, 1969, 2009), pp. 128–129.

9 *Ibid.*, p. 95.

10 *Ibid.*, p. 3.

11 Lewis Hyde, *Trickster Makes This World: How Disruptive Imagination Creates Culture* (New York: Canongate, 1998), p. 205.

12 Rainer Maria Rilke, *Rilke on Love and Other Difficulties: Translations and Consideration*, trans. John Mood (New York: W. W. Norton, 2004), p. 55.

[13] Mario Jacoby, *Longing for Paradise: Psychological Perspectives on an Archetype* (Toronto: Inner City Books, 1985, 2006), p. 112.

[14] Joseph Cambray, *Synchronicity: Nature and Psyche in an Interconnected Universe* (College Station, TX: Texas A&M University Press, 2009), pp. 57–60.

[15] Aldous Huxley, *Brave New World* (New York: Harper and Brothers, 1946), p. 97.

[16] *Ibid.*, p. 100.

[17] For a full discussion of Popenoe and marriage therapy, see Jill Lepore, "Fixed: The Rise of Marriage Therapy and Other Dreams of Human Betterment," *New Yorker*, March 29, 2010.

[18] Hannah Arendt, *The Origins of Totalitarianism* (New York: Harcourt Books, 1966), p. 463.

[19] As quoted in Arendt, *The Origins of Totalitarianism*, p. 463.

[20] Christopher Hitchens, *God Is Not Great: How Religion Poisons Everything* (New York: Twelve, Hachette Book Group, 2007), p. 247.

[21] The author wishes to thank Julie Bresciani, Ph.D., for the colorful image: a sea of denim, personal communication.

[22] Arendt, *The Origins of Totalitarianism*, p. 466.

Chapter Five

Sacrifice:
Blood Payments and Open Wounds

> The ideal passes through suffering like gold through fire.
> —Dostoyevsky, *The Brothers Karamazov*
>
> To kill a god or an ideal, go for the joints.
> —Lewis Hyde, *Trickster Makes This World*

Whether we like it or not, there seems to be a relationship—if bloody and costly—between dreaming of totality and sacrificial action. There is a dynamic movement between making taboo and scapegoating what lies outside totality's magic circle and the reentry of these disenfranchised elements or of what is simply new. Sacrificial dramas negotiate these passages from one form of organization to another. As we saw in chapter 2, for example, in the rituals of divination unity and harmony are restored by means of specific sacrifices. As we saw in chapter 3, the sacrifice of adolescent forms of the beloved other opens the way for a larger vision, as do innumerable other sacrifices of appetites and gratification. And as we saw in chapter 4, many historical and social changes are initiated and maintained by sacrifice, and this is no less true as we move into an era of information and communications. The way that sacrifice is negotiated is the decisive factor. Or put another way, it is the nature of our sacrificial dramas that makes the difference between truly primitive destruction and the humane death of our idealizations. It is to this that we now turn.

Sacrifice used to be simple—if deadly. Bloody sacrifice was always part and parcel of the public life of the state and especially of religion. The ancient Aztecs reputedly tore open the chest of a living person, removed the beating heart, and gave it to the gods every day so that the sun would continue to rise. In many cultures the blood of firstborn children was also given to presumably hungry gods, who were renewed by the new life's vitality. In the ancient and not so distant past, nothing was undertaken without a sacrifice, and the tribal leaders or their priests were specifically charged with carrying out the correct sacrificial acts. Failure to do so carried a heavy price, and still does, because there is an enduring platform in the psyche for sacrificial action as a part of creation. This is evidenced in all sorts of propitiatory deaths (or in just being booted out of democratic office), in "eye for an eye" punishments, in suicide and martyrdom, in the at-one-ment sacrifices of great culture heroes, and in the violence of myths and fairy tales, everyday dreams, and our own life dramas.

Seen through a less grisly lens, it was also the case that everything in the ancient world was consecrated and endowed with soul through sacrifice. As we saw in chapter 1, figure 15, the world itself was mythologized into existence through the sacrifice of a primordial being, a Creator whose body was transformed by dismemberment into the many different plants and foods for humanity's consumption. As Eliade suggested, this dynamic seems to be a prototypical creation myth, wherein the rites of construction are repetitions of the mythic acts of divine destruction and creation. Individuals also construct new interior worlds in this way. Acts of personal sacrifice either restore psychological and emotional order, reinvigorating an exhausted dream of totality, or give birth to a new one. In either case, sacrifice is a powerful psychological dynamic, a hedge against death and stagnation and a creative act unlike any other.

We can look down our noses at the so-called primitive societies that held themselves together by ritual sacrifice, or we can recognize that some form of sacrificial killing is how cohesion is created, maintained, and ultimately destroyed. Everything draws on the blood of what went before—in our contemporary world, where malignant dictatorships that draw their life from the blood of the many are increasingly untenable, we still, however, fell many trees for new construction. One of the challenges that we face in contemporary global culture is to become fully aware of two related aspects of collective sacrificial dramas that continue to be enacted. The first are the perils of scapegoating and disenfranchisement. These seem easier to recognize and stand against than in the past—and here the exposure available via social media is a distinct advantage. The second, which seems more difficult to come to terms with, is the challenge we face to dismantle our identification with creator and destroyer gods. Although we come to know ourselves and what matters to us through our acts of slaughter and sacrifice, what we sacrifice and how we go about it are always the deciding factors. It is, as we will see in what follows, the nature of our sacrifices that determines the integrity of our dreams of totality.

To sacrifice, from the Latin *sacrificare*, meant "to make sacred by action." Sacrificial killing is a conscious act. Animals don't do it. Although it's partially conditioned by physical circumstance—like animals, we do kill to eat, and it's also true that rising food prices often spark revolutions—ritual slaughter is uniquely human and related to making culture. As Wolfgang Giegerich argued in *Soul Violence*, both sacrificial killings and the fight against them are imagination's inventions. As deep as the need for ritual slaughter and scapegoating seems to be for preserving a sense of psychic and cultural integrity, so also is the need to turn away from blood sacrifice, and to be emancipated from sacrificial cults. Consequently, we recognize that the moment when Yahweh stayed Abraham's mythic hand, no longer demanding the sacrifice of an actual firstborn son, was a story that signaled a turning point in our negotiation of creation and destruction.

Around the world, making new culture is portrayed in the mythologies of heroes, who are heroes because they sacrifice themselves rather than others. The story, for example, of Christ's sacrificial death is about starting to pull inward, converting violence against others into conscious suffering. That the church has often foreclosed on this move does not belie the psychological truth and sophistication of the story. A culture hero is a hero precisely because he is willing to die or sacrifice himself, thus being reborn into another type of awareness about what constitutes self-preservation. This awareness is portrayed in myths as being capable of changing the entire human situation. This is the same idea behind the mystery initiation motif, wherein the initiate "dies" to a sensibility of life as strictly bound to the literal and is reborn into a sensibility of the unseen, that is, into a spiritual or symbolic attitude. This is also the same sensibility that informed Jung's maxim: "a defeat of the ego is a victory for the Self." The transformative agent is imaged as death—and often a violent sacrificial death. Sacrifice is the point of entry into another way of living.

Sacrifice, however, is never a metaphor, never just an "as if" act or merely symbolic. Sacrifice has to be real, and it has to touch something outside ourselves. It embodies a mythopoetic truth; it shares essentials. While seemingly pedantic on one level, questions such as whether there is real Judaism without Shabbat or true Christianity without the crucifixion are not entirely beside the point. We must actually lose our innocence, we must actually give things up, we must incur real guilt by making decisions. Falling apart means really coming undone. We "kill ourselves into being," Giegerich wrote, and "if dismemberment is only a metaphor, then the transformation that it is supposed to bring about is only metaphorical."[1]

In the contemporary world, blood payments continue to be acted out and suffered in our communities, from the wholesale scapegoating and genocide in Africa to the press for less consumptive lifestyles in the Western world. There is also a sacrifice of the sense of wholeness and identity that continues to be exacted from individuals and cultures as we experience breakdowns and splits in every area of life, including in our connections to each other, in our kinship ties. Exhortations for a return to so-called family values or national and economic imperialism notwithstanding, splits, ruptures, and despair proliferate in contemporary life. There are gaps and disconnects everywhere—severings among ourselves, between our ideals, and between cultures. We all know that the jig is up, that the old way of living is over. This is often experienced as the fear of getting cancer—"getting" in the sense of passively acquiring something—but we don't look at how our profligacy could kill everything. Doing so might lead to the conclusion that what needs to be sacrificed is the recurrent fantasy that we are kin to creator and destroyer gods.

Instead, as things come undone, as economic and social boundaries become more fluid and are transgressed with increasing frequency, hard and fixed centers and dogma form in reaction. We can hear the wounds of betrayal as old dreams of totality are lost: in the destructive cacophony of political rage, in the madness and fury that comes with continuing ruptures, and in the righteous but futile attempts to reclaim golden ages, which, if they ever existed at all, have passed into history. Or we quickly renew our identification with creator gods—skipping lightly and blindly over the chaos and distress all around—and imagine that a new utopia is right on the horizon in the form of globalization, or some sort of spiritualized Webworld, or an ever-green planet. Rather than bearing with death and decay, rather than helping with the pain of the dying, rather than burying the dead—and our own adolescent desires with them—we try to force more in vitro birth. But as mythology and world events have repeatedly illustrated, if not given its due by proper sacrifice, the fury of wounding and betrayal usually has the last word—in vengeance—even if it brings the whole house down.

Our autoerotic demands for perfect mirroring or the nostalgic clinging to essentials projected backward onto tribal living or forward into a technological utopia are being sacrificed at a dizzying speed. Suffering these fault lines, leaving their wounds open, is imperative. That's the good news: that the blood spilled as old forms of attachments and dreams of totality are sacrificed can fertilize the ground from which mature relationships with one another can grow. Empathic discourse between individuals and groups only sprouts on the bones of the dead. Sacrificing collective longings for binding identifications and attachments—including the attachment to ourselves as creator and destroyer gods and the ensuing externalization of endless freedom—may be our contemporary sacrificial drama, as potent a sacrifice as any that humanity has enacted thus far.

Sometimes dreams of totality fall under their own weight. Sometimes the Perfect One contains its own demise and collapses naturally, even gracefully, with the unfolding of time. But usually sacrifices must be made, to both the old and the approaching gods. This blood payment often begins with the fury and rage that comes from a threat to a dearly held dream of totality. These difficult emotions open a fissure in the psyche, a fissure that leads into the heart of darkness of human experience, into further fragmentation, not only into prophecy and futuristic vision. It may be the ancient Greeks who understood best that the play of the gods of destruction and creation usually draws blood. So in due deference to the ancestors and the dead, at this juncture I'm going to go forward by first looking backward.

Fury's Wound

In the Greek tragedies that make up the *Oresteia*, the ancient Furies were depicted as avenging all betrayals and sins against primal relationships with a ruthless, relentless, implacable intensity that showed no pity.[2] We still find the ever-grudging Furies at the interstices of all kinship conflicts: those initiated by blatant disregard of others through envy or greed, but also in the accidental insufficiencies of love and in our genuine struggles between relationship and independence. The fury and wounding that erupts when dreams of totality are threatened with betrayal can't be denied but rather must be suffered through to their conclusion. These betrayals are inevitable, part and parcel of the mind's moves toward new unitive experiences. What we try to escape from is drinking the dregs of fury's rage, our own and others'. But taking in this bitter brew can be part of the move toward inclusivity, leading us below into what has been called the underworld initiation, into the down-and-dirty essentials of human experience whose dark fruit is a blood-bond of communion and empathy.

First, a little mythology: the Furies genesis story lies very close to the beginning of time and creation—they were imagined simply as daughters of the night, or daughters of sky and earth, of the primordial parents Uranus and Gaia. The way Hesiod tells it, when the Titan Kronos flung the severed phallus of his father Uranus toward the sea, the blood that fell onto the earth fathered the Furies, and the blood that reached the sea fathered their sister, Aphrodite. The Furies still speak to the dark side of the binding power of love and eros, and it is to this bond betrayed that the Furies always return. They emerge from their underground lair to punish the most heinous crimes, particularly blood guilt within a family, and especially matricide.

Their names, Allecto, Tisiphone, and Megaira, mean "unceasing," "vengeance," and "strange dark memory." They were also imagined by the Greeks as unpurified spirits of the dead, the ghosts of those whose murders went unavenged, appearing as dark-colored doves in tune with all the other goddesses of fate and death who appeared as black birds—crows, vultures, ravens—the Celtic Morrigan, the Egyptian Nekhbet, and the wrathful Valkyries. The Furies' frightful wailing was called a binding hymn, and like the Sirens' song it had the power to grip its victims, weaving a curse and casting a spell that reached all the way into the blood, chilling and drying it up, and driving its victims mad. Only Orpheus, it seemed, was able to bring tears to the eyes of the Furies with his music, and only temporarily.

Like Nemesis and the Fates, the Furies personify emotions that bind us to what is most basic and elemental in our natures: the body, the mythopoetic mind, and to a deep response toward integrity, however painful. The Furies' binding, primitive though it may be, is nevertheless, like all bonds and vows, an expression about what is most valuable. Belonging to the magic circle and psychology of the Great Round of the Goddess, it is no mere conceit to say of the Furies that "what goes around comes around." The gods of Olympus and their favored heroes were heroic precisely because they halted, at least temporarily, this great round of compulsive repetition. Millennia later, the early heroes of psychoanalysis would continue trying to break these bonds, both freeing and severing us from this single-minded devotion to the psychology and emotions of blood order—with unsettling and ambivalent consequences.

We meet the Furies in their full glory in the *Oresteia* trilogy by Aeschylus, particularly in *The Eumenides*, a tragic drama about the curse on the house of Atreus, a curse inflicted by the gods for the sin of hubris. The story goes that when King Agamemnon returned home after the Trojan War, his wife Clytemnestra murdered him because she was enraged by Agamemnon's sacrifice of their daughter Iphigenia to the goddess Artemis, a sacrifice he had performed in return for the goddess granting him favorable winds home. Artemis's brother, the god Apollo, commands Orestes, the son of Agamemnon and Clytemnestra, to avenge the murder of his father by killing his mother. Orestes protests, and although he is reluctant he is also deeply afraid of Apollo's curse and of his father's unavenged ghost. In the end he is compelled to side with his father. He murders his mother, knowing full well that the Furies will drive him mad, and they do. They rise up immediately from deep underground and begin their ferocious pursuit and persecution of this most repulsive crime—matricide. Blood payment must be paid for this blood crime, a crime deemed by the Furies infinitely worse than killing a king or a mere husband:

> Your mother's blood is on the ground . . . The moist liquid is gone. But you in return must give to me to drain from you alive the red fluid from your limbs. From you would I take nurture . . . and having dried you up alive I will lead you below. Over our victim consecrate, this is our song—fraught with madness, fraught with frenzy, crazing the brain, the Furies' hymn, spell to bind the soul, untuned to the lyre, withering the life of mortal man.[3]

Orestes tries to escape them, but he can't—the Furies have a lock on his soul. He finally attempts to take refuge in Apollo's temple at Delphi, but Apollo orders him on to Athens to appeal to that city's patron goddess, Athena, to protect him. The play climaxes in the trial of Orestes on the hill of the Acropolis before a tribunal of Athenian citizens. This is actually the first known depiction of a human jury. At the trial Apollo defends Orestes, citing the ultimate primacy of paternity and the oracles of Zeus against mother right. The Furies defend themselves,

> When we were born such lots were assigned for our own keeping. So the immortals must hold hands off. Is there a man who does not fear this, does not shrink to hear how my place has been ordained, granted and given by destiny and god, absolute? Privilege primeval yet is mine, nor am I without place, though it be underneath the ground and in no sunlight and in gloom that I must stand.[4]

The vote by the Athenian citizenry is an uneasy tie, a tie that Athena breaks in favor of Orestes. He is freed from the Furies' curse. Not so fast though—at this Olympian acquittal the Furies become completely enraged. They threaten to destroy everything—the fertility of the earth, every infant in the womb,

> Gods of the younger generation, you have ridden down the laws of the elder time, torn them out of my hands. I, disinherited, suffering, heavy with anger shall let loose on the land the vindictive poison dripping deadly out of my heart upon the ground.[5]

Athena intervenes once again, answering that although the Furies can't be allowed to descend endlessly into future generations and have to be moderated by reason, she also acknowledges the wisdom in their claims, declaring that "these women have a work we cannot slight" and agreeing

SACRIFICE: BLOOD PAYMENTS AND OPEN WOUNDS

that the fear they inspire is even a good thing. So she gives them a sanctuary near the Acropolis and places the newborn children they threatened under their protection. The spirits of violent revenge are persuaded to accept a new dwelling in Athens, and reformed but honored they become known as the Eumenides, the "kindly or gentle ones." Blessing the land and its people, the Furies are led off the stage in a dignified procession to their new abode. At the beginning of the play, the Furies were clothed as beasts, crouching doglike creatures brought to life by the smell of blood. At the end they stand tall, clothed in robes given to them by the citizens of Athens and appearing to the audience as human women. So began a psychological fashion trend: in later Greek tragedies their role became less and less deadly until in Sophocles's *Electra* there are no Furies at all to pursue Orestes and his sister. The curse of the house of Atreus seemed to be over.

The *Oresteia* is often understood as expressing a turning point in humanity's relationship with blood sacrifice, as the true beginning of Western civilization, wherein reason, the justice of the jury, and to some extent even mercy all supersede the compulsive justice of the Furies, however right those ancient claims may feel. The new dream of totality—paternity and reason—goes so far as to pay a price to the old matriarchal world in the form of honor and recognition. The pact with the Furies represents meaningful contact with the archaic rumblings of the heart, not just a triumph of reason over the alien darkness of our deeper natures. Sounds friendly and rational, doesn't it?

But we may have reason to be suspicious of this exchange. As William Barrett commented in *Irrational Man*,

> The easiest way to escape the Furies, we think, is to deny that they exist... The conspiracy to forget them, or to deny them, thus turns out to be only one more contrivance in that vast and organized effort by modern society to flee from the self.[6]

Indeed, why would the Furies accept the deal at all—are they suddenly that easily flattered? How quickly they seem to succumb to the song of reason and respect. Isn't it a lot more difficult to reach an empathic relationship with the instinctive insistence on blood payment? Friedrich Nietzsche, famously challenging the optimistic Greek solution, suggested that it was precisely suffering with these emotions, not getting beyond them, that was "the essence of all the prophylactic healing forces."[7] The psychological questions can be framed as follows: Has the fury of betrayal been converted, actually changing its essential nature and becoming well disposed, or has it been merely silenced and appeased? Does the final act of the *Oresteia* depict the integration of one dream of totality with another—matriarchy with patriarchy—or a cover-up which will not hold? Has there been a "marriage of heaven and hell" in the sense of William Blake and Jung—forming something new and different—or merely one of arrangement, of coercion and convenience? What has actually been sacrificed?

One implication of the friendly interpretation is that rather than the gods hounding us, they somehow yearn to be on our side—something we still hear loud and clear in the vehement political rhetoric that advocates either a return to the good old days or a leap into utopia. Even in antiquity, the fragility of the Greek solution was acknowledged. It was imagined as easily reversible. Euripides, coming after Aeschylus, makes a dramatic point of inverting the process: in his plays, like *The Trojan Women*, noble women with kindly intentions become doglike furies thirsty for blood, and reason becomes a defense inside the dynamics of revenge. The robes of humanity, Athena's stock in trade, are easily removed.

The figures of the Furies personify deep primal emotions held in a magic circle, the old order of mother right. The classical Greek psyche imagined its development out of this magic circle as a progression from matriarchal consciousness into patriarchal consciousness, the "lower and darker" into the "higher and more temperate." The Furies expressed a cry of betrayal for this wound to one's very substance and identity, a betrayal that is not mitigated by anything else. In this type of experience, also characterized by an inability to hold ambiguity, the tension of opposites remains just that: a tense balance, an eye for an eye, a crime for a crime, blood pays for blood. The clash of mother right with patriarchal reason, with its spilling of blood, guilt, and retribution, was placed in the context of civilizing progress. The reconciling symbol, the new dream of totality, was personified as Athena, whose motherless paternity replaced the ancient fatherless maternity and who, in her particular blend of reason and emotion, embodied the androgynous spirit of the classical Greek psyche. It was no coincidence that she was a goddess of warfare, particularly well-reasoned "justified" warfare, whose roots nonetheless grow deep in the underworld of fury's rage and betrayal.

The Furies as we knew them at the start appeared to pass into the figure of Athena—much as Medusa's head appeared on Athena's shield.

They were transmogrified into a blessing through their subordination to the new Athenian solar law of Olympus, the patriarchal dream. Did this represent an integration of mother right with father right, an integration of one dream of totality into another, or an uneasy and ominous attempt at denial and marginalization through what would be termed in modern parlance *memorialization*?[8] Much as we may fear it, psychology and history both suggest that without a deeper sacrifice of identity, without suffering anxiety, disintegration, raw need, aggression, and even active forms of destruction like hate, there is no space in which dreaming of totality can really do its restorative work. In the case of the fury that arises in individuals and groups when there is a break in the fabric of totality, without suffering it all the way down, so to speak, there is no real movement into a more inclusive dream.

The other path—identification with the Furies' destruction—brings its own type of narcissistic catharsis, a pseudo-healing through the so-called free expression of anger and rage, but in the end, in an effort to avenge their wounds, the Furies continue to wound in turn. As historian Arno Mayer noted,

> There are certain affinities between . . . the Furies of [Greek tragedy], religious crusades, revolutionary terrors, overseas civilizing missions, and . . . the Furies of the killing fields, firebombing, and atomic discharges of the two world wars. The ultimate genius of these ordeals of twentieth-century war was less the deadliness of modern weapons than their *sacralization* along with the causes they were made to serve.[9]

But if stripped entirely of its destructive function, fury's claims become more, rather than less, potent. They eventually erupt. The collective question which no society has yet to answer is: Do we enlist fury's rage and wounds in the service of a righteous ideal—a seemingly "damned if we do, damned if we don't" proposition—or do we trust in its corrective potential? If the latter perspective shines through, we can understand fury's wound as creating a space, and creating the distress signal by which dreaming of totality is set in motion. There are telling etymological relationships between fury, frenzy, rage, passion, song, storms, possession—and prophecy. In the madness that fury brings when a dream of totality is broken, in the mad and passionate dynamics of primitive emotions and cold-blooded vengeance, exactly when pain and chaos reigns, there is fertile ground that allows new connections to be made.

Returning to the *Oresteia* for a moment, the pursuit of Orestes by the Furies on behalf of his mother pushes for a deeply ethical response, pushes him to take ownership and responsibility for the entirety of his humanity. The Furies bring him face-to-face with death, guilt, fear, and despair, with everything that appears hostile, everything that belongs to the darker matriarchal worldview. Difficult as it is to be pulled apart, this is a first step; dissolution provides the seeds for reconstruction. Having broken the simplicity of the original matriarchal world—and this is his fate as well as ours—the more Orestes is dismembered and bound by the Furies' hostile rage, the more firm and solid, the better and more complex he is challenged to become. The Furies' demand for blood payment stimulates the alchemy of dissolution and coagulation that they relentlessly demand. Thus, as Martha Nussbaum wrote in *The Fragility of Goodness*, "Orestes is not mad, but at his most sane, when he recognizes that the Furies are in pursuit."[10]

It is impossible, even delusional, to close prematurely the ruptures in broken dreams or to silence the distress and fury that come with that shattering. As we still witness in the contemporary world, the furies of terrorism and fundamentalisms are outgrowths of deep attachments to earth, family, and clan. Furious fundamentalists of all persuasions, literal and limited as their inner worlds may be, definitely have their hearts in their work, acting to protect and defend their deepest values, appearing in the guise of a god-given birthright. On a different note, this fantasy of reclaiming birthright has a mirror in the individual dynamics of fury and rage often encountered in psychotherapy, where what is frequently at issue is a seemingly lost or irreclaimable golden age of childhood. The Furies protect this golden age, a fantasy usually projected backward onto imaginary and idealized parents, and fury allows nothing to deconstruct this fantasy. Just as in the social arena where we try to adjudicate the Furies, sending them to war or to court or turning them in service to collective ego ideals, in therapy we often try (again, insanely) to turn fury's ruptures into the service of ego ideals such as empowerment or self-assertion.

In this scenario, the sacrifice of idealizations that fury's wounds could exact from us never actually takes place. And so instead, from out of the shadows of our optimistic (and sometimes seemingly God-given) dreams come furious fundamentalists whose absolute and spiritual identification with their chosen dream of totality allow them to be the very agents of vengeful justice. The bomb-laden terrorist traveling freely on public transport, the cyber terrorist or religious zealot who has unhampered access to massive communications networks—these are our frightening postmodern apparitions. They destabilize the dominant culture, they bloody our collective idealization, they pierce through our magic circles. When this is going on, "God" is on everyone's side.

What's not new is that the fury of the disenfranchised has always disrupted the collective ideal. Emancipation of the other at the bursting point in the dominant dream of totality upsets oppressive regimes in the way that, for example, feminism upset patriarchal organization in the latter part of the twentieth century. Remember WITCH, the Women's International Terrorist Conspiracy from Hell, aka Women Inspired to Tell their Collective History, aka Women Interested in Toppling Consumer Holidays? In the case of twentieth-century feminism, suffering with the wounds and fury that were expressed, without retaliation, and making the appropriate societal sacrifices was integral to the creative aspect of the destabilization prevailing and to the formation of a more inclusive cultural matrix that seems to have real staying power.

That time seems almost quaint now. Would the Greeks have understood as omens the events of September 2001, when burning birds fell from the sky alongside the people jumping to their deaths from the World Trade Center in New York City? In an explosion of murderous rage the Furies had burst into flame once again. That wound may have opened the eyes of the Western world to the blind faith in which we pursue our cherished dreams. We may have seen the seemingly bloodless expansion of the free market and the rising tide of Westernization threatening to flood the world as the destructive shadows of those dreams, perhaps even as the shadow of our beloved secular democracy. But our bewilderment bore witness to our collective resistance to seeing the hate, envy, and fury of what had been deemed the other. Both our faith in our dream and its shadow—the Western hegemony—arose from broken bonds of relationship to others. When those broken bonds were exposed, there was an opportunity to commune with the wounded soul of the world, to help what was dying, to pay attention to the decay and demise engendered in other places by many aspects of Western domination. But as the shadow of the evil other was cast back and forth in the vehemence of rhetoric and action, the Furies struck again and again at these very splits and betrayals of humanity. The fury of blood payments continued to curse the land.

Fury's destructive blood lust for revenge often begins as a defense against a broken dream of totality. It is a deeply ambivalent emotional reaction. Fury may both abase and transform us, just as cannibalism enacts a regressive fall into chaos and a communion of shared blood. If allowed to do their work, emotions like fury aim to correct by breaking down defensive structures until only the bones of identity remain, bones around which something new can form. Fury's lust has to be sacrificed, not for the sake of a cultural ideal or for collective standards—whether those be theocracy or secular democracy—but in order to face the other within and without. As individuals and societies we face into the process of converting the hatred and ecstasy that the Furies unleash—like the maniacal spectacle of Abu Ghraib—into a shared blood bond of communion and compassion. The critical turn and the moment of truth seems to lie in a willingness to take a chance, to let our dreams of totality and identity die, to choose communion over assimilation, to risk losing everything by keeping fury's wound open. Suffering our open wounds could connect us with the suffering in the world, with what the ancients called the *anima mundi*, the soul of the world. And it would seem the personification of the world's soul is no longer Athena or even a redemptive Christ. Embodying that soul in our time seems to mean suffering ambiguity and emptiness, not rushing to backfill the holes in our broken dreams with either rationality or redemption.

A comparison again with the work that happens in psychotherapy can illuminate what's at stake. Much of what takes place in treatment can be framed as a sacrifice of emotional attachment and behavior patterns, a sacrifice of what's called "incestuous desire," met before, for example, in the need for perfect mirroring. What I mean by incestuous desire is not sexual acts initiated by a parent toward a child—although it can take this form—but rather all manner of ways in which we wish to remain confined in repetitive self-reinforcing patterns, confined in a magic circle of feelings and thoughts that can be severely limiting and coercive to oneself and others.

In his essay "The Psychology of the Transference," Jung made the case that our first experience of kinship feelings is an unconscious instinctual one, often imaged as incest which, as he picturesquely put it, "like a sheepdog keeps the family group intact."[11] This pertains to actual family dynamics and can be understand intrapsychically too, as a tendency to keep the inner world protected within a magic circle—closed down and self-serving. Jung also pointed out, however, that there is a dilemma posed by the kinship instinct, which is that "it goes against nature to commit incest, and it goes against nature not to yield to an ardent desire."[12] This aptly expresses many of the seemingly unbearable tensions experienced in psychotherapy and even more so in life.

In treatment, both patient and analyst work against this pull of incestuous desire, sacrificing various forms of gratification so that the closed world of the magic circle is broken, opening up space for reconstruction, for new feelings and thoughts to take hold. Or, looked at from the relational perspective, the magic circle opens to admit an appreciation for and empathy with others. What has been made a scapegoat or taboo, whether elements in oneself or the reality of other people, is invited in. It is not, however, a matter of assimilating everything into oneself—the ubiquitous "it's a part of me" approach to therapy that seems like a kind of psychotherapeutic eating disorder—but rather, sacrificing the tendencies to either scapegoat or assimilate, in the service of communion. Rather than yielding to the ministrations of the sheepdog or, alternatively, just disappearing from an embodied life, keeping the family group intact has to be sacrificed at the altar of what I would describe as kinship with the unknown self, the unknown other, and the unknown story. This is a different form of yielding to desire. When the process goes awry, the magic circle is simply transferred into the therapeutic relationship, into an interminable therapy, into the folie à deux of shared transference/countertransference fantasies and collusions.

In the therapeutic encounter, success or failure stands or falls in great measure on keeping a sacrificial ethic toward the work, on keeping psychological and emotional space open for new experience, on keeping a tension in the therapeutic field between patient and therapist. This field comes to be experienced as a third player in the therapeutic encounter—it's where the sacrifice gets made and where new forms of experience take root. All the various dos and don'ts of therapeutic guidelines and strictures are a kind of proscribed ten commandments approach to keeping this space open, and they work as well or as ineffectively as most proscriptions do. When the open space of the symbolic field is appreciated as an arena that allows for the play of mythopoetic experience, both parties feel connected through it in a way that encourages both separateness and mutuality. Just as not making the appropriate sacrifices in therapeutic work leads to all sorts of abuse—sexual, financial, emotional—the same goes for not doing so in collective life. Power dynamics, often in the guise of assimilation, that is, malignant globalization and the like, substitute for communion and the genuine sharing of essentials.

The Beginning of the End of "Out"

Lucky for us, it is getting harder and harder to maintain our dreams of totality by scapegoating and taboo, the traditional mechanisms that controlled what belonged inside a dream of totality and what didn't—although we still try. In the mechanism of scapegoating, what's unwanted or feels impossible to live with is placed imaginally into the past by killing or banishing whatever has been designated to carry the projection of evil. Sometimes this is a one-time action, such as excommunication. Most often it needs to be maintained by periodic reenactments, such as intermittent resurgences of anti-Semitism. There are other, more direct forms of expulsion—war—and even benign ones, like the celebration of "out with the old and in with the new" on New Year's Eve. All these ritualized behaviors drive out what doesn't belong in the magic circle. The designated scapegoat can be the worst of the worst or the best of the best, the most ugly or the most beautiful, the oldest or the youngest (the gods like these equally well) or even just one's personal sacred cow, something that has been designated for sacrifice when disaster strikes. What doesn't belong inside the dream of totality is carried out by the scapegoat, to disappear into the mists of time.

In the dynamics of taboo, what is outside a dream of totality stays in real time, an ever present and potent danger that has to be contained and avoided by shunning, marginalization, or degradation, that is, racism or sexism. The offending people aren't literally banished or killed. They are placed under a taboo in a designated area of the psyche and society, remaining isolated and segregated within a magic circle of often elaborate rituals where a wary eye can be kept on them. There are also more benign forms of taboo, which are used, for example, in various healing traditions. In these rituals, sickness or distress is imaginally transferred into a person or system (therapist, head of state, justice system) deemed able to handle and metabolize it. The designated person or system then returns what was disturbing to the community, but metabolized into a safer form. While this is going on, the designated person or system is also taboo, isolated from others. If there is a failure to metabolize the danger, the person or the system may—by default—become a scapegoat. People who are victims of outright shunning and degradation like racism may also—by default and creative effort—metabolize some of the sickness projected onto them by the dominant culture, eventually returning it to the community in altered cultural and emotional forms. In this case, they are the sacrificial victims who live to tell the tale.

There is another form of sacrifice we enact that breaks totality's magic circle: apocalypse. In *Seeing Things Hidden,* Malcolm Bull describes the shift from a psychology of scapegoating and taboo to one of apocalyptic thinking, a shift that seems to characterize much of our contemporary situation. Bull describes how, for example, the situation that led up to the American Civil War began in the psychology of taboo—slavery— but gradually changed into recognition of the contradiction between slavery and democratic humanitarian values. This clash and return of what had been taboo—the people who had been enslaved—culminated in an apocalyptic "big bang" within American consciousness, the Civil War. In contrast to scapegoating or taboo, in apocalyptic thinking what isn't integrated seems to be "deferred," placed imaginally into the future when it will get reabsorbed at some later time.[13] The salient point about apocalyptic thinking, writes Bull, is that "apocalyptic does not merely invert the processes embodied in taboo or sacrifice, it also differs from these practices in that it positively welcomes the intrusion of chaos into the existing cosmos."[14]

Yeats expressed the apocalyptic sensibility of his time in the poem "The Second Coming":

> Turning and turning in the widening gyre
> The falcon cannot hear the falconer;
> Things fall apart; the centre cannot hold;
> Mere anarchy is loosed upon the world,
> The blood-dimmed tide is loosed, and everywhere
> The ceremony of innocence is drowned;
> The best lack all conviction, while the worst
> Are full of passionate intensity.

> Surely some revelation is at hand;
> Surely the Second Coming is at hand.[15]

In times of apocalyptic thinking, what's been kept out or deferred comes rushing in, urgently and recklessly. Rough beasts slouch toward Bethlehem, the creatures of Revelation reign supreme, stormy Leviathans rise from the sea, startling social and even genetic admixtures and contradictions abound, family values collapse, taboos are transgressed, forbidden unions are forged, and identities become fluid and alien. Sound familiar? There is a lot in this imagery that captures the flavor of change in the contemporary world and some startlingly bizarre symmetry reveals this unusual state of affairs. At the same time, for example, that genetic codes are being cracked in laboratories all over the world—allowing for hybridizing plants, cloning animals, even human organs—ultra-Orthodox Jews are still zealously trying to breed the pristine and mythical red heifer, which when ritually slaughtered on the Temple Mount will hasten the coming of the Messiah and the garden of paradise.

The prevalence of apocalyptic imagery that abounds in contemporary culture may be due in large part to the fact that there is simply no longer an out in which to banish or sequester what is unwanted. Everyone and everything are everywhere. This is true in many arenas of experience as the population continues to expand on the planet and in our minds and hearts via communications technology. As the notion of the stranger recedes, this also means that the enemy can seem to be anywhere and everywhere, even right next door, behind our eyeballs, or beneath our skin. Hence, our increasing concerns, even paranoia, about immigration, networks of terror, cancer, and the like. Even more difficult to come to terms with is that loss of structures and centers in our lives leads to a difficulty recognizing what constitutes transgressions—both creative and destructive ones. It's hard to know where the meaningful boundaries even are, much less when we have violated them. And at the other end of the spectrum, a more passive response to this apocalyptic state of affairs is to play dead, hiding from the chaos and our changing identities by disengaging—an unfortunately popular form of self-taboo that is aided and abetted by the stupefying stream of images and spectacles coming from the infotainment industry.

The features of postmodernity include the breakdown of taboos that used to keep people and things apart and the consequent appearance of people who defy the boundaries that those taboos held in check. There is growing acceptance in many quarters that scapegoating and expulsion of these people or of unwanted elements of self are no longer workable ways to regulate self or society. In any case, our time is not about the revelation of arcane beasts long forgotten or of a transfigured city of God in the form of a global village. What are revealed by our apocalyptic fantasies are the contradictions and uncertainties at the margins of contemporary experience. The limits of our worldviews, our identities, and our ways of coping are being uncovered very rapidly. For the apocalyptically minded, this chaos feels familiar—a prophecy come to fruition—and postmodern culture furnishes increasing "evidence" of it. This feels frightening or righteously maniacal, depending on one's affiliation.

But while it's not really that easy to destroy the world, a mass sacrifice of encapsulated dreams and forms of affiliation is indeed underway, and we can meet this with *amor fati*, "love of fate," as Jung once said, or be dragged to the sacrificial altar. Beat and bloodied, individually and as communities, both victims and players, our challenge seems to be facing into the prospect of sacrificing our prevailing attachments and dreams, with all their illusory safety and attendant destructiveness, into the freedom of an open wound. The fomenting this brings can also be a ferment that works like yeast, stirring things up if we can keep the wounds open. At the same time that the enemy can now be projected everywhere and anywhere, it could be precisely this that allows us to recognize that it is already in anyone and everyone, namely, ourselves. We may well be in the midst of an apocalyptic unveiling: an unveiling of what constitutes open psyches and open societies. There may be a new dawning, but it is not fated to be a return to ground zero.

Every age has its troublemakers, its transgressors and its sacrificial figures, who often play two roles: the bearer of apocalyptic woes and the savior who will end them. Christ was one such figure, a *pharmakos*; Galileo was another sacrificial victim who carried the poison and the panacea of his time, the spirit of scientific realism. Later, Nietzsche seemed to play a similar role in the collective imagination, initiating the tragic and liberating death of God and the birth of radical subjectivity with all its attendant ambivalence and suffering. Paradigm shifts are a bloody business, and now we are all playing the part of the *pharmakos*. Can we use our hard-won tools to cut our way out of afflicted identifications with creator and destroyer gods and suffer the wounds that engender empathy? The unmasking and decentering that drives our postmodern sensibility amplifies the feeling that there really is no Archimedean point from which to judge anything, and that is a good thing. With this unmasking comes the realization that as our identifications and projections fall away, in open societies and open psyches we are increasingly vulnerable—from the inside. What will play a defining role as we go forward is how we enact the sacrifices being exacted from us—and how we treat our wounds—what activities we are drawn into as the gods of modernism depart and both apocalypse and utopia seem to loom.

Notes

[1] Wolfgang Giegerich, *Soul Violence,* vol. 3, *Collected English Papers* (New Orleans: Spring Journal Books, 2008), p. 247.

[2] The author is indebted to Martha Nussbaum's *The Fragility of Goodness* (Cambridge, England: Cambridge University Press, 1986), for her interpretations of ethics in classical Greek tragedy.

[3] Aeschylus, *Complete Greek Tragedies,* vol. 1, *Oresteia: Agamemmnon, The Libation Bearers, The Eumenides,* trans. Richard Lattimore (Chicago: University of Chicago Press, 1953–1956), pp. 341–346.

[4] *Ibid.*, pp. 389–396.

[5] *Ibid.*, pp. 778–783.

[6] William Barrett, *Irrational Man* (New York: Random House, 1990), pp. 279–280.

[7] Friedrich Nietzsche, *The Birth of Tragedy* (New York: Dover Publications, 1927, 1995), p. 77.

[8] Svetlana Boym discusses the phenomenon of memorialization as a mechanism that institutionalizes a restorative nostalgia that fixes history in tradition, versus a reflective nostalgia that accesses imagination; see Svetlana Boym, *The Future of Nostalgia* (New York: Basic Books, 2001).

[9] Arno Mayer, *The Furies: Violence and Terror in the French and Russian Revolutions* (Princeton, NJ: Princeton University Press, 2000), p. 72.

[10] Nussbaum, *The Fragility of Goodness,* pp. 41–42.

[11] C. G. Jung, "The Psychology of the Transference" (1946), in *The Practice of Psychotherapy,* vol. 16, *The Collected Works of C. G. Jung* (Princeton, NJ: Princeton University Press, 1954), §431. In this essay, Jung amplifies a series of woodcuts from the alchemical *Rosarium* to illustrate the stages of increasing psychological differentiation that

characterize psychological maturation from a condition of unconscious merger to one of conscious relationship.

[12] *Ibid.*, §469.

[13] Malcolm Bull, *Seeing Things Hidden: Apocalypse, Vision, and Totality* (New York: Verso, 1999), p. 77.

[14] *Ibid.*, p. 78.

[15] As quoted by Peter Childs, *Modernism* (London: Routledge, 2007), p. 39.

Part III

Nothing at the Center

CHAPTER SIX

MASKING AND UNMASKING IMAGINATION: VIRTUALITY AND ITS TRANSGRESSIONS

I am thy creature.
—Mary Shelley, *Frankenstein*

Tryin' to make it real—compared to what?
—Les McCann and Eddie Harris, *Live at Montreux*

All the erasure and uncertainty that contemporary life allows us can also serve as a vehicle for creative disruption and as a stimulus for the call and response of creative imagination to come into play. The decentering and fragmented quality of contemporary life calls out in the imagination for integration and reconstitution—that is the dynamic of dreaming of totality. In answer to that call, there is a strong pull to default to the correctives of a mighty apocalypse or a new grail of global consciousness with its implicit promise of a global cybervillage. The technological carriers that took us into terra incognita just a few years ago were alien UFOs and homegrown spacecraft, products of the twentieth-century imagination—vehicles controlled by beings superior to us in either intelligence, as in *Close Encounters of the Third Kind*, or evil, as in *Invasion of the Body Snatchers*, or simply vehicles that represented the pinnacle of our own creativity.[1] The vehicles that now carry our projections of the new world order are our twenty-first-century technological creations—

cyberspace and virtuality. We cling for dear life to our laptops and smartphones, which have attained the status of containing self-objects or charged fetishes—prayer beads and connections to the dream of totality that is the World Wide Web.

Marshall McLuhan's Dilemma Redux

In this chapter, I explore the masking and unmasking of imagination in relation to transgression and to our dream of virtuality—to the ways we create culture in contemporary life. Media culture guru Marshall McLuhan, early in his career, famously proclaimed that "the medium is the message." But at the end of his professional life he was asking, "Is the medium the message or the massage?" As so much of our own experience is falling into the new medium of virtuality, we need to ask the same question about our relationship to it. Is the promise of virtuality another form of the fool's gold the alchemists warned against, or does it offer something more valuable? In a sense, it's an old question, like the tale of the Holy Grail. In that medieval story, which began during a time of interregnum, the land and its king had been withering away. One day Parsifal, a young boy, accidentally stumbled upon what all the knights in the kingdom had been hoping to find—deep in the forest he sees a vision of a mystical cup that could heal the moribund king and the kingdom. But Parsifal, untried and enraptured, under the spell of the grail vision, neglects to ask a crucial question about it: What does it serve? So it disappears. And that's how the quest for the Holy Grail began—with a disappearing act.

A quick and dirty interpretation of this story suggests that the vision of the grail grants a much-needed whiff of possibility, but that possibility disappears from view when we don't look at how it will be used. In our world, our projections onto cyberspace and virtuality are young and immature, like Parsifal, and like ourselves in relationship to them. They are still a vision, a glimpse of something around which we spin the fantasies and fears of the *pharmakon*. We don't know where we are going with it yet, and at the same time that we are logged on, happily contained in our new dream of totality, we also feel disoriented and frightened by the fabric of holes that are being exposed in what once felt whole. Most important, we usually don't ask what it's for, what it serves.

Experience in the virtual world is simultaneously real and imaginary—things are almost or nearly real. And although our experience there doesn't necessarily have a physical analog, it nevertheless exists in the imagination with profound effects and critical impact. The power of imagination to transgress into what is seemingly real is coming into sharp relief. At the same time, however engaging and realistic a virtual experience is, its imaginative origin still shines through. In what follows we will see how virtuality embodies—if we can even use that word—the *pharmakon* of totality in a way that does particular justice to its imaginal origin and its paradoxical effects. In addition, I will explore how the difficulty we have in recognizing what is transgressive—a difficulty that has come to light partly because of virtual experience—may also lay at the heart of our uneasiness about sorting through in what ways the Internet is beneficial, ushering in a whole new era, or bad, a case of garbage in garbage out.

Although the power of imagination has always been appreciated—at least in the arts and humanities, and often by common experience as well—recent developments in neuroscience have supplied another interesting perspective. Studies using brain PET and MRI have demonstrated that when people imagine they are walking down a street or pressing a button, the same brain areas that are active when they are actually walking down a street or pressing a button show signs of activity. Furthermore, imagining making a movement increases a person's subsequent skill in making the same actual movement. It appears that practicing in the imagination is almost as effective as training in actuality.[2]

It also appears to be the case that when people practice assertiveness, inventiveness, or compassion using virtual avatars and online personae, there may be similar crossover effects. There can be, of course, a huge downside to all this imaginary activity as it becomes real, something that we witnessed, for example, in Wall Street's mania for financial derivatives wherein investors were no longer buying anything actually real. Lest we were fooled into thinking that all this was merely imaginary and that the real values in life lay elsewhere, we only had to witness the real havoc and suffering caused by these imaginary instruments. I will return to the question of what happens when virtuality meets embodiment in the latter part of this chapter in conjunction with the ethics of transgression. First, we need to take a closer look at the *pharmakon* of virtuality.

Life in the global village of cyberspace purports to break down our fixed experience of time and location, connecting everyone and everything. It offers activities and imagery such as unlimited space, a home without boundaries, time without limits, utterly open access to information and unlimited connections—all of which is fueled by a kind of utopian posthumanist mindset about redemptive intelligent technology and global consciousness. Heraclitus's maxim applies to cyberspace: you never do step into the same river twice, and the ubiquity of virtuality will ensure that we are all immersed in the stream. Even now, the collective immersion in free-floating communities like Second Life and the widespread use of communication networks like Facebook and Twitter are everyday ways in which we are experiencing an alteration in our experience of what is real and what is imaginary.[3] At the same time, we definitely attribute qualities to the virtual world and to others in cyberspace that aren't really there. We project our minds and our feelings onto—some would say increasingly into—the virtual world, filling in the actual inconsistencies that abound there with what we imagine, rearranging fragments into wholes, restoring symmetry, fashioning a dream of totality. In part this is the message of the medium—that it allows us to do this so transparently—and it's also a massage.

Whether or not the nonexpert tweeting to thousands of followers has much of significance to offer the culture is in many ways beside the point right now. People are trying to contend with their experience. Everyone can now tell their own story in blogs and memoirs—not by accident the most popular narrative forms today—or archive and upload their purported real lives into virtual media. At the same time that these possibilities for genuine expression have materialized, the emphasis on style, the look of it all, has become the dominant mode of presentation and even of identity. We're trying to hold on to what feels real while simultaneously being overwhelmed by illusions. On the one hand, these popular genres feel genuine, but at the same time they embrace all the artifice and fictionalizing of contemporary life. To the extent that these forms, including the collective display of reality TV, actually manage to express mythopoetic truths, we accept them. When they don't, we think we can recognize the illusion, the manufactured spectacle. But is it so easy to tell the difference anymore, and more important, do we really care?

As the new technology offers avenues for greater awareness of the power of imagination, this cuts both ways. Our virtual world is also the ultimate illusionist, the "technician of sleight-of-hand," as Derrida described the *pharmakon*, even an embalmer—as many people caught in virtual life can attest.[4] *Pharmakon* also meant "color" (the high-definition kind of color), and virtual images are nothing if not colorful, simulacra sometimes so perfect that, like the sorcerer's *pharmakon*, they can bewitch and captivate, setting the imagination in motion as surely as the real thing. Traditionally, bewitchment was always considered to have been the result of a representation, an image. Like a cosmetic, the digital images that captivate us can conceal what's dead under the appearance of what's living. In the olden days, the antidote to the bewitching simulacrum used to be the science of measurement. As we used to say, "numbers don't lie." A considered and measured response stood against the intoxicating momentum with which a simulacrum could come alive. But with digitization and Photoshop, and as the stream of information and edited images becomes a steady deluge, it appears that even measurement can be enlisted in the service of illusion and manipulation. Measurement and facts are no antidote to the poison in virtuality. If we try to rely on the fact/fiction divide for our sense of reality, then we have to be careful to get our facts straight. But we sense that relying on the fact of facts now often seems like a form of quackery, in part because the lifetime and reliability of facts is shrinking so quickly. Facts are malleable and plastic; interpretation and meaning are relative. We accept illusion as an expression of reality, and reality as a series of illusions.

As we saw in chapter 3, this extends to ourselves, too. As experience becomes more complex and virtual in the contemporary world, we find ourselves at an interesting juncture regarding how we experience who we are. In addition to telling verbal stories, visual stories, and emotional stories, we tell ourselves virtual world stories—including a story about the author and user of the virtual world. Our contemporary experience seems to resemble the transparency, and also the masked quality, of a parallel series of as-if installation and improvisational art spaces, in which we are the installations and the improvisers, both revealed and hidden.

Meandering through these improvisational spaces we encounter ambiguity, a multiplicity of possible perspectives, and a plurality of possible personhoods. This can be cathartic in the same way that all theater is cathartic. Our virtual installations can provide consequence-free space in which we can experiment with identity and ideas—the creation of avatars and online personae being the most graphic examples. This free space for experimentation is crucial during adolescence and for creative processes at any age. Regarding self-identity in the virtual world, our virtual performance projects can foster what Robert Lifton identified as a fluid and protean self or what MIT psychologist Sherry Turkle referred to in *Alone Together* as a "collaborative self," a self continuously informed by other selves.[5] In addition to lauding the virtues of collaborative identity, Turkle also voiced concerns that for high school students "the years of identity construction are recast in terms of profile production."[6]

One way to reframe this dilemma is to consider a Facebook profile, for example, as a variation on the theatrical mask in the deepest sense—as both an experiment in identity and an expression of essence. Both masks and profiles are vehicles for catharsis and also the artifice that conceals it. Masks belong to the mythic arts of drama and storytelling—as do social profiling, avatars, and blogging. Masks have always portrayed the human life drama in all its manifold aspects, especially the compelling and often treacherous search for what we like to call the real self. Distillations of powerful emotions—love, envy, rage, disappointment, joy—are given impersonal artistic form in a mask. When a mask obscures the individual wearer, he or she can access the universal emotions that the mask evokes. As with traditional masks, a profile mask also provides this access, as well as a powerful protection from emotional states that might be overwhelming if experienced directly, "in your face."

By wearing a mask, universal emotions are also brought into a present context and can serve as models for social and psychological life. Masks have always been used for this sort of initiation into collective life or to maintain collective authority and social mores, and also to escape from that same collective authority. Looking both ways, they direct our gaze inward and also outward toward others. Masks can disguise, cover, veil, lie, capture, release, reveal, project, protect, disown, recollect, deceive, dissociate, embody, and even transform. The best Noh theatrical masks, for example, seem to have the ability to change the very emotions they express, appearing differently to the audience depending on how the light strikes the mask.

A mask, far from merely concealing its wearer, provides a bridge between the subjectivity of the wearer, universal emotions, and collective culture. No wonder then that Facebook profiling and constructing avatars is so appealing to adolescents. These activities provide all the ritual aspects of masks, and when creating profiles, adolescents are very busy being born (or dying) into adulthood. Another reason this works is that masks and profiles provide access to experiences that aren't ordinarily available. You can experience things in virtual life that you can't—or wouldn't—in real life. This can be both enlivening and terrorizing, as Facebook users, for example, can attest.

The terrorizing aspect of all tribal or cultic initiation rituals has always been designed to discipline and lock in behavior so as to maintain collective stasis—and sure enough, you must be "on" Facebook and "liked" or risk social death. But there is a similarly terrorizing aspect to being overidentified with one's persona, with one's tribal role and with the mask through which one enters and lives in the world, and Facebook users also take great pains to change profile pictures and comments constantly, to keep the persona updated. Not doing so risks psychological death.

On the enlivening end, both a mask and the social profile reflect an underlying drive toward adaptation and a creative participation in collective life. Lacking a social persona or mask makes one overly vulnerable, or it can be a childish and empty condition often reflecting failures of development and rendering one unable to be of service to society. Sorting this all out—becoming aware of one's masks and identifications, deciding what should remain hidden and what revealed, what is unduly pressured by conformity and what is unique, and finding one's place in the masquerade of life—is part of the work of adolescence and, really, of living well.

All the intrigues, the grand masquerade, the saving face, the Greek chorus, and the drama that take place in social media networks like Facebook are no accident and not inconsequential. Social profiling is a ritual as surely as any other masked performance. The big differences are that whole cultures now participate in the ongoing virtual performance and that the context doesn't appear to be a sacred one—although the devotion and attention paid to social networking often belies this assumption. On the one hand, we can applaud, for as Oscar Wilde quipped, "Man is least himself when he talks in his own person. Give him a mask, and he will tell the truth." On the other hand, we might ask ourselves what is it that we are protecting ourselves from so strenuously, what is it that needs the filter and catharsis of so much theater and masking? And on the other other hand—rare enough—there are also still those who are most themselves when they remove the mask completely.

One of the problems that emerges is similar to that posed by the venting offered by theatrical catharsis. Feeling good in our installations and virtual performances isn't the same as being good or doing good. We can feel connected without being involved; we can have relationships without being committed. We can do bad things and disappear easily. This brings us to the next point which is that, put starkly, the dream of totality we call virtuality is particularly nonethical. It's not that it's *un*ethical; it's just not concerned with ethics at all. Like theater, it provides an arena for evocation, but unlike most theater, not for the ethics of relationship. There is no moral to the story, there are no recognizable ethical mandates in cyberspace.

The Ethics of Transgression

The ethical dilemmas posed by masking in virtual life come into high relief if we look at the ways that virtuality is used as a contemporary confessional. In what seems like an almost apocalyptic gesture of unmasking, many people seem moved to tell all and reveal dark secrets online. For example, since 2005, Frank Warren, known on his website as "the most trusted stranger in America," has invited people all over the world to send him homemade postcards bearing secrets that they have never revealed before. These confessions are posted on his blog, PostSecret.com, described as "an ongoing community art project where people mail in their secrets anonymously," and may also become the content of an international traveling art exhibit, as well as text in five best-selling books.[7] PostSecret seems to be a virtual confessional space, but one that doesn't require the traditional sacrifices. It's free, it's not associated with wrongdoing or conflict, and it's a space without the embodied experience of apology or shame. On the one side, it seems like a kind of collective drainage system for what feels out of bounds, and many attest that their dark secrets really are turned to gold by virtue of being revealed and engaged with online. The other side is that virtual confessionals are just cyberdumps for a toxic waste of troubling feelings and for bad—even reprehensible—behavior. The fact that lots of money is being made by packaging these confessions is nothing new—many institutions have made a bundle from confessions and there is a kind of masking involved in those as well. What's new is the decorative ethic: you can dump your junk and also have it displayed at the same time.

Virtuality has been touted as a wonder drug for its facilitation of this sort of self-expression that also benefits society. This idea may be an outward rotation of the myriad psychospiritual techniques for self-renewal through inner work that were so popular during the later part of the twentieth century. And many people do find a sense of meaning and connection in the technology and techniques of online life. But making a fetish out of either inner life or virtual life can foster the same illusion of magical salvation. Or support the illusion that somehow those things can take care of us as well as—or even better than—other people can care for us. Actual people don't seem to have time to devote to caring, but the Web mother and the inner mother are always there, 24-7.

But we shouldn't blame virtuality for its lack of ethical sensibility. Virtuality exemplifies one of the avowed tenets of postmodernism, that it *should* lack verticality—no transcendent spiritual heights and no gritty unconscious depths necessary. Things are purely lateral and derivative, on a horizontal plane with no higher or lower vantage points and no need for any. The postmodern sensibility doesn't aim up or down for any sense of meaning. It aims instead toward a ground zero. What Malcolm Bull wrote about the postmodernists applies equally well to virtuality: "Derrida offered a reality of 'holes' rather then 'wholes' . . . and found insights in blindness rather than vision. Barthes attacked the ideology of the unified text; Bataille wrote of fleeing from 'the horror of reducing being to totality.'"[8] Nowadays there is an even greater cynicism about the possibility of knowledge (as opposed to information) and an increasing reliance on the streaming flow of information and images, although we compensate for this by resurrecting a whole—the Web as psychopomp of global consciousness.

It's important to remember though that virtuality is not the approaching singularity.[9] It is not a technological version of the Rapture, when AI (artificial intelligence) or the virtual world cross an imaginary line and merge with the human, each transcending their limits and/or destroying the other. If there is anything like a normative conscience in virtual life, it's imagined as being expressed in the ebbs and flows of the Web's content, purportedly narrating its own experience. Or to use other images, virtuality in the Web has been likened to an empty vessel—the no-thing of the Way in Buddhism—or to the ways in which self-organizing systems are constantly generating new, if fleeting, meanings. What's new, or at least what's old wine in an all-important new bottle, is that virtuality seems to offer the possibility of experiencing that we are the explicit and designated translators and transgressors of our experience. At the moment this can feel like a kind of glossolalia—a speaking in tongues that's both a disorienting babble and a kind of everyday ecstasy. And although some things do get lost in translation, a lot also gets across. One of the promises of the void of virtuality is a release that allows imagination to be appreciated as its own truth, part of but also separate from its creations.

What comes with this release, an appreciation of our shared imagination as being the ground of experience, is critical. For us postmoderns, dreaming of totality, for example, is no longer experienced in the objectivity of revealed wisdom or in the lone subjectivity of the exalted individual creator. What used to be called meaning now emerges in interdependence and interactivity, in an endless series of moves in a virtual and public state of mind. These moves toward meaning include the constant erasure of images, ideas, and identities. Another way to say this is that the virtual experience can make dreaming of totality's dynamic of the one and the many more transparent and accessible. We ourselves, with our mediums and our messages, and all the artifice of postmodern culture, have entered the vessel of imagination, which by virtue of its increasing virtuality has also disappeared into itself. Imagination let loose could come out into the open and lay claim to its dreams. And imagination is the ultimate transgressor. The shape-shifting play of our imaginal creations make noise and trouble, and they make change. Virtuality also plays very well with images and ideas—that's its element, its medium, and its comforting massage.

It's unclear though how well virtuality plays with others. A dramatic way to get at the transgressive character of virtuality is to look at it in relation to its extreme poison, a kind of psychopathy. Virtuality and psychopathy may have an affinity for one another—the evening news is full of flashes about psychopaths who thrive in the simulacrum atmosphere that the online world offers. The downside of the mockery and erasure shared by postmodern sensibility and virtual life is that the transgressions they permit also open the door to the *un*imaginative and the unempathic—to a psychopathy that finds its way in easily through the holes, the blind spots, and the uncaring flow.

But psychopathy and transgression are by no means the same. Psychopathic behavior is disengaged. It brings nothing new to the table, adds nothing new to the culture, opens no new doors, makes no new connections—it just severs them. This is the sense in which psychopathy is recognized as robotic and lacking in true imagination, and in fact, psychopaths, though they are masterful imitators of other people's emotions and motivations, usually cannot foresee even the consequences of their own actions. We sometimes anxiously label the transgressions in virtual life as psychopathic, but this is when we see the holes in the fabric of things that have been opened up in virtual life and try way too quickly to close them with a label. It's not always so easy to tell the difference however. A frightening development of this tension between psychopathy and transgression is, for example, the legal designation of people who look at child pornography online as sex offenders, even incarcerating them whether or not an actual crime has been committed, creating, in effect, a new species of fantasy offenders. The fact is that in the uninhibiting atmosphere of online life, people will do and say things that they wouldn't in real life, including abuse children. The great majority of people whose deviant activities occur online do not have the antisocial traits, such as lack of empathy, that characterize criminals.[10]

We are living in a really open society now, constrained by very little. Fabricators and prevaricators, entrepreneurs and con men, creators and destroyers, the artistic and the artless, the grandiose, the broken, and the genuine articles—all abide side by side offering opportunity and promoting opportunism. A lot of what we used to keep hidden or private is now exposed to the light of day for all to see. It's always high noon during summer on the Web—even if we log on in the dark. The Web doesn't care what we do, how we do it, why we do it, or with whom. Although we project all sorts of things onto it, the Web is completely indifferent to the words and images posted, equally welcoming of wonderful new ideas and child pornography, great works of art and junk, significant inventions, terrorist hubs, racist manifestos, inspiring essays, useful information, manipulative lies, instructions for self-improvement and for making toxic chemical agents. It permits any and all transgressions. It almost seems to be playing a game with us as we play games with it, allowing us to render and control the most intimate expression of self in relationship to another. YouPorn, for example, an amateur video site, is the most popular pornography site on the Web. But, interestingly, it's not exactly transgressive either, because it isn't really hidden or "dirty" anymore.

The indifference and the immediacy of virtual life is both liberating and undermining. The restraints and boundaries that were characteristic of dreams of totality seem to no longer apply. Everything seems possible and is accessible. The original and the forgery are equally appealing and hard to discern. As images and emotion enter virtual reportage, art and fact blend into a hybrid form that expresses the essence and uncertainty of postmodern life, as opposed to a canonical corpus into which we used to try and fit our experience. What we buy into (whether belief or brand name) is completely up for grabs, as is the option, "hey, I just don't buy that." The human psyche has been released further than ever from certainty, the unthinkable has become thinkable, along with the option not to think or feel at all—and we act, or don't, accordingly.

In *Trickster Makes This World*, Lewis Hyde made the compelling case that culture is created in large part by transgressive acts of all sorts. There's nothing wrong with embarrassing behavior, forbidden alliances, shameless appropriations, and just plain weirdness—in fact, without those and the disruptions that they initiate, vibrant culture would be finished. We saw transgression operate in an obviously progressive form in academia, for example, where after decades of struggle and experimentation—some successful, some not—the boundaries between traditional disciplines opened up, and much of the creative work in the academy and research now takes place at the interstices between disciplines. Even college curricula are moving in the direction of interdisciplinary education, with concentrations like cultural studies, brain, mind, and information, or interdisciplinary arts replacing single-discipline departments.[11] This is well and good, in large part because the transgressions were recognizable as such, and people struggled openly over them in a way that now appears almost picturesque.

Our current quandary lies in the fact that what usually precedes a transgressive act is the presence or the constitution of a center, an imaginal (or legal) structure that holds the prevailing values intact and is marked off by clear boundaries, even taboos. Unless this circle or boundary exists, it's hard to demarcate the territory of what's meaningful from what's meaninglessness. As a classic jazz riff puts it, "Tryin' to make it real—compared to what?" To transgress creatively you need to feel the press of limits. To move the boundary marker you need to know where it was. We are faced with a special quandary in contemporary life because the Web allows us to move across boundaries and transgress margins by erasing and blending them so easily. Without centers and boundaries, transgression becomes a very confusing affair. The popular pastime of Facebook stalking, for example—lurking obsessively on someone's Facebook profile, usually someone never spoken to—is, like YouPorn, a transgression that doesn't really transgress. It's not taboo; it's just a little creepy.

This kind of pseudo transgression falls right in line with the surveillance of Internet activity by advertisers and governments, which is also a transgression that doesn't really transgress by bringing anything new into culture. Instead, at best it invades privacy and at worst it consolidates control and access, doing both in the characteristic open disguise to which we have become habituated. Our surfing and buying profiles are being monitored all the time—we just choose to hide this fact from ourselves, even when the obvious pops up. If you sign up with an app that keeps track of your whereabouts, you become part of a magic circle by satellite. You can always be found in the loop, whether there is anybody who actually cares looking for you. It's a comforting and clever (if diabolical) way for us to keep ourselves in line. We won't need those rings of steel—the surveillance systems installed around cities in order to promote security—once this new state of mind becomes firmly implanted and implemented. It seems like we are free to connect and consume and transgress, but we are also just being stalked, by ourselves.

Another issue is that the immediacy of virtual life can lead us to feel that there's not enough space and time for us, and others, to make an ethical distinction between our thoughts and feelings and our actions. We don't allow time for longing and desire to develop or for anger and distress to ferment into something else. It's often during that delay between feeling and action that the journey toward the endgame reveals as much as or more than the goal. We miss out on that. The amusing side of all this is the ill-considered e-mail hastily or mistakenly sent or the cyber romance that bites the dust of a dull reality. The distressing side is the raw vitriol that can make its way into our minds and hearts every day we are connected to the Web. If everything is immediate and allowed, it's hard to be truly transgressive or, put the other way around, everything can be locked down as fantasy is mistaken for action. In this sense, even virtuality has its monolithic and hidden ideology that allows us—as usual—to act badly as individuals while subscribing to the new program.

We also sense something bogus and sad—even shameful—about the widening gyres without centers in which we live, where relevance replaces truth, where what feels right is right, and in the shifting multiplication of fractured identities that we must conform to and be deformed by. That disappointment often induces reactionary programs, cynicism, even a vehement valorization of virtuality. But if we look for signs of God in virtuality, we'll probably find that there's nothing there. Yet we also sense that the sacrifice and erasure of identity and affiliations, with all their past illusory safety and attendant destructiveness, can turn what are gaps between us, between our ideas, and between cultures into space for an approaching unknown. As in making a mosaic, the holes and spaces between things can be as important as the things themselves. Our imagination makes a beeline for the edges where things don't line up, and the more that transgressing those edges is tolerated, the more open our society and our psyches will be. The more the lines between in and out, sacred and profane, shameful and accepted can be redrawn, the more democratic things are. In an open society, social and psychological commerce proceeds freely across boundaries—boundaries that are more like herms, or road markers, than prohibitions, markers of the moments when we made a choice about something.[12]

Holding on to making a choice about things is critical, because both the quick and the dead come into being right at the edges between order and disorder. The erasures and the holes in our dreams of totality that get exposed by the *pharmakon* of virtuality are where creative transgression flourishes and where psychopathic responses find an open door. The "console cowboys" of iconic cyberpunk films like *Blade Runner* and the *Matrix*, who wrestle with their humanity and run amok in techno mania, are materializing. As we struggle with the ethics of transgression and with keeping the fabric of totality loose and open, what then do we do when there's nothing at the center?

Notes

[1] In 1958 Jung published one of his last essays, "Flying Saucers: A Modern Myth of Things Seen in the Sky," in which he makes the case that UFOs are the twentieth century's projections of unity and wholeness, not unlike other symbols of totality such as the Holy Ghost or the eye of

God. As with all archetypal symbols, Jung is careful to say that just because these are psychic in nature doesn't mean that they don't have an objective dimension; he makes a tentative case that the synchronicity attending the appearance of UFOs speaks to particular issues in the contemporary psyche and collective experience. C. G. Jung, "Flying Saucers: A Modern Myth of Things Seen in the Skies" (1958), in *Civilization in Transition*, vol. 10, *The Collected Works of C. G. Jung* (Princeton, NJ: Princeton University Press, 1964).

[2] Chris Frith, *Making Up the Mind: How the Brain Creates Our Mental World* (Oxford, England: Blackwell Publishing, 2007).

[3] See http://secondlife.com/whatis.

[4] Jacques Derrida, *Dissemination*, trans. Barbara Johnson (Chicago: University of Chicago Press, 1983), p. 140.

[5] Robert Lifton, *The Protean Self: Human Resilience in an Age of Fragmentation* (New York: Basic Books, 1993); Sherry Turkle, *Alone Together: Why We Expect More from Technology and Less from Each Other* (New York: Basic Books, 2011), p. 176.

[6] Turkle, *Alone Together*, p. 182.

[7] Samples selected from www.postsecret.com, August 23, 2011, read: "I like to leave Serenity coins in change slots for the next person"; "My wife is mentally ill, I want to have an affair with a woman whose husband is mentally ill so we can feel better"; "I am my ex-husband's mistress"; and "Laser hair removal on my BUTT! No regrets!!"

[8] Malcolm Bull, *Seeing Things Hidden: Apocalypse, Vision, and Totality* (New York: Verso, 1999), p. 170.

[9] The term *singularity* was first used in this context by futurist Ray Kurzweil in *The Singularity Is Near* (New York: Penguin Books, 2005).

[10] Rachel Aviv, "The Science of Sex Abuse," in the *New Yorker* magazine, January 14, 2013, discusses the research of Michael Seto at the University of Toronto, whose research critiques the infamous Butner study which influenced the incarceration of online sex offenders.

[11] See, for example, the curriculum of Hampshire College in Amherst, Massachusetts, at www.hampshire.edu/academics.

[12] Lewis Hyde discusses the herm as a boundary marker and a signpost, belonging to the culture-making and trickster aspects of the Greek god Hermes in *Trickster Makes This World: How Disruptive Imagination Creates Culture* (New York: Canongate, 1998).

CHAPTER SEVEN

THE R$_x$

In 1946 Aldous Huxley wrote a foreword to the second edition of *Brave New World* in which he said that although he didn't believe in rewriting works of art, there was one thing he did want to set straight. At the end of the story, Huxley's doomed hero, John Savage, was faced with two alternatives: an insane life in a dystopian techno-crazy utopia or the life of a dispirited primitive in an Indian village. It was a choice between insanity and lunacy, a choice that Huxley at the time found "amusing, and quite possibly true."[1] He has the Savage commit suicide instead. Years later, the middle-aged Huxley felt differently:

> Today, I feel no wish to demonstrate that sanity is impossible. On the contrary, though I remain no less sadly certain than in the past that sanity is a rather rare phenomenon, I am convinced that it can be achieved and would like to see more of it.... If I were to rewrite the book I would offer the Savage a third alternative.[2]

It can often feel that we are also operating within delusions, dreaming benighted dreams of totality in response to an overwhelmingly fragmented world or just giving up. Long ago Max Weber predicted something like "sensualists without heart" and "specialists without spirit." Today we encounter not only those, but everyman's misinformation delivered with plenty of spirit, while at the same time many still resonate with Heidegger's lamentation, delivered at the end of his life, that "only a god can save us." Nothing has turned up though, and it also seems too much of a truism to say that we are hurtling toward an abyss—that the new dawn to come is more like the Judgment Day of yore. We also have another choice. We can fulfill the promise of postmodernism and come to terms with imagination and the dreams of totality we spin.

Imagination really is more important than knowledge. It's the game we play and the ground we play it in. Our imagination is primed to integrate experience into wholes, particularly in response to stress or fragmentation, and the symbols of totality we create are capable of moving feelings and emotions in a way that rational thought is not. As we have seen, these symbols are not irrational but simply nonrational—an aspect of the mythopoetic mind, tied to the body and emotions. This tie to our bodies and emotions accounts for their deeply adaptive function, as well as for their propensity for fixation and compulsive behavior. They both open and close down the imagination, and they also come apart when they no longer contain our experience. The genius that dreams our dreams of totality is a capacity of mind and heart that we all share, a great medicine that's both panacea and poison, a capacity intimately responsive to the ecosystems of time and place.

Nowadays we dream about globalization and cyberspace. Once upon a time, we dreamed other dreams that expressed the depth and reality of our world and ourselves. Those dreams were up to date and expressed the spirit of their time, which is why they can't be re-created from whole cloth—their time has passed and they lack the objectivity of living experience. Many of them have little to add to the pressing questions of our time. Try as we might to compensate with authoritarian fundamentalisms and fanaticism or with a casual relationship to truth, the regressive nature of these nostalgic projects is exposed by their cognitive and emotional primitivity. There is no possibility of returning to "traditional values," to societies embedded in nature or organized around local customs, to theocracies, or to totalitarian systems; soon even unbridled free markets will no longer be an option. While we still imagine totality in images and events like globalization and the virtual world, we are also aware that our projections of wholeness and the centering function of social systems and self don't hold together very well anymore. We no longer integrate conflicting tendencies in contemporary life so much as we live them out. There's the satisfying reverberation of reality in this, and there are also feelings of arbitrariness and randomness, an open-ended anxiety, and fantasies of disintegration.

In some sense, we are now in trouble if things don't hold together but also if they do. In America, for example, *E pluribus unum* seems to be straining at the seams, threatening to break apart into dysfunctional pieces or close down under the umbrella of homeland security. All over the world, people are trying to refashion individual and cultural identities while at the same time moving toward assuming the responsibilities of cosmopolitan citizenship. Understanding the *pharmakon* of totality is crucial to going forward as we try to become psychologically capable of something like democracy and as we try to figure out how to be responsible to each other on a global scale. It won't help to simply default to a literal interpretation of our contemporary dreams of globalization or virtuality, just doing business as usual. Recognizing our shared predilection to dream of totality can engender empathy through the sharing of essentials it provides, and empathy is more important than simple identification with others, even more important than sympathy, because identification turns to anger or resentment when the other is revealed as different, and sympathy quickly becomes paternalistic.

At some level we know this. The dissociation and fragmentation we feel is not the problem. It's a sign of change, of the wheel turning. The real dangers would be a breakdown in our ability to dream of totality and, more important in the contemporary world, a failure to see through those dreams—the disaster would be a breakdown of imagination. Just as our planet is much wilder and mysterious than we think—after all, we've discovered only one quarter of the species on Earth—and much harder to destroy than we fear or imagine, we are also very resourceful. Taking a deep breath and stepping forward, we can appreciate both dreaming of totality and deconstructing those dreams as part of a larger opus—the project described most succinctly and poetically by Goethe in *Faust*: "Formation, transformation, eternal mind's eternal re-creation." In postmodern lingo, we could say that the psyche subjects itself to a continuous critique, and we can see the nodal points of this critique in our individual and collective dreams of totality and, most especially, in their demise.

The fact that our contemporary images of totality lack centers is not the problem either. The way that we fashion images of wholeness reflects our contemporary experience, binding and housing our feelings and perceptions in images that both reflect those feelings and compensate for them. That is the beauty of a dream of totality—it holds ambivalence together. While there may be nothing at the center of contemporary life, this is precisely what encourages us to see through our dreams of totality and allows the role of imagination to be more explicit. The increasing transparency still allows our need for integration to contain and renew individual and communal life, but in a different way. As their imaginary origin shines through, it is easier to dismantle our identification with particular dreams and to recognize that where we are when there's nothing at the center is in the imagination's endless series of calls, echoes, and responses. Even though complexity has been with us forever, we no longer have the option of waiting hopefully for the gods to speak with one voice again. Imagination has delivered its multiple messages and there is no going back, no filtering those out, no center beyond or behind that.

What is at stake though is staying ethical amid the flow and flux of images and identities. What's new is that being ethical is no longer dependent on a sense of meaning derived from a dream of totality. A sensibility about meaning doesn't have to come from a worldview, a belief system, or any dream of totality—be it family, culture, religion, or even our dependence on the natural world. Once upon a time these sufficed and were containing. Part of what we've seen is that desperate attempts at resuscitation or relocation are futile, beside the point, even downright dangerous. We are in the process of outgrowing such identifications. Equally problematic though is reacting to this by identifying with nihilism or with "whatever" thinking. This is hard, because it can often seem as if the portal into the creative imagination is now just a revolving door—and even that is closing fast, thanks to the glut of images surrounding us. It is as if what's most important stays hidden, obscured in plain sight. This is also part of our collective crisis of adolescence, but the more we identify with the fragmentation and the loss, the malignant transgressions and the simulations, the more ripe we become for takeover by totalitarianism of whatever stripe—corporate capitalism disguised as democracy or globalization or even the fantasy of a friendly green planet.

The fact that we often feel a loss of meaning is not the problem either, nor does the fact that we feel that way signify that we are ill. This is also a growing pain, which doesn't have to be replaced with a frantic search for meaning nor with giving up. It is surely strange indeed that we can go shopping in the "meaning mall," where a plurality of meanings are on display, meanings that we can buy into—

or not—including a choice about buying the whole meaning scenario, but this situation—confusing, liberating, and deceptive as it may be—is also part of where we are when there's no one thing at the center. Part of what we've seen is that as dreams of totality fall away, our imagination's provision to dream is revealed and can come fully into its own. In the same way, we can come to know that meaning is always just there, a part of us as we are a part of it.

Taking the Medicine

There is an old divination ritual called the poison oracle (*benge*), which the Azande people of sub-Saharan Africa use to ferret out the presence of witchcraft in their affairs.[3] The supplicant asks a carefully considered and phrased question. Poison is given to a young chicken. The *benge* answers through the action of the poison—if the chicken lives there is nothing to fear, if the chicken dies the supplicant's distress is warranted. Sometimes the poison is given to another chicken to check the accuracy of the first oracle. Some chickens live, some chickens die. This may go on for a while, until the question is answered to everyone's satisfaction. As in all truly difficult affairs, only the presence of doubt and ambiguity certify the authenticity of the answers we receive to our questions.

We're all just chickens when it comes to the great medicine of our imagination's dreams of totality. A lot depends on how we react. Staying ethical means staying grounded in empathy and imagination; that is the source of our contemporary discipline and stability. But to get to that ground we have to exercise our imaginal projections for all we're worth, handle all sides of the *pharmakon* of totality with care, and hold them together. There are things we can do with respect to this and things we can try to work against. Here then, by way of summary, are some recommendations for how to take the medicine of totality when there's nothing at the center.

Look both ways at our contemporary dreams of totality: at the ways we use them to defend and shut down or to include and open up. Fostering and maintaining the creative function of dreams of totality and minimizing their deadening effects depends on aligning ourselves with a symbolic perspective that looks at both progressive and defensive potentials. There is almost always a poison in the panacea, and a panacea in the poison, and the images of totality that we cook up usually hold the ambivalence of the *pharmakon* together. It's when we put those images into action that we split them apart, leaving out one side or the other. And looking both ways also means resisting the pull toward passive or righteous identification with either utopian faith or dystopian demise.

Beware fantasies and forms of the singularity, the mythical event horizon of the future—often set quite soon at 2030—beyond which overwhelming technological changes like virtuality and artificial intelligence will create an intelligence explosion, at which point we will all be wired into a single superhuman intelligence, effectively making it impossible for mere humans to predict or understand much of anything. Along with this, don't look for transcendental signifiers anywhere. The postmodernists were right about this one. It hasn't led us anywhere but astray. Don't try to return to fundamentals and essentials as a defense against anxiety, and don't get lost in malignant nostalgia.

Treat nostalgia as a private detour into reflective reverie, not a destination.[4] How to tell the difference? Malignant nostalgia becomes focused on abstract truths and traditions; it tries to rebuild the past, to return to origins, to close up the holes and drifts in memory. This kind of nostalgia can be conspiratorial, paranoid about forces that undermine the past, delusional, even apocalyptic. Getting lost in reflective reverie, however, one sees things much less clearly. Reverie takes us toward longing and grief, not away from them. It keeps the anxiety and ache of displacement and loss alive; it values and plays with the shards and fragments of memory. Unlike the flatland of malignant nostalgia, nostalgic reverie accesses the virtuality of imagination. So by all means make a detour. And even though we can no longer identify with transcendental signifiers, fundamentals, or the good old days, don't get trapped into closing the gap that separates you from your longing and desire by buying into or immediately acquiring what is available and promoted for the enhancement of well-being. Stay hungry.

Live on the edge. We know that in order for new dreams of totality to emerge, the old ones have to be broken, and that this happens at the point of weak links, where disenfranchised elements create tension. Stay near this edge between order and disorder. Have empathy for what's dying and being born there, and separate creativity from psychopathy. Look for the difference between the dead letter and the living word with respect to symbols. Feel the pulse for the quick and the dead with respect to actions. Sometimes the path from trash to art can be a very direct road. Read the signs. This requires vigilance and moment-to-moment reflection.

Tolerate transgression. Get your hands dirty and keep them there—but not necessarily in the farmland of redemptive ecological fantasies. Transgression can make us lose moral compass, but even worse, faux transgressions are ruses, like the bread and circuses instituted before the fall of the Roman Empire to keep the populace sated and in line. But real transgression can also force us to make moral decisions for ourselves—it can act like a refiner's fire for our ethical sensibility. While we are invited now to tolerate everything we can imagine, it is still appropriate to think and talk about right and wrong. Turn up, not down, the anxiety and uncertainty about right action. Transgress, make choices, and care.

Make the appropriate sacrifices. Don't designate scapegoats or set up taboos. Pay attention to what no longer works, help the dying, grieve and bury what's dead with dignity. Sacrificing our identifications to particular dreams, whether personal, religious, antireligious, economic, or political, and participating with conscience in the continuous creation, dissolution, and reformation of our dreams of totality is key to both individual and collective vitality. Sacrifice guards against hopelessness and reification by lifting out the symbolic dimension in what has been made overly concrete and the concrete dimension in what has been deemed merely symbolic. This fundamental cycle of creation and destruction has a reflection in our body's basic mechanisms for survival and growth—it's an echo of the ins and outs of breathing, of metabolism. As dreams of totality are dissolved into this larger solvent, the image making behind the images comes into higher relief.

So don't identify with either the in or the out, with either a creator or a destroyer god, with either the valorization of new dreams or the sometimes gleeful sadism of deconstruction. It's often said, for example, that our newly acquired capacity to blow everything up with nuclear technology or destroy the climate with carbon emissions is what has led to the widespread fears about extinction and ecological disasters that abound nowadays. But those apocalyptic fantasies have always been around, as has genocide—all still thriving. And although it's true that we can do very serious damage, our fantasies about bringing everything to an end also reflect our ongoing identification with destroyer gods—as does the corrective (and sometimes equally controlling) creator god fantasy of fashioning an eco-pure planet. It's not that easy to destroy the world, nor is it necessary to overcompensate by imagining that we could rid it completely of our trash and excrement.

We may no longer wish to say, as did the Delphic oracle, "called or not called, the god will be present." I have found it increasingly difficult—although still appealing and seductive—to assume that the myriad gods who dreamed our dreams of totality are somehow still here, just materialized outside in the concrete world—in our consumer culture and goods, cloaked yet fully present in our stuff and in our personal and cultural ailments—living in these places now, rather than in their temples or within the sanctum of the self. On a lighter note, I often wondered though, what self-respecting god would consent to be consigned to a shopping mall or a DSM-5 diagnosis? It did not help me contend with contemporary psychological life to simply assign, for example, the spirit of Hermes to preside over the commerce of globalization, cyberspace, and all the trickery of postmodern life—although traces of that archetypal image and pattern remain.

It seems closer to our experience to replace making such pilgrimages with peregrinations. To simply travel and wander around—in ourselves, in our symbols, on the planet, and in the virtual world. With the loss of traditional symbolic centers comes a seeming loss of direct access to meaning—at least to the sort of meaning we are used to. But we can easily access the space between our narratives, between cultures and their texts, between each other, and around the fragments of experience that have managed to elude media manufacture. The interstices, the spaces between, are where psyche is still alive and thriving. Wandering around these places, we still tell stories about ourselves and our dreams of totality. It's just easier to see through them, and that's a very good thing. As the gyres get wider and wider, and as we go with them, keep looking for the shards and sparks of life. Look underneath the destruction of symbolic forms for the fragments left over after dreams of totality have been destroyed, merely restored, or cleverly manufactured. Look for them emerging at the edges of your imagination. In all the confusion, in all the new places, slipping through the loose connections, there's another story already being told.

Notes

[1] Aldous Huxley, *Brave New World* (New York: Harper and Brothers, 1946), p. viii.

[2] *Ibid.*, p. ix.

[3] For an extensive discussion, see Evans-Pritchard's classic *Witchcraft, Oracles, and Magic among the Azande* (Oxford, England: Clarendon Press, 1976).

[4] For a discussion of the difference between nostalgia that restores the past and nostalgia that stimulates the imagination, see Svetlana Boym, *The Future of Nostalgia* (New York: Basic Books, 2001).

Bibliography

Abraham, Lyndy. *A Dictionary of Alchemical Imagery*. Cambridge: Cambridge University Press, 2001.

Aeschylus. *Complete Greek Tragedies,* vol. 1, *Oresteia: Agamemmnon, The Libation Bearers, The Eumenides*. Translated by Richard Lattimore. Chicago: University of Chicago Press, 1953–1956.

Arendt, Hannah. *The Origins of Totalitarianism*. New York: Harcourt Books, 1966.

Armstrong, Karen. *The Great Transformation*. New York: Random House, 2006.

Aviv, Rachel. "The Science of Sex Abuse." *New Yorker*, January 14, 2013.

Barrett, William. *Irrational Man*. New York: Random House, 1990.

Bascom, William. *Ifa Divination: Communication between Gods and Men in West Africa,* 2nd edition. Indianapolis: Indiana University Press, 1991.

Blackmore, Susan. *The Meme Machine*. New York: Oxford University Press, 1999.

Booker, Christopher. *The Seven Basic Plots: Why We Tell Stories*. London: Continuum, 2004.

Boym, Svetlana. *The Future of Nostalgia*. New York: Basic Books, 2001.

Bull, Malcolm. *Seeing Things Hidden: Apocalypse, Vision, and Totality*. New York: Verso, 1999.

Bynum, Bruce. *The African Unconscious: Roots of Ancient Mysticism and Modern Psychology*. New York: Teachers College Press, 1999.
Cambray, Joseph. *Synchronicity: Nature and Psyche in an Interconnected Universe*. College Station, TX: Texas A&M University Press, 2009.
Childs, Peter. *Modernism*. London: Routledge, 2008.
Corbin, Henry. *Creative Imagination in the Sufism of Ibn'Arabi*. London: Routledge, 2007.
Coupland, Douglas. *Generation X: Tales for an Accelerated Culture*. New York: St. Martin's Griffon, 1991.
Dawkins, Richard. *The God Delusion*. New York: Houghton Mifflin, 2006.
Dennett, Daniel. *Consciousness Explained*. Boston: Little, Brown, 1991.
Derrida, Jacques. *Dissemination*. Translated by Barbara Johnson. Chicago: University of Chicago Press, 1983.
Dickinson, Emily. *The Collected Poems of Emily Dickinson*. New York: Barnes & Noble Classics, 2003.
Einstein, Albert. *Cosmic Religion: With Other Opinions and Aphorisms*. New York: Covici-Friede, 1931.
Ekman, Paul. *Emotions Revealed: Recognizing Faces and Feelings to Improve Communication and Emotional Life*. New York: Holt Paperbacks, 2007.
Eliade, Mircea. *The Myth of the Eternal Return*. Princeton, NJ: Princeton University Press, 1954, 2005.
Ellenberger, Henry. *The Discovery of the Unconscious: The History and Evolution of Dynamic Psychiatry*. New York: Basic Books, 1970.
Emerson, Ralph Waldo. *The Complete Works of Ralph Waldo Emerson*. New York: Houghton Mifflin, 2004.
Erikson, Erik. *Identity and the Life Cycle*. New York: W. W. Norton, 1994.
Evans-Pritchard, E. E., and Eva Gilles. *Witchcraft, Oracles, and Magic among the Azande*. Oxford, England: Clarendon Press, 1976.
Fauconnier, Gilles, and Mark Turner. *The Way We Think: Conceptual Blending and the Mind's Hidden Complexities*. New York: Basic Books, 2002.
Flournoy, Theodore. *From India to the Planet Mars: A Case of Multiple Personality and Imaginary Languages*. Princeton, NJ: Princeton University Press, 1900, 1994.

Freud, Sigmund. *The Future of an Illusion*. Revised and edited by James Strachey. Garden City, NY: Doubleday Anchor Books, 1927, 1964.
Freud, Sigmund, and C. G. Jung. *The Freud/Jung Letters*. Edited by William McGuire. Princeton, NJ: Princeton University Press, 1974.
Friedman, Thomas. *The Lexus and the Olive Tree*. New York: Random House Anchor Books, 2000.
Frith, Chris. *Making Up the Mind: How the Brain Creates Our Mental World*. Oxford, England: Blackwell Publishing, 2007.
Gell-Mann, Murray. *The Quark and the Jaguar: Adventures in the Simple and the Complex*. San Francisco: W. H. Freeman, 1994.
Giegerich, Wolfgang. *The Soul's Logical Life*. Frankfurt: Peter Land, 2001.
———. "The End of Meaning and the Birth of Man." *Journal of Jungian Theory and Practice*, 6(1):1–66.
———. "Closure and Setting Free, or The Bottled Spirit of Alchemy and Psychology." *Spring: A Journal of Archetype and Culture* 74 (2006): 31–62.
———. *Technology and the Soul: From the Nuclear Bomb to the World Wide Web*. New Orleans: Spring Journal Books, 2007.
———. *Soul Violence*, vol. 3, *Collected English Papers*. New Orleans: Spring Journal Books, 2008.
Griffiths, R., W. Richards, M. Johnson, U. McCann, and R. Jesse. "Mystical-type experiences occasioned by psilocybin mediate the attribution of personal meaning and spiritual significance 14 months later." *Journal of Psychopharmacology*, (2008): 1–12.
Grosskurth, Phyllis. *The Secret Ring: Freud's Inner Circle and the Politics of Psychoanalysis*. New York: Addison-Wesley Publishing, 1991.
Hamilton, Edith, Huntington Cairns, and Lane Cooper, eds., *The Collected Dialogues of Plato: Including the Letters*. Princeton, NJ: Princeton University Press, 2005.
Hillman, James. *Healing Fiction*. Woodstock, CT: Spring Publications, 1998.
———. *Re-Visioning Psychology*. New York: Harper Paperbacks, 1977.
Hitchens, Christopher. *God Is Not Great: How Religion Poisons Everything*. New York: Twelve, Hachette Book Group, 2007.

Huffington, Arianna. "Sarah Palin, 'Mama Grizzlies,' Carl Jung, and the Power of Archetypes." August 1, 2010, www.huffingtonpost.com.

Huxley, Aldous. *Brave New World*. New York: Harper and Brothers, 1946.

Hyde, Lewis. *Trickster Makes This World: How Disruptive Imagination Creates Culture*. New York: Canongate, 1998.

Hyde, Michael. *Perfection: Coming to Terms with Being Human*. Waco, TX: Baylor University Press, 2010.

Jacoby, Mario. *Longing for Paradise: Psychological Perspectives on an Archetype*. Toronto: Inner City Books, 1985, 2006.

James, William. *The Principles of Psychology Vol. 1*. New York: Cosimo Classics, 2007.

Jaynes, Julian. *The Origin of Consciousness in the Breakdown of the Bicameral Mind*. New York: Houghton Mifflin, 1976, 1990.

Johnson, Mark. *The Body in the Mind*. Chicago: University of Chicago Press, 1987.

Jung, C. G. "Commentary of 'The Secret of the Golden Flower'" (1957). In *Alchemical Studies*, vol. 13, *The Collected Works of C. G. Jung*. Princeton, NJ: Princeton University Press, 1967.

———. "Flying Saucers: A Modern Myth of Things Seen in the Skies" (1958). In *Civilization in Transition*, vol. 10, *The Collected Works of C. G. Jung*. Princeton, NJ: Princeton University Press, 1964.

———. *Memories, Dreams, Reflections*. New York: Vintage, 1963.

———. *Modern Man in Search of a Soul*. Orlando, FL: Harcourt, 1933, 1955.

———. *Mysterium Coniunctionis*, vol. 14, *The Collected Works of C. G. Jung*. Princeton, NJ: Princeton University Press, 1955.

———. *Psychological Types*, vol. 6, *The Collected Works of C. G. Jung*. Princeton, NJ: Princeton University Press, 1971.

———. *Psychology and Alchemy*, vol. 12, *The Collected Works of C. G. Jung*. Princeton, NJ: Princeton University Press, 1953, 1968.

———. "Psychology and Religion" (1938). In *Psychology and Religion*, vol. 11, *The Collected Works of C. G. Jung*. Princeton, NJ: Princeton University Press, 1958, 1969.

———. "The Psychology of the Transference" (1946). In *The Practice of Psychotherapy*, vol. 16, *The Collected Works of C. G. Jung*. Princeton, NJ: Princeton University Press, 1954.

———. *The Red Book: Liber Novus*. Edited and introduction by Sonu Shamdasani. New York: W. W. Norton, 2009.

Jung, C. G., and Wolfgang Pauli. *Atom and Archetype: The Pauli-Jung Letters 1932–1958*. Edited by C. A. Meier. Princeton, NJ: Princeton University Press, 2001.

Kawai, Toshio. "Postmodern Consciousness in Psychotherapy." *Journal of Analytical Psychology* 51 (no. 3, 2006): 437–450.

Kearney, Richard. *The Wake of Imagination*. London: Routledge, 1988.

Kelly, Kevin. *Out of Control: The Rise of Neo-Biological Civilization*. New York: Perseus Books, 1994.

Kristeva, Julia. *This Incredible Need to Believe*. New York: Columbia University Press, 2009.

Kurzweil, Ray. *The Singularity Is Near*. New York: Penguin Books, 2005.

LaGamma, Alisa. *Art and Oracle: African Art and Rituals of Divination*. New York: Harry Abrams, 2000.

Lepore, Jill. "Fixed: The Rise of Marriage Therapy and Other Dreams of Human Betterment," *New Yorker*, March 29, 2010.

Lifton, Robert J. *The Protean Self: Human Resilience in an Age of Fragmentation*. New York: Basic Books, 1993.

Martin, Stephen, and Aryeh Maidenbaum, eds., *Lingering Shadows: Jungians, Freudians, and Anti-Semitism*. Boston: Shambhala, 1991.

Mayer, Arno. *The Furies: Violence and Terror in the French and Russian Revolutions*. Princeton, NJ: Princeton University Press, 2000.

Meier, C. A. *Healing Dream and Ritual: Ancient Incubation and Modern Psychotherapy*. Einsiedeln, Switzerland: Daimon Verlag, 2003.

Mumford, Lewis. *The City in History*. New York: Harcourt, Brace and World, 1961.

Nietzsche, Friedrich. *The Birth of Tragedy*. New York: Dover Publications, 1927, 1995.

Nussbaum, Martha. *The Fragility of Goodness*. Cambridge, England: Cambridge University Press, 1986.

Onians, Richard. *The Origins of European Thought*. New York: Cambridge University Press, 1991.

Radin, Paul. *The Road of Life and Death: A Ritual Drama of the American Indians*. Princeton, NJ: Princeton University Press, 1991.

Ramachandran, Vilayanur S. *A Brief Tour of Human Consciousness*. New York: Pi Press, 2004.

Read, Piers Paul. *The Templars*. Cambridge, MA: Da Capo Press, 1999.

Rilke, Rainer Maria. *Rilke on Love and Other Difficulties: Translations and Consideration*. Translated and commentary by John Mood. New York: W. W. Norton, 2004.

Rizzolatti, Giacomo, and Corrado Sinigaglia. *Mirrors in the Brain: How Our Minds Share Actions, Emotions, and Experience*. Oxford, England: Oxford University Press, 2008.

Ronnberg, Ami, and Kathleen Martin, eds. *The Book of Symbols: Reflections on Archetypal Images*. New York: Taschen, 2010.

Rundle-Clark, Robert T. *Myth and Symbol in Ancient Egypt*. London: Thames and Hudson, 1959, 1978.

Sachs, Jeffrey. *The Price of Civilization: Reawakening American Virtue and Prosperity*. New York: Random House, 2011.

Saggs, Henry W. F. *The Greatness That Was Babylon*. London: Sidgwick and Jackson, 1991.

Salman, Sherry. "Blood Payments." In *Terror, Violence, and the Impulse to Destroy: Perspectives from Analytical Psychology*. Zurich, Switzerland: Daimon-Verlag, 2003.

———. "Breakdowns and Breakthroughs: Kinship and Psychoanalytic Theory." *Quadrant* 38 (no. 1, 2008): 32–41.

———. "The Creative Psyche: Jung's Major Contributions," in *The Cambridge Companion to Jung*, 2nd ed. Edited by Polly Young-Eisendrath and Terence Dawson. New York: Cambridge University Press, 2008.

———. "Dissociation and the Self in the Magical pre-Oedipal Field." *Journal of Analytical Psychology* 44 (no. 1, 1999): 69–85.

———. "Peregrinations of Active Imagination: The Elusive Quintessence in Postmodern Motion." In *Jungian Psychoanalysis*, 3rd edition, Murray Stein, ed. Chicago: Open Court Books, 2010.

———. "True Imagination." *Spring: A Journal of Archetype and Culture* 47 (2006): 175–187.

Samuels, Andrew. *The Political Psyche*. London: Routledge, 1993.

Serrano, Miguel. *C. G. Jung and Herman Hesse: A Record of Two Friendships.* New York: Schocken Books, 1966.

Shamdasani, Sonu. Introduction to Theodore Flournoy, *From India to the Planet Mars: A Case of Multiple Personality and Imaginary Languages.* Princeton, NJ: Princeton University Press, 1994.

Shields, David. *Reality Hunger.* New York: Alfred A. Knopf, 2010.

Steger, Manfred. *Globalization: A Very Short Introduction.* Oxford, England: Oxford University Press, 2009.

Stern, Daniel. *The Interpersonal World of the Infant.* New York: Basic Books, 1985.

Stevens, Anthony. *Private Myths: Dreams and Dreaming.* Cambridge, MA: Harvard University Press, 1997.

Turkle, Sherry. *Alone Together: Why We Expect More from Technology and Less from Each Other.* New York: Basic Books, 2011.

Turner, Victor. *The Ritual Process: Structure and Anti-Structure.* New Brunswick, NJ: Aldine Transaction, 1969, 2009.

Ulanov, Ann. "Losing, Finding, Being Found: At the Edge between Despair and Hope." *Quadrant* 37 (2007): 2.

Wilhelm, Richard, and C. F. Baynes. *The I Ching; Or, Book of Changes.* Princeton, NJ: Princeton University Press, 1967.

Wilson, Edward O., ed. *From So Simple a Beginning: The Four Great Books of Charles Darwin.* New York: W. W. Norton, 2005.

Wood, James. "God in the Quad." *The New Yorker,* August 31, 2009.

Yates, Frances. *The Art of Memory.* Chicago: University of Chicago Press, 1966.

Zweig, Connie. *The Holy Longing: Spiritual Yearning and Its Shadow Side.* Bloomington, IN: iUniverse, 2008.

Figure Credits

The author would like to thank the following for granting permission to reproduce images in this book; any images for which no permission or copyright information is provided are in the public domain. All efforts have been made to contact all copyright holders, but the author and Spring Journal Books would be pleased to correct any errors or omissions in subsequent editions.

page 31. Figure 1. Folio #129 from C. G. Jung, *The Red Book: Liber Novus.* Copyright © 2009 by the Foundation of the Works of C. G. Jung. Used by permission of W. W. Norton & Company, Inc.

page 35. Figure 2. The Callanish Stones. © Kenro Izu Photography 85 ST 2.

page 35. Figure 3. Mummy Cave. © Kenro Izu Photography 93 SW 3.

page 36. Figure 4. Advertisement for Rotating Magic Circle. © 2010 Julianus Nightfire, Tiphareth Designs, USA.

page 39. Figure 5. *Saturn Devouring His Son.* Wikimedia Commons.

page 40. Figure 6. Borobudur. © Kenro Izu Photography 96 INS 15.

page 41. Figure 7. *The Dream.* Digital image © The Museum of Modern Art / Licensed by SCALA/Art Resource, NY.

page 43. Figure 8. *Figures for a Trance Diviner: Couple.* © Metropolitan Museum of Art, New York, The Michael C. Rockefeller Memorial Collection, Gift of Nelson Rockefeller, 1969.

page 45. Figure 9. *The Creation of the World and the Expulsion from Paradise.* Photograph by Malcolm Varon. Image © The Metropolitan Museum of Art.

page 49. Figure 11. *Vitruvian Man.* Photograph by Luc Viatour, www.Lucnix.be, Wikimedia Commons.

page 52. Figure 12. *The Chakras of the Subtle Body.* © Sven Gahlin.

page 53. Figure 13. *Jacob's Ladder* or *Jacob's Dream.* © Trustees of the British Museum, London.

page 55. Figure 14. Romanesco broccoli fractals (2004), PDphoto.org, http://www.fourmilab.ch/images/Romanesco.

page 56. Figure 15. *Dismemberment of Watakame.* © Juan Negrin and Wixarika Research Center.

page 57. Figure 16. Human embryonic stem cells. © courtesy of the California Institute for Regenerative Medicine.

page 71. Figure 17. *Sibyl and Medicine Bowl* or *Yassi Society Figure.* © University of Pennsylvania Museum of Archaeology and Anthropology, Philadelphia, Penn Museum object 37-22-279, image #150632.

page 73. Figure 18. *Ifa Divination Tray.* © Ulmer Museum—Weickmann Collection, Ulm. Photo: Bernd Kegler, Ulm.

page 82. Figure 19. Helix Nebula. © NASA, NOAO, ESA, the Hubble Helix Nebula Team, M. Meixner (STScI), and T. A. Rector (NRAO).

page 93. Figure 20. *The Creation of the World.* Wikimedia Commons.

page 94. Figure 21. "The Blue Marble, East." NASA Goddard Space Flight Center. Image by Reto Stockli (land surface, shallow water, clouds). Enhancements by Robert Simmon (ocean color, compositing, 3D globes, animation). Data and technical support: MODIS Land Group; MODIS Science Data Support Team; MODIS Atmosphere Group; MODIS Ocean Group. Additional data: USGS EROS Data Center (topography);

USGS Terrestrial Remote Sensing Flagstaff Field Center (Antarctica); Defense Meteorological Satellite Program (city lights). (http://visibleearth.nasa.gov/)

page 96. Figure 23. Freud's Consulting Room. © Photo courtesy of the Freud Museum, London.

page 99. Figure 24. *Brain Story.* © 1994. Courtesy of C. San Roque, for the Commonwealth of Australia.

page 126. Figure 25. *Moscow at Night*, courtesy of the photographer, Alexey Kochemasov.

page 133. Figure 26. *The Wheel of Time, Kalachakra.* © Rubin Museum of Art, New York. C2001.1.1.

page 137. Figure 27. *Narcissus.* © Gallery Nazionale d'Arte Antica, Rome. Photograph: The Yorck Project: *10.000 Meisterwerke der Malerei.* DVD-ROM, 2002. ISBN 3936122202. Distributed by DIRECTMEDIA Publishing GmbH.

page 222 and back cover. About the Author and back cover photographs. © 2013 China Jorrin.

Index

Italic page numbers indicate an illustration.

A

Abu Ghraib, 162
academia, 184
Adam and Eve, 44
adolescence, 135–136
Aeschylus:
    Oresteia, 154–160
    Prometheus Bound, 68
alchemical imagery, 114
alchemical *Rosarium*, 168n11
alchemy, medieval, 69
alembic, 97–98, 114
al-Qaeda, 1, 62
America, symbolic of totality, 7
American Civil War, 165
Americanization, 18
anima mundi, 162
anti-Semitism, 138, 164
Anubis, 103
apocalypse, 45–46, 66n38, 165–168, 173, 195
Apollo, 68–69, 127

Arab Spring protests, 145–146
archetypal images, 20
archetypal patterns, 94
archetypes, 23, 38, 46
Arendt, Hannah, 123, 141–142, 144
Aristotle, 22
Armstrong, Karen, 128
artificial intelligence, 145, 181, 194
Asclepius, 68–69
astrology, 40
atomic bomb, 138
authority, sacrificed, 10
Avatar (movie), 6, 41, 60, 119
avatars, 3, 175, 177–178
axis mundi, 40
Aztecs, 150

B

Babylon, 38, 125
Barrett, William, 157
Barthes, Roland, 181
Bataille, Georges, 181
Baule people, 42, *43*
behaviorism, 129
beloved, dream of, 135–137

bewitchment, 177
Bible:
    Genesis, 44
    Luke, 67
    Revelation, 8
bicamerality, 100–101
birther movement, 84
black magic, 74
Blake, William, 158
    Jacob's Ladder, 51, *53*
blogosphere (blogging), 10, 117, 120, 176, 178
blood payments, 152–153, 155, 162
blood sacrifice, 150–151, 157. *See also* sacrifice
Booker, Christopher, 50, 60
Borobudur, 38, *40*
Bosch, Hieronymus, *The Garden of Earthly Delights*, 92, *93*
Boym, Svetlana, 168n8
brain, 97–100, 102, 119
Buddha, 128
Buddha Mind, 51
Buddhism, 80, 128, 181
    Tantric, 133–134
Bull, Malcolm, 116–117, 165, 181
Bush, George W., 26

C

Callanish Stones, *35*
Cambray, Joseph, 64n5
capitalism:
    corporate, 143–144, 192
    free-market, 18, 24, 58–59, 124
Caravaggio, Michelangelo, *Narcissus*, 137–138, *137*
catharsis, theatrical. *See* theater, as catharsis
cathedrals, European, 125
Catholicism, 138
centering function, 29, 190
centers, and boundaries, 184–186, 191

chakras, 51, *52*, 98
Christ, 26, 69, 97, 162, 167
    his sacrificial death, 83, 151
Christianity, 47, 92, 127–128, 152
cities, 125, 128
    ancient, 101, 126
Citizens United v. Federal Election Commission, 143–144
city life, 126
climate crisis, 61. *See also* global (climate) meltdown
cognitive fluidity, 21
cognitive psychology, 19, 24, 118
communications:
    satellite, 146
    technology, 4, 44, 47, 120
communitas, 130–131
complex adaptive systems, 63n5
complexes, 103, 111
conceptual blending, 20–22
confessions, 180
Confucius, 128
consciousness, 109–110, 112
    emergent, 117
    global, 181
consumerism, corporate, 141
contemporary life, 12, 117, 190. *See also* postmodernism
    decentered and fragmented, 173, 191
Corbin, Henry, 123
corporate culture, 143
corporate personhood, 59, 144
cosmologies, 40
cosmos, Aboriginal, 98
Coupland, Douglas, 118
creation:
    myths, 129, 150
    religious versus scientific views, 128
creativity, 19
cultural narrative, 83

INDEX

cyberpunk, 145
cyberspace, 41, 47, 174, 176, 180, 190, 196
cybervillage, 26, 119, 173

D

da Vinci, Leonardo, *Vitruvian Man*, 48, *49*
Dante, *Inferno*, 92, 103
Darfur, Africa, 138
Darwin, Charles, *The Expression of the Emotions in Man and Animals*, 95
Darwinism, 142
Dawkins, Richard, 8, 79–81, 87n13
de Paolo, Giovanni, *The Creation of the World and the Expulsion from Paradise*, 44, *45*
death:
    and composting, 58
    and renewal, 42
    sacrificial, 152. *See also* killing, sacrificial
decentering, 118, 167, 173
deities, world-creating, 47
Delphi, 38, 125–128, 146
Delphic oracle, 104, 127–128, 196
democracy, 9, 20, 58–59, 143, 146, 191–192
Derrida, Jacques, 75–78, 177, 181
desire, 138–139
Diagnostic and Statistical Manual of Mental Disorders (DSM–5), 5
dialectic materialism, 134
Dickinson, Emily, 100
digital archiving, 117
Diocletian (Emperor), 127
discipleships, 37
disenfranchisement, 151, 161
dismemberment, 152
dissociation, 5, 11, 44, 86, 103, 120, 191

dissociative states of mind, 104, 106, 110–112
divination, 72–73, 101, 104, 193
DNA, 47
dogma, 5
Dostoyevsky, Fyodor, 149
Dracula, 135
drama, 77, 178, 155, 179
    life, 125, 150, 178
    sacrificial, 149–150, 151, 153
dreams, 103, 107
    healing, 69
    in therapy, 42
    of a dog show, 114
    of a dragon, 2
dreaming, 21, 96, 107
    REM, 117
dreams (dreaming) of totality, 3–9, 17, 86, 123–125. *See also* images of totality
    adolescent, 132
    and sacrificial action, 149
    as a system of exclusion and suppression, 34
    creative function, 10–11
    gone bad, 129
    psychology's, 120
drugs:
    recreational, 68, 70, 76, 78, 139. *See also* psychedelic substances
    war on, 68
dualism, 81
dystopias. *See* utopias and dystopias

E

Earth, from space, 92, *94*
ecology, 42, 44, 116
education, interdisciplinary, 184
Einstein, Albert, 17–18, 32
Ekman, Paul, 95, 121n3
Eliade, Mircea, 28, 38, 150

Emerson, Ralph Waldo, 84
emotion, 96, 178
emotional communication, 24–25
empathy, 137, 144–145
end-times, 3, 18, 45
Engels, Friedrich, 142
entanglement, 33
entertainment, 76
epidemics, mass, 1
Erikson, Erik, 112
Eros, 131
Eshu, 74
ethics, 12, 85–86, 180–181, 192–193, 195
   of transgression, 175
ethnography, 95
Euripides, 158
evil, 135, 161
   projection of, 164
evolution, 8, 80–81, 84–85
exhibitionism, 143
exorcism, 9
eye of God, 17, 82–83

F

Facebook, 176, 178–179
   stalking, 185
facism, German, 138
fact/fiction divide, 177
fairy tales, 48–49
family life, 5
fanaticism, 190
farming, organic, 61
father, insane, 115
Fauconnier, Gilles, 20
feminism, 116, 161
Fitzgerald, Ella, 76
Flournoy, Theodore, 104–105
fractal geometry, 55, *55*
fragmentation, 120, 191–192
   and wholeness. *See* wholeness, and fragmentation

free markets, 20, 190. *See also* capitalism, free-market
Freud, Sigmund, 8, 79–81, 94, 101, 103–106, 109–111
   consulting room, *96*
   Interpretation of Dreams, 92, 105
   secret committee, 37
Friedman, Tom, 18, 20
fundamentalism(s), 5–8, 12, 80, 82–85, 141, 160, 190
   American, 13n3
Furies, 154–162

G

Galileo, 48, 167
Garden of Eden, 44
Gell-Mann, Murray, 63n5
gender, 5, 116
genius, 22, 97
genius religiosus, 79, 84
genocide, 124, 138, 152, 195
Giegerich, Wolfgang, 32, 151–152
Gilded Age, 62
global (climate) meltdown, 1–2, 45. *See also* end-times
global village, 1, 6, 146, 167, 176
   virtual, 41
globalization, 3–6, 10–11, 18, 20–21, 46, 61–62, 63n2, 119, 153, 190–192, 196
   corporate, 59
   images of, 59
God, 47–48, 84–85, 87n13
gods, 92–93, 100–102, 104, 196
   identification with creator and destroyer, 151, 153, 167, 196
Goethe, Johann Wolfgang von, *Faust*, 191
Golden Mean, 54
golden ratio, 54
Grosskurth, Phyllis, 36–37

H

Hale-Bopp, 66n38
hallucinations, auditory, 100–101
Harris, Eddie, 173
head, as the locus of consciousness, 96–98
healing, 70, 72
health, 50, 69–70
    psychological (psychic), 93–94, 106, 118
    and wholeness, 114
health care, universal, 144
heaven, 20, 120
Heaven's Gate, 66n38
hegemony, Western, 161
Heidegger, Martin, 189
Heisenberg, Werner, 32
Helix Nebula, 82, *82*
Heraclitus, 176
Hermes, 196
    and the herm as a boundary marker, 187n12
Hermes Trismegistus, 103
heroes, 151
Hesiod, 154
Hillman, James, 116
Hinduism, 47
hippies, 142
hippocampus, 2
history, 134–135
Hitchens, Christopher, 8, 79–80, 83, 143
Hitler, Adolf, 34
hive mind, 146
holistic functioning, 98
Holy Grail, 97, 101, 174
hubris, 68
Huffington, Arianna, 23
humanism, 11
    scientific, 129
Huxley, Aldous, *Brave New World*, 60, 139–141, 189
Hyde, Lewis, 7, 74, 131, 149, 184, 187n12
hyperreality, 88n25

I

I Ching, 72
identity, 112, 117, 119–120, 135–136, 177, 186. *See also* self-identity
    collaborative, 178
    cultural, 5
    ego, 70, 96, 107, 111, 113, 115, 118
    individual, 5
    sacrifice of, 159
    social construction of, 116
identity formation, 114
ideologies, 62, 123–124, 136, 141–143
Ifa, 72–74
Ifa (Yoruban) divination tray, 72, *73*
illness, 69–72
illusions, 3, 11, 78, 118, 176
    as an expression of reality, 177
image industry, 8, 76
image schemata, 22
    body-based, 19–22
images, 23, 25, 76–77, 192
    digital, 177
    spinning of, 5–6
    of totality, 12
imagination, 7–12, 63, 64n5, 81, 100, 115, 118–119, 137, 144–145, 190–192
    adaptive and cohesive function, 3–5
    as the basis for rationality, 19
    as something public, 22
    breakdown of, 141, 191
    call and response dynamic, 26, 61
    collective, 6, 17, 26, 41, 46, 61, 86, 104, 123

creative, 17–18, 25, 78, 106–108
and magic, 30–31
mythopoetic, 22, 27, 74, 80, 83
power to transgress, 175–176, 182
immigration, fears of, 4
immortal animal, 135
incestuous desire, 162
incubation ritual (mysteries), 69–70, 93, 111
Indra's net, 1, 3, 51, 55
industrialization, 60
infotainment industry, 5, 59, 140, 166. *See also* media industry
initiation rituals, 24, 152, 178–179
instinct, 79–80, 95, 127
kinship, 162–163
sexual, 94
instinctive responses, 27
integration, 3–4
interiority, 100, 102, 104, 109, 119
Internet, 18, 25, 61, 77, 146, 175
surveillance of, 185
interregnum, 26–27, 104
introversion, 5
Islam, 47, 92
isms, 12–13, 101, 132, 138, 142
Israel, and Palestine, 124

J

Jacoby, Mario, 132
James, William, 32, 67, 80, 104, 110–11
Jaynes, Julian, 100–102
Jericho, 125
Jerusalem, 38
Jesus, 83, 85
Job, 69
Johnson, Mark, 19
Jones, Ernest, 37
Judaism, 47, 92, 152
Julian (Emperor), 128
Jung, C. G., 20–21, 23, 79, 84, 91, 94–96, 103–106, 109–115, 117, 124, 152, 158, 167
and National Socialism, 34, 65n30
break with Freud, 27, 37, 110
breakdown, 27–32
collaboration with Wolfgang Pauli, 32–33, 65n24
in Africa, 109
interview with John Freeman, 87–88n13
military service, 29
on mandala symbolism, 66n42
Jung, C. G., *works*:
"Flying Saucers: A Modern Myth of Things Seen in the Sky," 186n1
"The Psychology of the Transference," 162–163, 168n11
Psychological Types, 29
Jurra, Rachel Napaljarri, *Brain Story*, 98, *99*

K

Kalachakra, 133, *133*
Kawai, Toshio, 118
Kearny, Richard, 11
killing, sacrificial, 151
knowledge, 190
as opposed to information, 181
Kohut, Heinz, 37
Kremlin, 126
Kristeva, Julia, 110
Kronos, 38, 57–59, 127, 154
Kundalini yoga, 51, 65n22, 127
Kurzweil, Ray, 187n9

L

Lacan, Jacques, 37
Ladies Home Journal, 140
LaGamma, Alisa, 42
Leibniz, Gottfried Wilhelm, 48

life:
> collective, 4, 11, 28, 103, 112, 124–125, 130, 164, 178–179
> postmodern, 184, 196. *See also* contemporary life
> virtual, 10, 177, 179–185

Lifton, Robert, 42–44, 112, 178
liminality, 130
London Society for Psychical Research, 104
love, 131, 135–136, 138–139
> romantic or spiritual, 132

M

Machu Picchu, 125
magic circles, 17, 33–38, *35*, *36*, 44–50, 62, 134, 143, 163–165
> of time, 41

"mama grizzlies," 23–24
man, as a microcosm of the universe, 20, 110
mandalas, 29–30, 34, 37, 50–51, 54, 62, 66n42, 82, 114–115
> Kalachakra, 133–134
> sand, Tibetan Buddist ritual, 54

mandala symbolism, 29, 51, 106
manifest destiny, 58, 124
Maria Prophetissa, 50
Marx, Karl, 142
Marxism, 141
masks, 178–180
matriarchy, 158
matricide, 155
Matrix, The (movie), 25, 60
matter, spiritualizing, 52–53
Mayans, 47
> calendar, 45

Mayer, Arno, 159
McCann, Les, 173
McLuhan, Marshall, 174
meaning, 8, 182, 192–193

relational quality, 116
measurement, 177
media industry, 10. *See also* infotainment industry
media spectacles, 6
medicine, 68–70
mediums, 104
Medusa, 68
Melville, Herman, *Moby-Dick*, 60
memeplexes, 81
memoirs, 108, 176
Memorex tape, commercials for, 76–77
memorialization, 159, 168n8
memory, 107–108
> art of, 75, 77
> playing with, 73–74

memories, accessed in therapy, 108
Mercurius, 2
metaphors, 19–22, 25, 95, 107, 152
mind:
> mythopoetic, 102, 104–105, 107, 120, 129, 131, 190. *See also* thinking, mythopoetic
> savage, 131

Mind, universal, 98
mirror neurons, 24
mirroring, 136–138, 153
> perfect, 153, 162

Mnemosyne, 107
modernity, 119
monomyth, 109
monotheism, 92, 128
moralism, 142–143
Moscow, 126, *126*
mother-child couple, 132
mouth, ancient Egyptian ritual of washing and opening, 121n12
multiculturalism, 11
Mumford, Lewis, 125
Mummy Cave, 34–36, *35*

mundus imaginalis, 123
Myers, F. W. H., 104–105
mysticism:
    apocalyptic, 9
    reactionary, 7
mythologizing, 75, 150
mythology:
    creation, 58
    Indian, 40
mythopoetic awareness (experience), 94, 102, 163. *See also* imagination, mythopoetic; thinking, mythopoetic

N

narcissism, 137, 139
narrative, 4, 13, 22, 24, 83, 107–108, 111–113, 196
    collective, 124
    historical, 128
narrative theory, postmodern, 25
narrative transport, 24
National Socialism, 34, 138
nationalism, 5
Nazism, 34, 138, 141
neuro disciplines, 98
neuroscience, 24, 81, 119, 175
New Atheism, 80–81, 83–85, 101
New Jerusalem, 124
New York City, 126, 161
Nietzsche, Friedrich, 91, 157, 167
nihilism, 7, 192
Noh, 178
no-self, 118
nostalgia, 3, 41, 101–102, 168n8
    malignant, 194, 197n4
nuclear holocaust, 45
number magic, 48–50
numbers, in storytelling, 48
Nussbaum, Martha, 86, 160

O

Obama, Barack, 1, 25–27, 84
occultism, 105
Odu Ifa, 72–74
one and the many, 54–55, 58, 110
oneness, 67. *See also* wholeness
online personae, 117, 175, 177
opportunity, and opportunism, 183

P

Palin, Sarah, 23, 27
paradise, 17
Parsifal, 174
Pascal, Blaise, 48
patriarchy, 158
patriotic fervor, 76
patterns, 19
Pauli, Wolfgang, 32–33, 65n24
personality, 113, 116
    fragmented and unified, 110–111
phantom limb pain, 136
pharmakon, 9, 11, 68, 75–79, 85, 106, 112, 114
    meaning color, 177
    question, 111
    social, 124
    of totality, 74, 83
Philo, 48
philosopher's stone, 114
philosophical rationalism, 128
Plato, *Phaedrus*, 74–75, 78
pluralism, 116
plurality, in the oneness of totality, 54. *See also* one and the many
poison oracle (*benge*), 193
Popenoe, Paul, 140
population, global, 61
pornography, 62, 140–141
    child, 183
postmodernism (postmodernity), 4, 11, 84, 166–167, 181–182, 190. *See also* contemporary life

PostSecret.com, 180, 187n7
post-traumatic stress disorder, 29
power, democratized, 146
primitive societies, 150
primitivity, 83, 102
profiling. *See* social profiling
projection, 50, 72, 92, 96, 102, 120, 132, 138
prophecy, 127
psilocybin, 68
psyche, 13n6, 21, 27, 31–32, 38, 76, 84, 98, 100, 106–107, 111, 113, 115
   adolescent, 141
   archaic, 94, 109
   collective, 59, 61, 119, 130
psychedelic substances, 68. *See also* drugs, recreational
psychic energy, 30, 32, 51, 54, 127
psychic fields, 32
psychoanalysis (psychoanalytic theory), 27, 36, 70, 94, 103
psychological experience, 7, 25, 79–80, 83, 88n13, 105, 132
psychological process, 4, 80, 93, 103, 108, 112–113, 116, 118
psychology, 11, 92, 96, 102–104, 112, 116, 119–120
   depth, 42, 104, 107
   founding fathers, 105, 110
   its identity crisis, 118
   of the child, 103–104
   postmodern, 116
psychopathy, 182–183
psychopomps, 26, 102–105, 119–120, 128, 130
psychotherapy, 96, 112, 115, 163
Pythagoras, 48

R

racism, 164–165
Radin, Paul, 24

Rapture, 46, *46*
rationality, 19, 21
reality, 23, 47, 60–62
   virtual, 10. *See also* virtuality
reality TV, 5, 176
Red Book, 28–32, *31*, 37
religion, 54, 67, 79, 80–81, 84–85, 129, 150
   as a fiction, 8
religion/science debate, 8
religious freedom, 58
revenge, 157–158, 162
Ricoeur, Paul, 123
Rilke, R. M., 17, 63, 131
rite de passage, 132
Rousseau, Henri, *The Dream*, 41, *41*
Rubens, Peter Paul, *Saturn Devouring His Son*, 38, *39*

S

Sachs, Jeffrey, 61
sacrifice, 73, 78, 85, 149–153, 195
salvation, 6, 41, 66n38, 79, 136, 181
Samuels, Andrew, 19
Sanchez, Jose Benitez, *Dismemberment of Watakame*, 56, *56*
scapegoating, 9, 77–78, 85, 142, 149, 151–152, 164–165, 167, 195
   intellectual, 84
science, 54, 129
Second Life, 176
self, 116–120
   decentering of, 118
   narrative nature of, 119
   real, 178
Self, 110–115
   as a dream of totality, 3, 91
self-identity, 34, 178
self-organization, principle of, 47
selves, fugitive, 116
September 11, 2001, 161

serpent mandala, 30–32, *31*
serpent power, 31, 127
Serrano, Miguel, 3
Seto, Michael, 187n10
sex offenders, 183, 187n10
sexuality, 103, 105, 131, 136, 139–141, 143
Shamdasani, Sonu, 105
Shangri-La, 125
Shelley, Mary, 173
   Frankenstein, 60
sibyl, 70, *71*
sickness. *See* illness
singularity, 82, 181, 187n9, 194
skulls, as sacred drinking cups, 97
slavery, 165
Slick, Grace, "White Rabbit," 67
social media, 146, 151, 179
social networking, 179
social organization, multiple modes, 119
social profiling, 178–179
social systems, human, 130–131, 144
socialism, 143
Socrates, 74–75, 78, 128
Sophocles, *Electra*, 157
sorcery, 76, 78
specialization, 98
spirit, materializing, 52–53
spiritualism, 104
Stalin, Joseph, 124
standing stones, 34, *35*
Steger, Manfred, 63n2
stem cells, 56–57, *57*
   research and application, 68
Stevens, Anthony, 117
storytelling, 48, 178
structure, and anti-structure, 130–131
symbols, 23, 27
symbol formation, 83, 129
symbol systems, 21
symbolization, 27, 63, 85, 96

symmetry, in the human form, 136
synchronicity, 32, 65n24, 72

T

taboos, 10, 36, 78, 85, 103, 149, 164–166, 195
Tao (Taoism), 47, 50–51
technology, 3–5, 18, 61, 77. *See also* communications technology
technology, digital, 22, 120
Teotihuacán, 125
terror networks (terrorism), 1, 3, 135, 143, 160
theater, 180. *See also* drama
   as catharsis, 177–180
theory of special relativity, 32
therapeutic relationship, as a magic circle, 163
thinking:
   mythopoetic, 21–22, 106
   rational and nonrational, 21
threshold people, 130
time:
   and space, sacred, 38–40, 44
   circular images versus linear images, 134–135
totalitarianism, 9, 131, 138–139, 141–144, 192
Tower of Babel, 54, 59
traditional values, 138, 190
transgression, 131, 166, 182–185, 192, 195
   creative, 147, 186
   of boundaries, 5, 10, 152
tribal societies, and individual freedom, 6
trickster, 103, 131
truth, 9, 11, 101
   casual relationship to, 6
   mythopoetic, 152, 176
Turkle, Sherry, 178
Turner, Mark, 20

Turner, Victor, 123, 130–131
Twilight series, 135
Twitter (Tweeting), 120, 176

U

UFOs, 186n1
unconscious, 92–93, 95, 103, 105–106, 109
    as a projection of the imagination, 96
    collective, 95
United States, motto and seal, 58, 144, 191
unity. *See* oneness; wholeness
unobtainium, 6
unus mundus, 47
utopias and dystopias, 3, 141, 145, 153, 168

V

vampires, 135
verticality, 19
village of truth, 42
violence, 38
Virgil, 92, 103
virgin birth, 83–84
virtuality, 5, 11, 59, 174–177, 180–182, 186, 191, 194. *See also* reality, virtual; life, virtual; world, virtual
visions, 1, 9, 27, 79, 83, 107
voodoo, African, 127

W

Wall Street, and financial derivatives, 175
war, 8, 27, 124
Warren, Frank, 180
Watakame, 56–58
Web archiving, 77
Weber, Max, 189
Webworld, 153
Wheel of Time, 133–134, *133*
Whitman, Walt, 67, 91
wholeness, 11, 68, 114
    and fragmentation, 112–113
Wilde, Oscar, 179
Wilhelm, Richard, 29
Wilson, Edward O., 8, 128–129
Wired magazine, 1
WITCH, 161
witchcraft, 193
Woodroffe, John, 65n22
world clock, 33
world community, 42
World Health Organization, 70
World War I, 27–28, 34
World Wide Web, 1, 3, 6, 18, 20, 61–62, 146, 174, 181, 183, 185. *See also* Internet
world, virtual, 6, 175–178, 181, 190, 196
writing, 74–75, 77

Y

Y2K, 45
Yeats, William Butler, 3
    "The Second Coming," 165
YouPorn, 183, 185

Z

Zabriskie, Beverley, 65n24

About the Author

Sherry Salman works as a psychoanalyst and is an internationally recognized author and speaker. Her area of expertise is the imagination in postmodern culture and psychological life. She has been a teacher, lecturer, and author for thirty years and has served as an associate editor for three professional journals and a consultant for the Archive for Research in Archetypal Symbolism. She was a founding member and the first president of the Jungian Psychoanalytic Association, a nonprofit educational community that fosters the training of psychoanalysts and promotes the creative understanding and applications of psychology in professional, cultural, and scientific communities. She received her B.A. from Vassar College and a Ph.D. in neuropsychology from the City University of New York, did research in psychosomatic medicine, and completed training as a Jungian analyst in 1985. Her work has appeared in numerous journals and in the popular press. Recent contributions can be found in *The Book of Symbols: Reflections on Archetypal Images* (2010), *The Cambridge Companion to Jung* (2008), *Jungian Psychoanalysis* (2010), and *Terror, Violence, and the Impulse to Destroy* (2003). She lives with her family in the Hudson Valley of New York.

CPSIA information can be obtained at www.ICGtesting.com
Printed in the USA
LVOW01s0957260314

378999LV00011B/95/P